About Island Press

Island Press is the only nonprofit organization in the United States whose principal purpose is the publication of books on environmental issues and natural resource management. We provide solutions-oriented information to professionals, public officials, business and community leaders, and concerned citizens who are shaping responses to environmental problems.

In 1998, Island Press celebrates its fourteenth anniversary as the leading provider of timely and practical books that take a multidisciplinary approach to critical environmental concerns. Our growing list of titles reflects our commitment to bringing the best of an expanding body of literature to the environmental community throughout North America and the world.

Support for Island Press is provided by The Jenifer Altman Foundation, The Bullitt Foundation, The Mary Flagler Cary Charitable Trust, The Nathan Cummings Foundation, The Geraldine R. Dodge Foundation, The Charles Engelhard Foundation, The Ford Foundation, The Vira I. Heinz Endowment, The W. Alton Jones Foundation, The John D. and Catherine T. MacArthur Foundation, The Andrew W. Mellon Foundation, The Charles Stewart Mott Foundation, The Curtis and Edith Munson Foundation, The National Fish and Wildlife Foundation, The National Science Foundation, The New-Land Foundation, The David and Lucile Packard Foundation, The Surdna Foundation, The Winslow Foundation, The Pew Charitable Trusts, and individual donors.

Structural Economics

Structural Economics

Measuring Change in Technology, Lifestyles, and the Environment

FAYE DUCHIN

The United Nations
University
UNU / IAS
Institute of Advanced Studies

Published in cooperation with the United Nations
University/Institute of Advanced Studies

ISLAND PRESS

Washington, D.C. ♦ Covelo, California

Library of Congress Cataloging-in-Publication Data
Duchin, Faye, 1944–
    Structural economics : measuring change in technology, lifestyles, and the environment / by Faye Duchin.
        p.   cm.
    Includes bibliographical references and index.
    ISBN 1–55963–606–8 (cloth : alk. paper)
    1. Economic development.   2. Technological innovations—Economic aspects.   3. Infrastructure (Economics)   4. Economic development—Environmental aspects.   5. Indonesia—Economic conditions—1945– 6. United States—Economic conditions—1981–   I. Title.
    HD75.D83   1998   98–13576
    333.7—dc21   CIP

Printed on recycled, acid-free paper

Manufactured in the United States of America
10 9 8 7 6 5 4 3 2 1

Contents

List of Tables and Figures

Tables

Figures

Preface

Structural economics is a body of theory and methods relating changes in technology, lifestyles, and the environment, an approach that makes it possible to address, and begin to answer, some of the most challenging questions of our time. This volume brings together for the first time a full description of structural economics and provides new material that develops not only its technological but also its social dimension. The effort involves integrating qualitative understanding into a flexible quantitative framework intended for describing and analyzing how people live in households and earn their livings producing goods and services on farms, in mines, in factories, and, increasingly, in offices. The framework also deals with how technologies change and how the lifestyles of different kinds of households change in the process of development. The case of Indonesia has been used in this book both for illustration and to test and improve new concepts by applying them to factual information.

This work has in part been supported by the program in sustainable development of the United Nations University in Tokyo. The program sets out to explore how it might be possible to ensure adequate protection of the natural world while satisfying the objectives of accelerated economic development in industrializing countries and maintaining current standards of living in the developed world. A distinctive feature of this effort of the United Nations University is its focus on the perspectives, challenges, options, and active participation of developing countries, especially those in the Asia Pacific region.

Many dimensions of structural economics have been developed over a period of decades, in particular its power for analyzing the implications of technological change. A relevant body of work is described in some detail in this book. New research about the social dimension of sustainable development seeks to conceptualize and describe different categories of households and their lifestyles and to develop a framework for analyzing scenarios about alternative prospects for lifestyle changes. This is achieved by extending existing concepts, databases, and models in ways that parallel the treatment of technological change.

The present volume consists of nine chapters written over the past five years. Each chapter is intended to be self-contained in the treatment of some part of the overall subject while touching on most of the other themes as well. The reason for this approach is that the different aspects—classifications, data, mathematics, scenarios—are highly interdependent to such an extent that the research itself has moved in an iterative fashion from one to the next. To the extent possible I wanted to avoid a highly technical treatment that would isolate the topics in separate chapters. While most chapters thus take up overlapping material, I have tried to avoid redundancy and to provide the flow and integration that a reader has the right to expect.

The book is addressed to the general reader who is concerned with the public good, believes that substantial changes in how we live and work may be in store, and is convinced that a deeper understanding of our options is needed if we are to make reasonable decisions. Yet, while I strive for a clear presentation and avoid jargon, the book is not light reading and includes some mathematics.

I have two reasons for aiming the exposition at a general reader. First, at a time of extreme specialization within mutually exclusive academic disciplines, one of the few ways to try to address a variety of social scientists is to write for a general reader. Second, this work is based on the conviction that specialists, generalists, and ordinary (that is, nonexpert) citizens are reliant upon each other in effecting social change. For this reason, I want to point out that there is a pathway through the book, simply skipping chapters 5 and 6, that tells a coherent story while bypassing the most technical material.

The mathematical formulation of chapter 6 recapitulates the entire story of structural economics in a succinct form that makes it possible to carry out experiments. The nonmathematical reader, who will already be familiar with the story, may not be interested in the equations but may want to peruse the list of variables to get an intuition about the formal representation.

While all chapters include references to a scholarly literature, many of the cited books and articles may well be of interest to a general reader. This is least likely to be true for the references to the social accounting literature in chapter 5. That work is nonetheless included because it serves as a major stimulus, and also a point of comparison, for the somewhat different approach that I propose.

◆

This book marks a main turning point in my intellectual work. At the time I began the manuscript, I had no idea that the completion of the first draft would exactly coincide with my leaving the Institute for Economic Analysis at New York University, where I had been for twenty years, for a different kind of challenge.

In September of 1996 I moved to Troy, New York, to become the dean of the School of the Humanities and Social Sciences at Rensselaer Polytechnic Institute, a technological university and the home of the first school of engineering to be established in the United States (in 1824). The fresh perspective provided by this change, coupled with the detailed and incisive comments of Frank Ackerman of Tufts University, Bert Steenge of the University of Twente, and Reid Lifset of Yale University, informed a substantial revision of the scope of the manuscript. I am grateful to my editor at Island Press, Todd Baldwin, for his interest in this work and his substantial help in improving the text. The book is a synthesis of my work of the past twenty years and provides a point of departure for moving, with the collaboration of new colleagues, in fresh directions.

I want to thank Dr. Fu-chen Lo, deputy director of the Institute for Advanced Studies at the United Nations University in Tokyo, for his support of this project and his commitment, more generally, to the interplay of theoretical and empirical research. I gratefully acknowledge the collaboration of Glenn-Marie Lange in drafting an early version of chapter 5 and that of Karim Nauphal in carrying out the computations reported in chapter 8. I am extremely fortunate to have worked for two decades with Wassily Leontief, who shared with me his passion for understanding how economies function.

Introduction

For twenty years I carried out detailed studies about changes in ways of producing steel, generating electricity, manufacturing cars, and growing rice. I supervised the construction of large databases from information collected mainly by national statistical offices and oversaw the development of mathematical models and computer systems to analyze the data. I was especially interested in the similarities and differences in production techniques among various societies, and in the effects of those techniques on employment, income, and the use of raw materials. Over the past decade I focused increasingly on the generation of pollution and ways of reducing wastes, use of materials and energy, and erosion. I wrote many technical reports and articles and a few books describing the results of various analyses. Finally, I realized (with the urging of a number of friends and colleagues) that it was time to give a name to this body of theory and methods and provide a systematic description of the approach, along with examples that would demonstrate its power. In this way, other researchers might take it up.

I chose the name structural economics because the theory and methodology emphasize the structure of an economy, the fundamental ways in which various industrial sectors relate—to one another, to the households that constitute the labor force and consume industrial products, and to the environment, which is both source for materials and sink for wastes.

I had come to see that while mainstream academic economists had different concerns, my basic approach was highly valued in other quarters. I had discovered strong common interests with engineers in life-cycle analysis and state-of-the-art technologies, with applied physical scientists in energy and materials, and with ecologists in the effects of human activities on the environment. But it was clear to me that structural economics needed to be rooted in eco-

1

nomics, the field that deals with what is produced and how, what is consumed and by whom. I thought that a department of economics at a technological university could be a hospitable home.

The central feature of a technological university, such as the one at which I now work, is its school of engineering, which makes use of the methods and results of science while imparting to the entire campus community a pragmatic, problem-solving orientation. The humanities and social sciences constitute the largest academic unit at a liberal arts college; at a technological university the school of the humanities and social sciences is relatively small and generally includes only a subset of the independent disciplines and departments that are within its scope. This fact makes for a looser affiliation for its researchers with the mainstream disciplines in which they received their formal training and far more readiness on their parts to cross disciplinary borders. The technological university provides a suitable setting for studying all aspects of life and work in a technological society.

At New York University I had found myself at a large, diversified institution, but one with a conventional department of economics and no school of engineering. I chose to move to a technological university after many years of trying to collaborate with engineers and other economists from a distance.

To throw more light on my motivation, I will describe the kinds of questions that have interested me in recent years. The major source of environmental degradation in an industrial society lies in the ways in which materials and energy are used. I have attempted to understand the extent to which it is realistic to reduce the scale of use of fuels and major materials or to substantially increase recycling of the latter. A serious examination of these prospects requires investigating the basis for people's lifestyle decisions—in the case of materials, particularly in terms of the items they use and discard. But it also requires understanding facts about the potential substitutions of reprocessed for virgin materials on the basis of their physical characteristics. This knowledge, which is in the domain of engineers and applied physical scientists, is necessary for evaluating the feasibility and economic viability of alternative strategies. Among materials, an especially difficult challenge is posed by the proliferation of nondegradable plastics. My work on plastics (discussed in chapter 2) benefited from collaboration with engineers.

Like other private and public institutions before them, American universities are now under substantial pressures for change.

The main reason is economic. There have been major shifts in the composition and needs of the population seeking university-level training. Many prospective students who are from modest socioeconomic backgrounds would not in past decades have aspired to a college degree. The need to supplement the limited financial means of a more diverse group of students is obviously costly.

Like corporations before them, financially pressed universities resort first to cutting costs across all functions, but economies achieved in this way generally prove inadequate. In response to changes in students' needs and in management practices, new kinds of institutions are proving popular. Nonresidential programs delivered via satellite or on the Internet, on-site corporate programs, and community colleges are among the alternatives that are vastly expanding the range of training and diplomas available. This environment poses a severe challenge to those attempting to create new programs within a university setting committed to maintaining a community of scholars.

In the twenty-first century, research universities that do not have enormous endowments will change in order to survive. Many institutions will combine departments rather than try to cover every discipline and subdiscipline. Economics and the other social sciences will move away from abstract theorizing and toward a more pragmatic, problem-oriented focus—in particular, they will use the communities in which they are located as their laboratories. Virtually all communities are preoccupied with economic development. Local officials, businesspeople, and community leaders are concerned about maintaining the tax base and municipal services and expanding employment, while preserving and improving the local quality of life. Meeting challenges like these requires an understanding of social realities, physical facts, and technological alternatives. In short, the strengths of a school of the humanities and social sciences at a technological university place it in a position today to pioneer the kinds of programs, especially in economics, that we are likely to see at many universities in the future.

University-based research agendas about social problems, such as those experienced in the local community, involve generalists, specialists, and people in their capacity as citizens. The generalists and citizens are well placed to formulate the problems but may need to work with experts to identify options for resolving them. A collaboration of social scientists, engineers, and citizens could develop solid waste or sewage treatment and disposal options that are well suited to the population density and other characteristics of a particular community, for example. Or a study of where people live and work and shop could be conducted and used as a basis for replacing some use of the car with convenient public transportation.

It is legitimate to inquire as to whether this kind of approach, while it may be of both educational and social value, belongs to the tradition of theory-based science. There are, to be sure, approaches to problem-oriented analysis that have little to do with science. One can take positions of principle that are plausible but have no empirical support, or conduct empirical investigations that take on important questions but vastly oversimplify them. An example of the former is the declaration that "material throughput" in a community (or a nation or the global economy) should be minimized. This exhortation sounds prudent, economical, and environmentally sound, but it provides no basis for action: When you get down to specifics, like how to reduce the use of plastics, it will generally be necessary to increase the use of some materials in order to decrease that of others. An example of an oversimplified empirical study is one that concludes that waste plastics should be incinerated or, for that matter, that they should be recycled. A substantial body of work will be needed before questions of this scope can possibly be answered in such categorical terms. Most studies of this type simply reflect the a priori conviction of the analyst rather than the weight of evidence.

Depending on the degree of specificity, economic reasoning based on general principles has been called pure theory (abstract theorizing by critics), applied or policy analysis, or outright advocacy. All of these have their place. These analyses are able to deliver an enviably simple message. Especially the applied analysts also often exhibit great tolerance for different theoretical perspectives and methods.

This tolerance is called pluralism, and pluralists are reticent to criticize the work of their colleagues, a characteristic that makes for congenial social relations and enjoyable conferences. Furthermore, espousing pluralism is simpler than building a new theoretical framework. Nonpluralists, or researchers with an unwavering preference for a specific theoretical framework and methodological practice, are open to criticism for reductionism, rigidity, and a misplaced concern with rigor.

It is a mistake of historic dimensions, however, to forgo the power of science in addressing society's major challenges. A distinguishing characteristic of scientific inquiry is its openness to unexpected conclusions. By contrast, it is distressingly common among issue-oriented analysts to conduct a study in order to demonstrate their convictions. Advocates believe they know what needs to be done, but it behooves the scientist to be more skeptical and demanding of evidence.

I believe that the fundamental challenge facing civic society today is to figure out what our options are for dealing with social and environmental problems. This requires acts of imagination—the ability to describe novel, untried, but plausible solutions that could represent dramatic departures from present practices. The gift of this type of imagination is probably equally distributed among generalists, specialists, and citizens. Interestingly, the scientific tradition explicitly acknowledges the importance of curiosity about how things work, but not of imagination—the ability to conceive of how things might work differently.

Subsequently, the alternative options, based on imaginative scenarios, require systematic analysis to determine their feasibility and other characteristics. The scientific method is a demonstrated approach for formulating this kind of investigation.

The particular approach that I will develop in the course of this book, structural economics, involves the kind of inquiry that I have been describing. The first step is determining the scope of the inquiry, which I take to be the production and consumption of goods and services and the social and environmental issues surrounding those activities. Then the variables of interest are identified; these include quantitative measures of the amounts of production and consumption of specific goods and services in a particular economy. This specificity makes it possible to distinguish, for example, plastic from steel and uranium or coal from wood. Next a model, or symbolic representation, of the relationships among these variables is needed. Building a model is the familiar process of developing theory, in this case determining the relationships among the production and consumption of plastic, steel, wood, and other inputs and outputs. A mathematical, and therefore formalized and simplified, version of the conceptual model is then developed and used with a body of descriptive data to assess the implications of alternative scenarios about the future. Methodology is needed, as in other scientific endeavors, to assure quality control over the collection and manipulation of the data, which provide empirical content to an analysis. The scenarios are a translation of the acts of imagination about what could be done into the language of the model.

Structural economics bears a family resemblance to neoclassical economics, but there are striking differences between them. In a hypothetico-deductive science like neoclassical economics, most research effort is devoted to stating and proving theorems and testing hypotheses. Hypothesis testing is a way of evaluating the truth or falsity of a more general theory from which the hypothesis is deduced. As a result of the test, it may be possible to reject the hypothesis, implying that the theory is false. In laboratory sciences, experiments are used for a similar purpose. This is not true for structural economics, which is more about constructing solutions than deducing proofs.

In structural economics each scenario about the future could (if one wished) be viewed as a hypothesis or an experiment. But the feasibility at issue is mainly that of the scenario itself, or perhaps of a family of related scenarios, rather than the validity of the theory or model. It is only after cumulative experience with interpreting the results of many such experiments that the researcher might be moved to change or extend the theory—and, in turn, the form of the model. Not only imagination but also inductive reasoning and intuition play a large and explicitly recognized role in the development of theory in structural economics. Research consists of bringing a broadening set of ideas and an expanding body of data into closer correspondence in the process of evaluating alternative prospects for action. This is what I mean by exploiting the power of science for issue-oriented research.

Structural economics represents an effort to apply the power of science to the social domain. It is rooted in economics but requires the participation not only of economists but also of engineers, sociologists, and anthropologists in addressing questions of common interest. At a time when the number of economics majors at universities is falling precipitously, I believe it can help interest young people in taking on these challenges.

Two societies are discussed in this book, those of the United States and, especially, Indonesia. This choice is consistent with the desire to create an analytic framework sufficiently general that it can be useful for both developing and developed countries. Indonesia is the fourth most populous country in the world (after India, China, and the United States) and has a resource-rich economy that was growing rapidly until the financial crisis that began in 1997. These facts, and its geographic location in Southeast Asia, account for its importance among developing countries. Information is available because the Central Bureau of Statistics of Indonesia collects large volumes of economic and social data on a regular basis. Finally, my colleagues and I have been studying strategies for sustainable development in Indonesia for a number of years, and that work provides the point of departure for the analysis described in this volume. My own familiarity with the American economy, its relative size and importance, and the abundant information available about it make it a logical candidate, as well.

From the outset of my team's involvement, the objective of the work in Indonesia was to build a dynamic input–output model and database and a capability for using this modeling system to analyze alternative strategies for environmentally sound economic development. In broad outline this procedure is familiar; there are numerous models, and even several other input–output models, of the Indonesian economy that are used in a similar way. But the limitation of many modeling exercises is that they are far too formal, based on scenarios that are too simple and models and data that are too schematic, to exploit the full potential contribution of economic modeling to the development process. We have tried to increase the realism of this type of exercise.

In Indonesia, as elsewhere, each ministry has its own objectives, but the consequences of each ministry's actions inevitably spill over and have important effects that ripple into the areas of responsibility of other ministries. Our principal challenge in Indonesia was to help institutionalize an iterative process of dialogue among various ministries. Spokesmen would describe their concerns and strategies in a general way. Using this input we would build a scenario, analyze it, and report back the results. In the process, individual objectives and agendas could be confronted and to some extent reconciled. Development strategies need to be built bit by bit, based on the contributions of many people. The broader the constituency involved in the discourse, the more diverse and potentially useful the scenarios will be.

The main themes of this book are introduced in chapter 1. The second chapter describes the analysis of technological change within the structural tradition of input–output analysis. It demonstrates the widely used industrial classification scheme and describes the representation of an industry's technological structure, indicating the nature of collaboration with engineers and other technical specialists. It highlights examples of important empirical results in this area.

Chapter 3 develops the striking parallels in the social significance of changes in technology and changes in lifestyle. Compared to the body of analysis of technology, lifestyle has received extremely little systematic research attention. In this chapter, I discuss the importance of classifying households as a basis for distinguishing their lifestyles and propose a new kind of classification system that has not previously been used in economic analysis.

Structural economics is described in chapter 4 as a representation of the interdependency of the different parts of an economy. I stress its capability to integrate concrete empirical content about technology and lifestyle into a systematic, quantitative data and modeling framework.

Two key components of structural economics are input–output economics and social accounting. Chapter 5 proceeds to describe in detail the social accounting approach. The scholarly literature includes applications of this approach to investigating the role of households in the Indonesian economy. The most important of these studies are reviewed to illustrate these roots of structural economics.

Chapter 6 presents the formal mathematical framework of structural economics, which integrates the social accounting matrix into an extended input–output model. The resulting model is more general than any of those described in the previous chapter and is presented here for the first time.

The households of Indonesia are described in chapter 7 through the use of both qualitative and quantitative information. This information, which should prove interesting to a general reader, is arranged so as to demonstrate the features and the advantages of increasing amounts of structural detail. The final section shows a social accounting matrix for Indonesia in 1985.

Chapter 8 presents a hypothetical scenario about structural change in Indonesia between 1985 and 2000 and analyzes it using the social accounting matrix and the new formal framework. An interpretation of the results is provided.

The final chapter reviews what has been accomplished, points out some shortcomings, and draws conclusions at a number of different levels. The appendices show the classifications and the raw data.

Chapter 1
Origins and Objectives

The term *structural economics,* used to denote a body of theory and empirical research, is not today familiar among economists or other social scientists. There is ample history of a structural approach in the human sciences, however, notably in linguistics, anthropology, and psychology, and development economists since the 1950s have been clearly influenced by the intellectual traditions of structuralism. A number of contemporary economists, including myself, claim to take a structural approach. There is even a professional journal, *Structural Change and Economic Dynamics,* that includes the work of a variety of "heterodox" economists, most of whom would identify with a structuralist tradition. In none of these cases, however, has there been a systematic effort to provide motivation for a structural approach and describe what is meant by economic structure—that is, to bring together objectives and strategies, theory and practice.

Unlike earlier challenges to neoclassical economics, structural economics provides not only a detailed and coherent story that extends an umbrella over diverse lines of inquiry but also a powerful formalism for quantitative evaluation. This approach makes use of familiar ideas and techniques as well as some new ones. The combined power of the story and the formalism is amplified by a purpose that is avowedly pragmatic—as distinguished from the typical objective of theorists, which is to reveal truths and laws that are assumed to be independent of time and place. Namely, structural economics aims to understand and help resolve the important social and environmental challenges of our time. As a by-product, it broadens the scope of conventional economics and invites collaboration with other disciplines.

Numerous attempts have been made to increase the realism of neoclassical economic theory; a celebrated example is institutional economics, which regards markets as substantially governed by rules and norms embodied in social institutions (like laws or labor unions). While many researchers are sympathetic with the critique implicit in institutional economics, when they wish to make computations, they return to the neoclassical framework, which they believe to be the only game in town. Structural economics is a practical construction rather than a critique, in that it offers a computational framework that makes use of mathematics and quantitative information in the fundamental ways that have proven useful in other areas of scientific investigation.

Structural economics is concerned with describing the state, or structure, of an economic system and with the quantitative and qualitative changes that take place in that structure with the passage of time. The structure is defined in terms of production and consumption activities, the considerations important for those social units engaged in production and consumption, and the physical input and output flows involved in those activities. The economy is treated as a system, in that it is a set of interrelated component activities. The theory about the working of this system can be called operational in the sense that it is faithfully represented by sets of mathematical equations, or models. The models consist of equations containing variables, corresponding to important activities, and constant parameters, whose values describe the relations among the variables. Like the variables, the parameters are directly measurable. The practical significance of the mathematical equations is that they permit quantitative evaluations.

The main variables in structural economic theory describe the activities carried out in industrial sectors and in different kinds of households. Each sector or household type is said to have a structure. The electric power sector, for example, procures and prepares fuels, generates electricity, and then distributes power. It has a specific mix of inputs and a particular distribution of its output to users—this is its structure. Change takes place when a new set of inputs, processes, and outputs, one out of various possible alternatives, is substituted for the old one. For example, it might change its

materials that could be anticipated if specific kinds of households started purchasing homes constructed in different ways, or changed their diets.

The attributes of models depend on their mathematical formulations. They may be linear or nonlinear, deterministic or probabilistic, discrete or continuous. Neoclassical models are nonlinear, probabilistic, and continuous. Some of the models of structural economics are nonlinear (the dynamic ones), but all are deterministic and discrete.

A model is said to be deterministic if the key relationships are represented explicitly and directly (as in the simple equation above). It is probabilistic if the assumptions allow randomness in the distribution of the variables. After the deterministic aspects have been described in a structural model, an unexplained residual will undeniably remain. For example, in the wood equation given above, there is no way to describe variations in wood requirements from one house to another. Such variations exist, but their significance is small relative to the quantities that are explicitly captured in the equation.

The wood equation represents production requirements at one point in time—say, in the course of a given year. A more complicated equation (actually a system of equations) is required to represent changes in production from one year to the next. A discrete model represents distinct states and can show the changes from one state to another, changes not only in the strengths of relationships (e.g., the amount of wood to make an average house) but even in the identity of important variables (like a switch from wood to steel). A continuous model, by contrast, is less concerned with the relations among variables at a given time than with the rates of change of the same variables over time.

The Origins of Structural Economics

Structural economics makes full use of the thought, mathematical formulations, and applied work of two twentieth-century economists, both Nobel laureates: Wassily Leontief, who created input–output economics and applied it to studying technological change, and Richard Stone, who extended input–output economics into social and demographic areas. It integrates those frameworks and substantially extends them in terms of scope, mathematical formalism, and empirical content. Structural economics is also influenced by ideas that have arisen largely outside of the economics profession. It adopts the problem-oriented pragmatism, a disregard for disciplinary boundaries, and respect for imagination and the experience of nonspecialists that are characteristic of ecological economics. Finally, structural economics overlaps with another new field, industrial ecology, in the importance it accords to the use of energy and materials in production and consumption activities and to a life-cycle approach to assessing costs and benefits.

In most of these ways structural economics is readily distinguished from neoclassical economic theory and practice, the dominant paradigm for academic economics throughout the twentieth century. Neoclassical economics is highly specialized and intolerant of "amateurs"—i.e., noneconomists. Despite the nominal importance accorded to technology, it can hardly be said to incorporate the expertise of engineers in its framework, and representation of technology is mainly symbolic. Neoclassical economists' view of individuals and what is important about their lives in society appears to have little if any common ground with the concerns of sociologists and anthropologists. Their emphasis on economic laws and theorems about rational decisions is based exclusively on stylized, utilitarian considerations, which are assumed to transcend specific social settings. Neoclassical economics treats production and consumption decisions as subject to small, continuous changes and in practice relies on the indirect approach of statistical inference about the values of random variables to quantify parameters. No variables are considered relevant unless they are—or at least in principle can be—measured in money units. For the neoclassical economist, the dominant feature of an economy is the set of so-called equilibrium prices toward which it is assumed to be moving.

A powerful example of a structural model that uses bold simplification to highlight important variables and relationships is the original input–output formulation of Wassily Leontief. He developed a linear, deterministic model and accompanying database to depict production and consumption activities using a set of equations like the one described earlier. The input–output framework will be described in substantial detail in subsequent chapters.

The early development economists valued input–output economics because it represented the interdependency of the major parts of an economic system. In addition, the 1950s and 1960s saw a considerable flurry of interest among prominent economic theorists (many of whom were students of Leontief's at Harvard) in the mathematics of the dynamic input–output formulation. Nonetheless, the input–output model was subsequently stripped of academic respectability for one main reason: It fails to honor the central conviction of neoclassical economics, namely, that the most important economic effects (if not all of them) are reflected in and follow predictably from changes in prices. The unfortunate reality is that many input–output economists have actually accepted this indictment and are apologetic about what in fact is their greatest strength.

The great strength of input–output models is that they feature a physical description of production and consumption activities in terms of inputs per unit of output. Changes in the values of inputs need to be explained by a physical logic, such as a change in combustion technology (or in packaging practices) that is adopted when the prices of fuels (or landfill fees) change. Physical quantities do not in some mechanical way "equilibrate" following changes in prices. Instead, the analyst needs to provide an explicit logic about technological alternatives to link changes in prices with associated changes in physical input structures. In neoclassical models, these changes are automatically governed by a set of "elasticity" parameters. Despite their criticisms, however, neither practitioners with, say, policy responsibilities nor even applied neoclassical modelers have failed to exploit the practical usefulness of input–output economics. Virtually all large macroeconomic or general equilibrium models include an input–output portion, which serves to disaggregate results but is not treated as part of the theoretical structure.

Input–output economics makes the mainstream economist uncomfortable. When included in textbooks, it is classified sometimes as part of microeconomics and sometimes as part of macroeconomics. Since these two major subfields of neoclassical economics are considered non-overlapping, it is clear that input–output economics, and the structural economics that builds upon it, does not fit in to neoclassical economics. The time has come for establishing structural economics as a viable, independent field that provides an alternative to neoclassical economics.

Structural Economics and Development

An explicit focus on how people live brings social and demographic phenomena, and the material aspects of everyday life, into the analysis of structural change. Such a focus has been largely absent from work on sustainable development and from the main body of economic studies more generally. Structural economics provides an approach for situating economic activities in a broader environmental, technological, social, demographic, and cultural context that can support quantitative as well as qualitative analysis. The analyst can explore alternatives available to different industries and social groups along with the major structural changes to which they are exposed. The framework is applied in this book in a case study of Indonesia, which has already served as a model for similar studies in other countries.

Development poses challenges not only at the local and national levels but also at the global level. The drastic differences in the material standards of living in the rich and the poor countries create a potentially explosive social situation. The strenuous pursuit of new technologies for industrialization is likely to succeed in raising the standards of living in developing countries substantially. However, it will also put increasing pressure on social organization and on the physical environment—the fundamental long-term problem for life on earth.

Virtually all work to date by economists about reducing pressures on the environment is focused on ways of changing the money costs of making alternative decisions, for example by shifting the burden of taxation away from income and employment toward the generation of pollution. The resulting change in relative costs can stimulate the adoption of cleaner production techniques that are cost-effective under the new but not the old regime of taxes, licenses, permits, and so on. It is assumed that such techniques will be forthcoming, but no attempt is generally made to specify what they might be.

I believe that the fundamental challenge is a different one: the actual specification of less polluting techniques for generating energy and transforming materials. It is not economists but engineers and applied physical scientists who have followed this route. New fields concerned with the development of environmentally benign techniques, such as industrial ecology, are beginning to articulate viable technological alternatives. This work can make available new options for which the relative costs would presumably be lowered by the economists' incentive schemes.

The potential to substantially reduce all forms of environmental degradation, however, depends not only on economic instruments and new technologies but also on legislation, education, and the cooperation of citizens in their various public and private capacities.

One of the clearest lessons about economic development is the importance of involving in the decision-making process those whose lives are affected by the changes; otherwise, change will come very slowly if at all. Understanding how to do this effectively and on a large scale poses a challenge to social scientists (among others) that remains largely unmet in the absence of a systematic approach to the lifestyle decisions of households.

For the past half century, economic development has been the goal of a wide variety of countries that share a perception of themselves as poor and far distant from the various frontiers that define the modern world. Their objectives have been to increase national wealth and reduce poverty by benefiting from all the perceived advantages that the Industrial Revolution conferred on the rich, industrialized societies. The latter have encouraged this orientation by providing a willing role model, technical and institutional advice of many sorts, and financial assistance—as well as commercial loans, marketed goods and services, and direct investment. Naturally, traditional societies have undergone substantial transformation in the course of these historic events. Under the tutelage of the United Nations they have created statistical offices to collect information of prescribed sorts to help them, as well as interested parties in the rich countries, to gauge the nature and extent of the changes.

Thoughtful observers of structural change readily acknowledge that economic development eludes a simple definition. There are various measures of success or failure, but they tell only fragments of a complex story. Nonetheless, the idea of growth in its various manifestations has become tightly linked with economic development. Growth in the size of the population is an attribute of all developing countries today, and it is relatively easily measured. But the real objective of development is the expansion of those economic activities that are considered modern. A common measure used to assess the latter is gross national product (GNP). GNP can be measured in one of two ways: the sum of incomes paid to citizens in wages, profits, and resource rents; or, alternatively, the total value of those goods and services that are sold to final consumers. (That these two quantities should be equal is a definition that drives the national accounting system.) A major deficiency of GNP as a measure of beneficial development has been widely noted; namely, it fails to adequately reflect relevant activities and phenomena, both desirable (like the produce from community gardens) and undesirable (like pollution), that are not monetized. Of course, even for the activities that are counted, the sum of incomes paid out is only an indirect measure of the volume and importance of an enterprise. This oversimplified index is popular because it is much easier to measure GNP and growth in GNP than it would be to sort out the actual significance of the cataclysmic social changes that accompany growth. At the present time it is common in many circles to envy a country with GNP growing at, say, 8 percent a year, without probing into the social and environmental changes that are necessarily also taking place.

In the rich countries, population growth has leveled off, and so has economic expansion—at least relative to many developing countries. There is substantial concern in those countries about inadequate numbers of jobs, immigration pressures, and antisocial behavior that often takes violent forms. The statistical offices of the rich countries track unemployment, immigration, and crime as well as production, consumption, taxes, trade, pollution, and so on. However, a great deal of their attention, and that of economists and other analysts, is still focused on measuring growth—based on the lingering conviction that the best way for a country to resolve social and environmental problems is to grow out of them.

There is no doubt that the developing countries are undergoing substantial restructuring and not only expansion and that the rich countries are concerned with growth as well as restructuring. As the former are incorporated into the emerging global economy through their reliance on imports and promotion of exports, the prospect for continued growth of the rich economies acquires an increasingly obvious international significance. The rate of return on investment tends to increase with the rate of growth of an economy, and the fastest-growing economies today are the so-called newly industrializing ones. Thus profits in the rich countries will rely more and more on investing in the faster-growing, poor countries. An integrated conception of global development will describe the changes experienced by any economy as a consequence of its attempts to improve its material situation, and it needs to encompass both a quantitative and a qualitative dimension. A common approach to development is more powerful than two less general ones, one for industrialized economies and another for nonindustrialized ones. Structural economics provides a single framework that is equally suited for analyzing development scenarios about developed and developing economies. Naturally, detailed objectives and outcomes will be specific to each place and time.

Sustainability

In the 1980s the ambiguities already surrounding the meaning of economic development became vastly compounded when a widely discussed document, often called the Brundtland Report,[2] popularized the term *sustainable development*. Sustainable development is, broadly speaking, development that does not harm the natural world. But, given the ambiguities surrounding development, it will come as no surprise that a rigorous, concise definition for sustainable development has eluded ecologists, the specialists who might have been expected to produce an appropriate interpretation for sustainability. Thus, the attempt to come to consensus on a definition for sustainable development has a double air of unreality. One could probably fill a book with refinements of, objections to, and replacements for the definition offered in the Brundtland Report.[3] This spectacle has led many observers to dismiss "sustainable development" as a vacuous term.

There can be no formulaic prescription for development in any particular time and place, nor can there be a simple formula for deducing its impact on the natural world. More fundamentally, there are no unambiguous criteria for judging the degree of success or failure of any specific development effort. Despite this dilemma, reasonable guidelines do exist for recognizing environmentally sound economic development.

There are various evaluation frameworks for determining whether sustainable development has taken place. A simple method is to create an "indicator" of sustainability to place alongside GNP or some other measure of economic development. Sustainable development could be said to occur if both indicators increase simultaneously. Aggregate indicators like these, and even more detailed ones (such as the number of species lost in an ecosystem), have the appeal of comprehensive coverage, as each one takes the net effects of many subsidiary activities into account. A great deal of effort is being devoted to the creation of new indicators. However, a mathematical model of the economy, which not only identifies the key economic, social, and environmental variables but also describes the relationships among them, is required for a more elaborated evaluation framework. While indicators can be helpful in evaluating past courses of action, models are needed for analyzing prospective future ones. Structural economics is concerned with model-based analysis and not only with indicators.

It is important to recognize that the authors of the Brundtland Report took on a different challenge from that of evaluation. They started from the conviction that sustainable development is in most instances not taking place. They then proceeded to describe in substantial detail the kinds of actions that would need to be taken in the future in order to reconcile continued economic growth in both rich and poor countries with reduced pressures on the environment. I initially became involved with this set of recommendations when asked by the government of Norway and the United Nations to evaluate their plausibility as part of the preparations for the Earth Summit that took place in Rio de Janeiro in 1992.

In the course of that work my colleagues and I examined and documented the technologies currently in place in all geographic regions. Then we constructed scenarios about the rapid phasing in of cleaner, more efficient technological options in all regions of the world. The scenarios were evaluated using a model and database of the world economy, the first versions of which had been developed for the United Nations under the direction of Wassily Leontief (Leontief, Carter, and Petri 1977). On the basis of this work, we concluded that the outlook of the Brundtland Report was unrealistically reassuring. The kinds of means that were being proposed—such as more extensive recycling of materials and more fuel-efficient cars—could achieve the economic objectives that had been targeted for many individual countries and for the world as a whole, but they could not also achieve the environmental ones. As population and affluence increased, pollution could also be expected to grow—although not nearly as steeply as if no corrective actions had been taken.

The book that resulted from this research (Duchin and Lange 1994) contributed to the methods and ideas developed in the present volume. In particular, our evaluation concluded that much bolder technological and social changes would need to be envisaged than those discussed in the Brundtland Report and mentioned a few possibilities, focused mainly on technological approaches, like increased use of fuels and materials from renewable sources. Another option we mentioned was the reduced use of cars, which would require changes in the layout of communities. It already occurred to us that achieving these kinds of objectives would not begin with new general principles but rather would require digging more deeply into the specific situations in different parts of the world (Duchin and Lange 1994, 8–9).

The Industrialized World

In pondering the results of this analysis, I became increasingly convinced that there were two main avenues for bolder scenarios: technological change and change in the lifestyles of households. The most promising prospects seemed to require both kinds of changes to reinforce each other. But who might take the initiative for instigating these kinds of changes? Automobile manufacturers would produce more fuel-efficient cars if they thought the public would buy them at the prices they would need to charge, especially if prodded by government incentives or regulations. The individual consumer in a rich country would weigh the purchase price, the annual cost differential for gasoline, and in many cases the desire to reduce pollution, and then select which car to buy. In this kind of case, the interlocking incentives are evident. A well-defined set of actors would be involved in well-defined decisions, with restricted prospects for truly surprising outcomes.

Consider the contrast between an objective of more fuel-efficient cars and one of reducing automobile use through the spread of communities of relatively high density based on the spatial integration of residential, commercial, and business activities. Even in the simplest conception, mixed-use communities require the design skills of various specialists, political processes such as zoning changes, expensive public infrastructure, and the buy-in of businesses and residents. Powerful vested interests are invariably challenged. Many kinds of actors would need to collaborate in undertakings based on long-term thinking involving fundamental uncertainties. Clearly, the first efforts would need to be the work of pioneers. And one would need more than a few isolated successes to create a viable, generalizable model. The effectiveness of a limited number of demonstration projects would need to be very strong indeed in order for a geographic region supporting millions of people to be able to deal in this way with the transformation of its transportation networks.

A scenario about reduced reliance on cars in all parts of the world is substantially more interesting but harder to construct than one about fuel-efficient cars. Would mobility be maintained but furnished by other modes of transportation? Would changes in the layout of communities make it convenient for people to reduce their mobility without lowering their satisfaction? It would be foolhardy to try to construct a global scenario about reduced automobile use at the present time because there are too many missing pieces in the story. I believe that we should approach this challenge by first gaining experience in building and analyzing more tractable scenarios. Alternative economy-wide approaches to the handling of plastics (see Duchin 1994; Duchin and Lange, 1998) are a good example. A substantial effort is required to make them concrete, as they rely on actions taken by producers of polymers, a large variety of manufacturers using plastics for goods or packaging, municipalities in their waste-handling practices, governments establishing standards and regulations, and consumers making purchases and disposing of wastes. The familiar element of technological choice is apparent in these scenarios, as is the role of government in providing services and possibly incentives and regulations.

But the old notion of the consumer concerned only with getting the most products for the least money and effort needs to be replaced by a more complex actor. Citizens want a decent quality of life in the form of a way to make a livelihood, clean air and water, reduced traffic delays and congestion, and reasonable ways of disposing of smaller amounts of wastes. Most decisions affecting an individual's lifestyle reflect the characteristics of the household in which he or she lives, and household lifestyle decisions, while a fundamental part of social change, have so far been absent from all of the scenario-based economic analyses about sustainable development.

The potential importance of household lifestyle decisions, as distinct from decisions made passively in response to changes in incomes and prices, was highlighted in one of the major debates at the Earth Summit. Many representatives of rich countries identified the large and growing populations of developing countries as the principal problem requiring redress, and the developing countries countered with charges of "overconsumption" in the rich countries, pointing out that one American in his or her lifetime consumes as much as do several dozen Indians, for example. In the years since then, the consumption patterns of the middle classes in affluent countries have received increasing attention, at least in the United States, from private foundations, a vanguard of social scientists, and popular authors. In addition, there is evidence of a voluntary reexamination of consumption priorities by individuals and citizen groups, although the scale of this phenomenon is hard to assess. The idea is that citizens of the rich countries might be ready to work less, earn less, and consume less, in part to reduce pressures on the environment and set a better example for the developing countries to follow. Analysis by social scientists of alternative lifestyle options could capture people's imaginations as much as environmental concerns have.

Sustainability and Growth in Industrializing Nations

While discussing the consumption practices of the middle class in the rich countries with other economists, and increasingly with anthropologists and sociologists, I thought in parallel about household lifestyles in poor countries. Following our analysis for the Earth Summit, I had been asked to apply this approach of building and analyzing scenarios about sustainable development to the specific problems of developing countries, starting with Indonesia, a country with an exemplary official economic database. Senior officials at the Ministry of Planning specified the basic ideas behind the development strategies for Indonesia. The scenarios assumed rapid expansion of manufacturing based on modern technologies. They also assumed growth of selected exports, an upgrading of the diet (more animal products and vegetables) for a growing population on a contracting land base, and more intensive management of forests and plantations to support an expanded pulp and paper industry.

The main economic objective is rapid growth. But the fastest-growing industries are less labor intensive than are those in which employment is contracting, notably agriculture. Thus, there is concern that the number of future jobs may be inadequate to support an expanding and increasingly urban population. The main environmental preoccupations are to assure the availability and quality of water and to slow the erosion of land.

Our analysis pinpointed the substantial difficulties that are likely to be faced in addressing environmental challenges over the next decade (Duchin, Hamilton, and Lange 1993; Duchin and Lange 1993). With respect to employment, however, we came to a reassuring conclusion. It is true that modern industries are less labor intensive than agriculture. However, the rapid growth assumed in the industrialization scenarios, which seemed plausible based on the history of recent years, more than offset the relatively low labor requirements of the fastest-growing industries. As a consequence, employment would grow fast enough to absorb not only new labor force entrants but also virtually all of the "disguised unemployment" in both rural and urban areas.

There was an important reservation, however. This would be

true provided that those available for work were able to do the kinds of tasks expected of them in industrialized settings. Clearly, meeting this challenge would be much more difficult than training old workers in new skills. There is no contemporary equivalent in industrialized countries to the difficulty of incorporating tribal peoples and peasants into modern work settings not only in rural locations but also in urban factories and offices. The result is a very large, ill-defined "informal" economy, which exists in virtually all developing countries. Informal businesses tend to be very small, avoid taxes, and have difficulty obtaining loans from banks. Their workers have no job security, and many of their activities are outside the formal economy. Most informal workers are engaged in construction activities, transportation services, or retail trade in cities and agriculture in the countryside. These crucial activities, which provide a buffer between traditional and modern ways, are only beginning to be studied, in part because they are ill described using the kinds of concepts that have been borrowed from the rich countries, where "informal" means mainly illegal for most economists.

Problems associated with industrialization include new forms of environmental stress and dependence on the rich countries for new technologies. In the social realm, market-based institutions tend to be imported along with aid, investment, and goods and services. Even when markets are only incompletely developed and barely integrated, market relations tend to displace traditional social practices and institutions.

With industrialization, there has historically been a transformation of the size and composition of households and of the balance between household and community work and different types of work for money wages. In a widening circle, the changes affect working-aged men, working-aged women, their old and young dependents, and community relationships. New needs and activities emerge: for example, changed child-care arrangements, or the purchase of kerosene for cooking in place of the collection of firewood.

Even in rapidly industrializing countries like Indonesia, a significant share of the population will continue to rely on agriculture for their livelihoods over the foreseeable future. Modernization generally entails the intensification of agricultural activities, often with increased use of chemicals and machinery for a given yield. Such changes pose both continuing and new environmental challenges and displace many peasant households whose members will need to find new forms of livelihood and in the process transform the social support networks on which they have traditionally depended. If there are not adequate opportunities to make a livelihood in rural areas, they will migrate to cities in numbers far too large to be absorbed in an orderly way. The government has tried to act through bold social policies like the relocation of very large numbers of households under the "transmigration" program. The program is only nominally voluntary and at best marginally successful. Clearly, other kinds of options are needed, especially for those households in both rural and urban areas that are only loosely associated with the monetized economy. Through a better understanding of the different categories of households and their lifestyles, and of alternative industrialization scenarios, it is possible to anticipate the kinds of social changes at the local, regional, and national levels that might accompany alternative patterns of development. Many governments attach substantial importance to social and cultural objectives, yet their policies strongly favor the modern over the traditional and they focus more attention and resources on achieving economic growth than on anticipating, in order to mitigate, undesirable social consequences.

The Crucial Importance of Household Choices

For most contemporary economists, the primary engine of development and growth is market exchange. In this view, the producer seeks to expand sales and reduce costs, while the consumer wants to earn and consume more and pay less. New technologies and a more efficient allocation of resources make it possible to satisfy both of these desires. Government agencies provide some social services and play a role in coordinating and regulating private activities. Consumers set the goals for both business and government in a highly decentralized fashion—as an outcome of how millions of individuals spend their dollars and cast their votes.

Unlike economists, sociologists recognize the importance of social movements as a fundamental force behind social change. Both individually and in more or less organized groupings, people perceive discrepancies between how things are and how they would like them to be and act on those perceptions. In some situations they have leaders and a vision and take some initiative; in others, they are passively responding to changes largely beyond their control.

Economists' treatment of development ignores social movements in part because they are based on social and political motives (e.g., the women's movement or the civil rights movement) rather than mainly economic ones. The economic outcomes (like improved wage rates for women and minorities) are naturally recognized, but the noneconomic aspects of the decision-making processes of the social actors are ignored.

People as citizens are agents of change. People live in households, and households are grouped in communities. Perhaps the most important reason for elaborating the treatment of households within structural economics is to facilitate an analysis of the transformative capability of ordinary people as part of the communities and social contexts in which they live and act. Social scientists are interested in different aspects of people's behavior: Economists study their consumption patterns, and political scientists study their voting patterns, while policy makers attempt to influence their decisions. What has been missing is a systematic body of research and development (analogous to the R&D provided to businesses) to help people make lifestyle decisions based on an in-depth consideration of their alternatives. A necessary step in this direction is to create the framework for such analysis.

My objective is to develop a framework suitable for representing lifestyle options. I refer to the collection of roles a person plays as a lifestyle and focus on the lifestyles of households, thus replacing the economist's usual unit of the individual as consumer with a socially more inclusive one. A related objective is to classify households in ways that illuminate each category's distinctive social and economic roles and behaviors, options, and inclinations. Then it will be possible to build alternative scenarios about different lifestyle options for different categories of households. This kind of analysis could prove as useful to the decision-making processes of households and larger social organizations, namely communities, as the extensive specialized and popular literatures about technological options are to corporate decision makers. In a more general way, an understanding of the implications of such changes in lifestyles is important for corporations selling goods and services, government agencies providing services and collecting taxes, and citizens concerned about the overall quality of life in their society.

In the rich countries there is the real possibility that over the next several decades, households and other social units will take the initiative in changing important features of today's lifestyles. In the developing countries, the next several decades will probably be a period of even more substantial changes in households' lifestyles, but changes that reflect survival strategies for adapting to changed circumstances. Both kinds of situations would be well served by a common conceptual framework that does not now exist, one that starts with an appropriate classification of households in a given place and time and a description of the lifestyle of each kind of household. An example category in the United States would be the household of an individual over seventy-five years old, retired from a professional job and living alone in an urban area. This category is probably too small to be of interest in Indonesia. There a relevant category might be a rural household of four adults and four or more children, in which one adult is a paid government employee and the others are unpaid agricultural workers. In each case, the average pattern of consumption and the mix of income sources would be part of the description of that household category's lifestyle.

The most important contribution of economics to sustainable development is the provision of a system-wide framework that is suitable for comparing the implications of alternative future courses of action. Economists may simplify the determination of what should be measured, how it is measured, and the relations assumed in mathematical equations; but because they are able to come to conclusions that are concise and concrete, they can hope to provide a basis for action.

Sociologists and anthropologists insist upon context-sensitive distinctions that provide a nuanced description of what is really happening, evocatively called "thick description" by C. Geertz (1973), but that eludes mathematical representation. They also have an understanding of households, lifestyles, and the social fabric that so far has been absent from the largely formalistic work of economists in the area called household economics. It would obviously be of great value to integrate empirical content from the other social sciences with what could be called the systems approach of economics. This has, of course, been tried but without resounding success as yet.

Structural economics provides a conceptual framework that captures the fundamental interrelationships among the economic, social, and environmental aspects of making a living in a particular society. It is *issue-oriented* in that the development scenarios to be analyzed provide the driving force behind it. Structural models rely on national accounting systems for input–output tables, which are now systematically collected in most countries on a periodic basis. They also use two sets of related data that national statistical offices around the world are beginning to compile: natural resource accounts and social accounting matrices.

The social accounting matrix is a generalization of the input–output table that includes additional detail about the income generated for institutions by the factors of production. Different categories of households (among the institutions) and of labor (among the factors of production) are distinguished. For each household category, a social accounting matrix describes its consumption of goods and services and its provision of labor to the different sectors of the economy.

Principles for classifying households in social accounting matrices have not yet been adequately developed, and analysis of households has focused exclusively on the distribution of income. Structural economics will require case studies that draw on all the social sciences to identify a basic set of household categories for a particular society and describe the dominant lifestyles of those households. Such a description will provide an anchor for alternative scenarios about changes in lifestyle.

I attempt in the following chapters of this book to take first steps in a few new directions. I start and remain within the framework of structural economics, extended here from a framework for studying technological change to one that also includes a more adequate treatment of households and their activities. The process involves interplay among several strands. A conceptual framework represents the activities of different kinds of households and their relations to various economic activities. The data are collected to describe household lifestyles. An analytic framework is developed for the mathematical analysis of these data. Finally, scenarios describe the kinds of lifestyle changes that could be analyzed. In each of these areas structural economics already provides an operational starting point.

NOTES

1. In a more detailed representation with dozens of sectors, this .2 might represent the amount of wood required (per cubic foot of wood output) to build a factory for processing wood.

2. The report of the World Commission on Environment and Development (WCED), 1987. G. Brundtland, prime minister of Norway, chaired the commission.

3. "Sustainable development seeks to meet the needs and aspirations of the present without compromising the ability to meet those of the future" (WCED 1987, 40).

Chapter 2

The Analysis of Technological Change

Humans, unlike any other forms of life, have devised techniques for evading the confines of the local environment and inhabit the globe as if it were a single ecosystem (Eldredge 1995). This problematic achievement has convinced prominent life scientists that, for the first time, social decisions are as important as biological evolution in influencing the future prospects for life on Earth.

Technology is the fundamental determinant of the impact human society has on its environment. The Industrial Revolution launched an era of remarkable progress in focusing human ingenuity on the practical objectives of generating, storing, and transmitting energy and on extracting and transforming metals and other minerals. Since then we have come to expect increasing material comfort in everyday life and the endless technological innovation that makes it possible. The global networks of extremely mobile researchers, businesspeople, and financiers have assured relatively rapid international access to the ideas behind new technologies, independent of where they were developed.

While economics is about what is produced and consumed in a society and how those activities are carried out, structural economics goes a step further to provide a distinctive framework for describing production activities in terms of specific technologies and the inputs and outputs associated with each. The power of the approach is achieved through the structure provided by industrial classification schemes and a systematic way of representing inputs and outputs associated with the technologies in use in each industry. Assuming we know a society's requirements for consumption goods and services, and the technologies by which the individual goods and services will be produced, then it is possible to compute the total production volumes for items such as cement, paper, and automobiles. The need for different categories of laborers, from cement mixers to automobile mechanics, can also be determined and linked to the wages they earn and the goods and services consumed in their households. The energy and material requirements and the various wastes associated with production can also be quantified.

Input–output economics is focused especially on production technologies and changes in technology. It is a systems approach for describing technology and studying its effects. Wassily Leontief demonstrated its power in several important empirical studies carried out while he was at Harvard. In the late 1970s he founded the Institute for Economic Analysis at New York University and initiated a new set of studies to explore concerns that he had had for many decades. Leontief worried that technological change in the late twentieth century, mainly computer-based automation, would erode the material well-being of large numbers of people who depend on their wages by making it possible to produce more with far less labor. If empirical analysis confirmed this outcome, he was interested in investigating corporate and government policies that might promote, for example, worker ownership plans, so as to at least partially decouple income from labor.

However, when the results of our analyses suggested that technological change alone would not displace labor at alarming rates, the focus of the inquiry began to shift. I personally became increasingly convinced that the environmental consequences of technological choices and technological change were as important as the direct social implications.

A number of these empirical investigations are described later in this chapter. First, scenario assumptions from four studies (one on automation and three related to the environment) are reported to demonstrate how data are developed for input–output case studies. Then selected empirical results are presented. They range from the well-known Leontief paradox established in the 1950s (about the role of labor in American imports and exports), through the research on automation in the 1980s, to a sequence of studies in the 1990s

mix of fuels or start purchasing electricity from secondary producers, like pulp and paper mills. These would be changes in structure.
(This notion of structure and change in structure can be contrasted
with the slow, continuous, smooth changes in individual variables
that characterize neoclassical economics.)

A theory is described in words. A mathematical model translates
the words into a set of mathematical equations. The theory is necessarily richer than its formal transcription, but a model is needed
for numerical computations. It is ultimately a matter of judgment,
based in part on the ability of the model to produce more or less
compelling empirical results, whether the theory is sound and
whether the model is a faithful reflection of it.

The relationships among variables in an equation can be illustrated by the example of a simplified economy in which grain, wood,
and houses are produced. The equation for determining wood production might take the following, particularly simple form:

$$x_1 = 0.2x_1 + 0.5x_2 + 1,000x_3 + 25,000$$

There are three variables: x_1 measures cubic feet of wood produced,[1] x_2 is the number of tons of grain, and x_3 is the number of
houses. The equation states that this economy has the following
requirements for wood: 0.2 cubic feet for each cubic foot of wood
produced,[1] 0.5 cubic feet for each ton of grain, 1,000 cubic feet for
each house, and an additional 25,000 cubic feet delivered directly to
households, perhaps for their wood-burning stoves. The statement
that the equation is linear is illustrated by the fact that each additional ton of grain will require an additional 0.5 cubic feet of wood:
the requirement will not rise or fall depending on the level of grain
production. The figures 0.2 and 0.5 are parameters; this means that
they need to be provided by the analyst as part of the database and
may change under alternative scenarios. For example, the wood
parameter for houses will fall if houses begin to be constructed of
stone or brick instead of wood. The analyst has also provided the figure 25,000. That figure would fall if households started using other
heating methods, for example. The values of the variables are determined by the computation. If the parameters are changed, the variables will take on new values.

Now imagine a model with a hundred sectors instead of three,
and ten categories of households instead of a single one. One could
use this model to inquire into the change in the use of energy and

that examine the relationship between the choice of technology and environmental degradation.

Industrial Classification Schemes

Most technological choices are made in millions of individual business establishments when managers decide what to produce and how to produce it. Different establishments in the same industry may make somewhat different determinations even though they produce similar goods and services. Within any society, however, there will in practice be only a limited number of ways to grow grain, to make steel, and to generate electricity.

The systematic categorization of business establishments is indispensable for research and analysis in structural economics. The classification principles and associated codes that constitute the Standard Industrial Classification, or SIC, are widely used by businesses for reporting and analysis. The United Nations Statistical Office has produced an International Standard Industrial Classification, and most countries adopt a more or less customized version of it, which provides more detail for the industries in which they are active and less for the others. There are strong common elements in the schemes used in different countries, but they are far from identical.

A moderately detailed version of the Standard Industrial Classification scheme used by the U.S. Department of Commerce is shown in appendix A. A more aggregated version, of nine major industrial sectors that are intended to cover all economic activities, is shown in table 2.1. These activities include two extractive sectors (agriculture and mining), construction, manufacturing, and four service sectors. Both classifications have the important property of providing a *partition* of business establishments: that is, every establishment is meant to be assignable to one, and only one, of these sectors. Thus a farm falls under agriculture, and a steel factory under manufacturing. When the use of a partition is practical, as it is for categorizing business establishments, it offers advantages that no other classification principle can match.

Each of these major categories is subdivided into increasingly finer classifications. The classification in the appendix table, which partitions all of the several million business establishments in the United States into fewer than a hundred categories, is at the level of detail most widely utilized in analysis.

The SIC codes can be disaggregated to the four-digit level, which

TABLE 2.1. AGGREGATED INDUSTRIAL CLASSIFICATION

Sector	Codes
1 Agriculture, forestry, and fisheries	1–4
2 Mining	5–8
3 Construction	9–10
4 Manufacturing	11–62
5 Transportation, communication, and utilities	63–72
6 Wholesale and retail trade	73–74
7 Finance, insurance, and real estate	75–78
8 Services	79–89
9 Government enterprises	90–91

Note: Codes are consistent with those in appendix A.

includes over a thousand categories. Individual establishments will sometimes disaggregate these codes even further in order to make fine distinctions among their inputs or their outputs. An analyst might choose to use the two-digit scheme for most sectors but include greater detail for a part of the economy of particular interest, say, chemicals. A study might be carried out at the four-digit level but report results aggregated to the much smaller number of one-digit categories. Ease of customizing the degree of detail, and of readily aggregating and disaggregating categories, is made possible by the multileveled structure built into the Standard Industrial Classification. A slightly modified version of the two-digit classification is shown in appendix A. This simple but powerful structure incorporates numerous assumptions that are consequently shared by independently conducted studies, assuring that their results will be substantially compatible.

In April 1997, after several years of preparations, a major change in industrial classifications was announced in the United States: the Standard Industrial Classification, created in the 1930s and last modified in 1987, would be replaced by the North American Industrial Classification System (NAICS), which will be used for the first time in 1999 to present the results of the Economic Census for 1997.

Based on a fresh assessment of economic structure rather than modification of an existing classification, the new system differs from earlier industrial classifications in several ways. The categories are intended to describe equally well the structures of three different economies, those of Canada, the United States, and Mexico, while also being compatible up to a certain level of detail with the International Standard Industrial Classification of the United Nations.

The system explicitly distinguishes modern manufacturing industries that had not previously been identified, as well as an enormously expanded array of marketed services. In its most compact form the NAICS covers the economy in terms of twenty sectors, compared to just nine for the SIC; these are shown in table 2.2.

The NAICS expands the twenty two-digit sectors to six-digit codes describing some twelve hundred industries, compared to the approximately one thousand four-digit codes of the SIC. The intention of both numerical schemes is to achieve a logical structure that describes the current state of the economy while leaving room for modification and future expansion. The new industries that will be added in the U.S. version of the NAICS reflect the nature of technological change in the late twentieth century. Paging is part of an entirely new, two-digit information sector. This sector (#51 in tables 2.2 and 2.3) is intended to group together industries that create or disseminate products with "intellectual property" content. Likewise, arts, entertainment, and recreation (#71 in table 2.2) includes twenty-five industries, nineteen of which are new. The NAICS scheme includes 359 industries that were not distinguished in even the most

TABLE 2.2. NORTH AMERICAN INDUSTRIAL CLASSIFICATION SYSTEM (NAICS)

	Sector	2-Digit Codes
1	Agriculture, forestry, fishing, and hunting	11
2	Mining	21
3	Utilities	22
4	Construction	23
5	Manufacturing	31–33
6	Wholesale trade	42
7	Retail trade	44–45
8	Transportation	48–49
9	Information	51
10	Finance and insurance	52
11	Real estate and rental and leasing	53
12	Professional, scientific, and technical services	54
13	Management of companies and enterprises	55
14	Administrative and support, waste management and remediation services	56
15	Educational services	61
16	Health care and social assistance	62
17	Arts, entertainment, and recreation	71
18	Accommodation and food services	72
19	Other services (except public administration)	81
20	Public administration	92

Note: Compare with the system in table 2.1.

TABLE 2.3. EXAMPLES OF SECTORAL DISAGGREGATION IN THE NORTH AMERICAN
INDUSTRIAL CLASSIFICATION SYSTEM (NAICS)

Example #1		Example #2	
NAICS code	Description	NAICS code	Description
31–33	Manufacturing	51	Information
334	Computer and electronic product manufacturing	513	Broadcasting and telecommunications
3346	Manufacturing and reproduction of magnetic and optical media	5133	Telecommunications
33461	Manufacturing and reproduction of magnetic and optical media	51332	Wireless telecommunications carriers, except satellite
334611	Reproduction of software	513321	Paging

Source: NAICS Website: http://www.census.gov/epcd/www/naics/usr.html#NEWSECTORS
Note: In example #1, the five-digit level provides no more information than the four-digit level.

detailed SIC classification. A selection is shown in table 2.4. These
include, for example, the reproduction of computer software and
paging (see table 2.3 for their positions in the classification hierar-
chy). While the new classification poses practical challenges for
the analysis of changes from before 1999 to later years, it clearly
facilitates a research focus on crucial areas of change, such as environmentally motivated technologies and the use and processing of
information.

The Representation of Technology

A number of different techniques can be used to produce the characteristic outputs of each industry. Grains can be grown on irrigated lands with substantial amounts of chemicals and mechanized
equipment and relatively little labor. Alternatively, production of
essentially the same output can be achieved using mainly human
and animal labor. There are many variations of these "modern" and
"traditional" agricultural technologies, and instances of the entire
range can sometimes be found in a single society. Nonetheless, the
dominant technologies used to grow rice in the United States and in
Indonesia, for example, do not overlap because of differences in culture and history, natural endowments, and industrial development.

Electric arc technology is distinguished from other techniques
for producing steel by its reliance on recycled scrap and electricity.
By contrast, iron, coal, and lime predominate among the inputs to
other modern steel-making technologies. Most electricity today is
generated in large, centralized plants from fossil fuels or nuclear

TABLE 2.4. SELECTED NEW INDUSTRIES IN THE UNITED STATES

Semiconductor machinery manufacturing
Fiber optic cable manufacturing
Reproduction of computer software
Manufacturing of compact discs except software
Convenience stores
Gas stations with convenience foods
Warehouse clubs
Food/health supplement stores
Pet supply stores
Pet care services
Cable networks
Satellite communications
Paging
Cellular and other wireless communications
Telecommunication resellers
Credit card issuing
Temporary help supply
Telemarketing bureaus
Hazardous waste collection
HMO medical centers
Continuing care retirement communities
Casino hotels
Casinos
Other gambling industries
Bed and breakfast inns
Limited service restaurants
Automotive oil change and lubrication shops
Diet and weight-reducing centers

Source: NAICS Website: http://www.census.gov/epcd/www/naics/usr.html#NEWSECTORS.

materials and distributed over a common grid. Photovoltaic cells provide a very different way to generate and deliver electric power, one that is decentralized and depends on solar radiation.

In all of these cases, a specific mix and quantity of inputs corresponds to a particular technological choice. Choices among alternative technologies are made on a regular basis, and names—such as electric arc technology, nuclear power, or wet-rice cultivation—are associated with many specific technologies. The name is part of the language used by engineers, technicians, and other experts who work with specific production processes. Structural economics provides a means to organize specialized knowledge about named technologies associated with different industries to make it useful for economic analysis.

Specific technologies are already in place in existing establishments, and they reflect decisions made in the past. In business and government databases, which report purchases and sales distinguished by SIC (or in the future NAICS) codes, the technologies are not named, but they are nonetheless described implicitly. I will use the device of an input–output table to demonstrate the use of the classification schemes for representing technologies.

Input–output tables are described in considerable detail in chapter 4, but an intuitive introduction is provided by the seven-sector version shown in table 2.5. Each figure is located in a row, named at the left, and a column, named at the top; it quantifies the dollar amount of sales from the row sector to the column sector. The matrix in section b of the table shows each input (from the row sector) per unit of output (of the column sector). The matrix is obtained by dividing every number in a particular column, say the third one, construction, by the total output for the corresponding row ($165,998 for the construction row). Official input–output tables and matrices (i.e., those published by government agencies) follow the same logic but are substantially more detailed.

Consider, for example, the figures in table 2.5 reporting the inputs to and outputs from manufacturing (in the fourth row and column, respectively). These figures are taken from the questionnaires of an economic census. Each figure represents a set of transactions, which can be seen from the seller's (the row industry) or the purchaser's (the column industry) point of view. The figures in row 4 record the volume of manufactured goods sold to producers of manufactured goods and all other sectors. But it is often more interesting to view the table columnwise. The fourth column of figures records the purchases of the manufacturing sector. These purchases reflect the input requirements for the manufacturing technology (actually, the mix of technologies) in use. A comparison of the columns in the input–output matrix shows the systematic differences in the input structures of different sectors.

The input structure for manufacturing is shown in table 2.5, but this classification is far too aggregated to reveal information about technologies. In a two-digit SIC classification of about one hundred sectors, the input structure does convey real technological distinctions. Table 2.6 shows the main features of the input–output structures (i.e., the largest figures in the columns of the input–output matrix) for steel and for livestock in the United States in 1987. There would be no mistaking the steel input structure for, say, that of food processing, another manufacturing industry. A practiced eye could further distinguish the steel column for the United States from

TABLE 2.5. HIGHLY AGGREGATED INPUT–OUTPUT TABLE OF THE U.S. ECONOMY

a. Inter-industry Transactions in 1972 (millions of dollars)

	Sector	1	2	3	4	5	6	7	Final Demand	Total Output
1	Agriculture	26,369	10	468	41,263	183	2,944	23	12,696	83,956
2	Mining	158	1,649	1,498	22,417	73	6,113	314	-1,837	30,386
3	Construction	583	858	47	3,244	3,125	16,464	2,672	139,005	165,998
4	Manufacturing	12,046	2,866	58,441	285,096	12,286	49,841	1,249	339,430	761,255
5	Trade and transportation	4,323	710	16,833	48,238	16,196	13,429	1,126	190,308	291,163
6	Services	8,123	5,196	12,133	59,466	46,106	113,905	3,827	364,363	613,118
7	Other	189	216	471	5,892	2,218	5,785	118	141,646	156,533

b. Direct Requirements ($ input per $ output)

	Sector	1	2	3	4	5	6	7
1	Agriculture	0.3141	0.0003	0.0028	0.0542	0.0006	0.0048	0.0001
2	Mining	0.0019	0.0543	0.0090	0.0294	0.0002	0.0100	0.0020
3	Construction	0.0069	0.0282	0.0003	0.0043	0.0107	0.0269	0.0171
4	Manufacturing	0.1435	0.0943	0.3521	0.3745	0.0422	0.0813	0.0080
5	Trade and transportation	0.0515	0.0234	0.1014	0.0634	0.0556	0.0219	0.0072
6	Services	0.0967	0.1710	0.0731	0.0781	0.1583	0.1858	0.0244
7	Other	0.0022	0.0071	0.0028	0.0077	0.0076	0.0094	0.0008

Source: R. Miller and P. Blair. *Input–Output Analysis: Foundations and Extensions*. Englewood Cliffs, NJ: Prentice-Hall, Inc, 1985, p. 424.
Note: Totals may not add due to rounding.

TABLE 2.6. MODERATELY DETAILED INPUT–OUTPUT STRUCTURES FOR TWO SELECTED SECTORS, STEEL AND LIVESTOCK, IN THE UNITED STATES IN 1987 ($ INPUT PER $ OUTPUT)

Steel			Livestock		
5	Metallic ores mining	0.029	1	Livestock and livestock products	0.192
6	Coal mining	0.021	2	Other agricultural products	0.272
10	Maintenance and repair construction	0.020	4	Agricultural, forestry and fishery services	0.046
24	Industrial and other chemicals	0.025	12	Food and kindred products	0.132
35	Iron and steel	0.150	64	Motor freight transportation and warehousing	0.022
36	Primary nonferrous metals manufacturing	0.022	73	Wholesale trade	0.044
70	Electric services (utilities)	0.041	78	Real estate and royalties	0.034
71	Gas production and distribution (utilities)	0.028		All other goods and services	0.086
				Factor inputs (labor and capital)	0.172
73	Wholesale trade	0.063	Total		1.000
84	Advertising	0.030			
	Scrap	0.038			
	All other goods and services	0.160			
	Factor inputs (labor and capital)	0.373			
Total		1.000			

Source: *Survey of Current Business*, May 1994, pp. 64, 66.
Note: Only values greater than .02 are shown. Codes are consistent with those in appendix A.

the one for Brazil or Japan on the basis of knowledge about labor intensity, capital intensity, and degree of recycling in the three societies. These types of data about input structures, which implicitly describe the technologies in use, are compiled regularly for dozens of industries in over a hundred countries.

It would be desirable if every input–output table were accompanied by supplementary information that provided a name for the most important technologies in use in each industry, showed the corresponding input structure, and reported weights showing their relative importance. For example, it could be useful to know the relative importance of electric arc and other steel-making technologies underlying the steel column in table 2.6. This is not now done in any country: the data that are collected record purchases and sales. Such figures reflect technological requirements indirectly, but they do so without explicitly identifying the mix of technologies.

Use of Case Studies to Describe Technological Alternatives

The technologies that will be put in place in the future will depend on decisions that are made today. Decision makers will generally want to consider several options and make at least a cursory comparison of their relative costs and other trade-offs. Descriptions of explicit alternative technologies for each industry, in terms of inputs and outputs and other related considerations, can be systematically compiled and described by the analyst. Within structural economics, these technological alternatives are developed in the form of highly structured case studies.

The empirical studies that were carried out at the Institute for Economic Analysis over the past two decades provide examples of combining the use of historical databases, with their implicit descriptions of technologies already in place, with case studies that explicitly describe alternative scenarios for the future. My colleagues and I began a series of studies in the early 1980s to examine technological changes in the U.S. economy over the period starting around 1960 and extending to 2000 and, in particular, to assess their implications for workers. The scenarios about the future were based on case studies covering the automation of manufacturing (using computers, robots, and numerically controlled machine tools), office automation, technological changes in the major service sectors such as education and health care, and the use of computer-based automation in households (Leontief and Duchin 1986). Scenarios about the future were constructed by assembling and documenting an interlocking set of assumptions, organized into dozens of tables, about future changes in input coefficients. Table 2.7, which shows how the adoption of robots was assumed to affect other inputs under two

TABLE 2.7. IMPACT OF ROBOTS ON PAINT REQUIREMENTS IN 1990 AND 2000

	Slow-Adoption Scenario		Fast-Adoption Scenario	
	1990	2000	1990	2000
Portion of paint saved (a)	0.20	0.20	0.20	0.20
Portion of painting tasks performed by robots (b)	0.15	0.25	0.25	0.40
Paint coefficient as portion of 1977 coefficient ($1 - ab$)	0.97	0.95	0.95	0.92

Source: Leontief and Duchin 1986, p. 57
Note: Under both scenarios, application of paint using industrial robots requires 20% less paint than manual application in 1977. Under the second scenario 25% of all industrial painting tasks in 1990 and 40% in 2000 are carried out by robots, compared to only 15% and 25%, respectively, under the first scenario. Thus, the industrial system would require 8% less paint by 2000 to produce a given volume and mix of output than the techniques in place in 1977. The original study made scores of assumptions at this level of detail and documented the reasoning behind them.

alternative scenarios for 1990 and 2000, provides an example of the level of detail.

In a subsequent study of alternative scenarios about sustainable development, projections were made about the future adoption of relatively clean, economical technologies in each of sixteen regions of the world economy over the next several decades. Case studies were carried out for pollutant emissions, electric power generation, industrial energy conservation, processing and fabrication of metals, construction, household energy conservation, and the production and use of cement, pulp and paper, chemicals, and motor vehicles.

The case study for construction illustrates the nature of these projections. This industry makes intensive use of materials, and processing them requires large quantities of energy and generates substantial pollution. The case study tabulated the importance of maintenance and repair relative to new construction in all parts of the world and the predominance of residential compared to other types of new construction. Then it described the different materials used for each purpose and likely future changes in material requirements. Based on these detailed assumptions, projections about changes in material inputs to construction are shown, for an illustrative scenario, in table 2.8.

Another set of case studies was carried out for scenarios about the sustainable development of the Indonesian economy. The subjects included alternative techniques for growing rice and other food crops, estate crops (like rubber) and livestock, and forest products and their transformation to pulp and paper. Other case studies were carried out for electricity and industrial and household energy use; the food, beverages, and tobacco sector; cement and construction; and textiles, leather, and wearing apparel. The final set was about the use of labor, land, and capital and water use; water pollution; and atmospheric emissions. Special attention was focused on alternative ways of providing inputs to the rapidly growing pulp and paper industry. Table 2.9 shows major aspects of the reliance on natural forests in 1985 and coefficient changes to describe two options for 2020: a more sustainable system of logging natural forests and the reliance on cultivated tree plantations. The plantations require more chemical inputs, labor, and capital per unit of output. However, assuming they can be established on suitable land that is not now forested, they involve far less soil erosion in the long term and can show dramatic yields on short rotation periods.

Yet another set of studies focused on the production, use, and

TABLE 2.8. CONSTRUCTION INPUTS BY GEOGRAPHIC REGION IN 2020 (AVERAGE ANNUAL RATE OF CHANGE IN INPUT PER UNIT OF OUTPUT AFTER 1990)

	Copper	Aluminum	Iron	Finished Chemicals	Cement
High-income North America	−1.50%	0.50%	−1.00%	1.00%	−0.50%
Newly industrialized Latin America	−1.50	0.50	−2.00	1.00	−1.00
Low-income Latin America	−1.00	1.50	−2.00	1.00	0.00
High-income Western Europe	−1.50	1.00	−1.00	1.00	−1.00
Medium-income Western Europe	−1.50	0.50	−2.00	1.00	−2.00
Eastern Europe	−1.50	1.50	−2.00	1.00	−1.50
Former Soviet Union	−1.50	1.00	−2.50	1.00	−1.50
Centrally planned Asia	−1.50	1.00	−2.75	1.00	−0.50
Japan	−1.50	0.50	−1.00	1.00	−1.00
Newly industrialized Asia	−1.50	1.00	−2.00	1.00	−0.50
Low-income Asia	−0.50	1.50	−1.50	1.00	0.00
Major oil producers	−1.50	0.00	−2.75	1.00	−1.00
North Africa and other Middle East	−0.50	1.00	−1.00	1.00	−1.00
Sub-Saharan Africa	−1.50	0.00	−2.00	1.00	2.00
Southern Africa	−1.50	0.50	−1.00	1.00	−1.00
Oceania	−1.50	0.50	−1.00	1.00	−1.00

Source: Duchin and Lange 1994, p. 134.
Note: Aluminum and chemical products (mainly plastics and paint) displace copper, iron and steel, and cement as building materials after 1990. The reasoning behind these assumptions is described in the original study.

TABLE 2.9. ASSUMPTIONS ABOUT NATURAL FOREST AND PLANTATION LOGGING IN 1985 AND 2020

	Actual 1985	Natural Forest 2020	Plantation 2020
Fertilizer and pesticides (Rp/Rp of output)	0	0	0.0016
Other manufacturing inputs (Rp/Rp of output)	0.0226	0.0226	0.0244
Labor (person years/Rp million of output)	0.0492	0.0499	0.1855
Capital stock (Rp/Rp of output)	0.2925	0.321	0.5634
Deforestation (proportion of land area)	0.26	0.15	0
Soil erosion (tons/ha)			
−before establishment (one-time)	0	0	15
−after establishment (ongoing)	79	30	10
Yield (m³/ha)	21.1	37.0	310
Rotation (years)	35	50	15
Area required (ha/10³m³)	47.4	26.5	3.22
Unit price (Rp/m³)	61,548	61,548	61,548

Source: Duchin, Hamilton, and Lange 1993, p. 106.
Notes: 1. Rp are rupiahs, the national currency of Indonesia (about 2,000 to the U.S. dollar in the first half of the 1990s). Land is measured in hectares (ha) and output in Rp or cubic meters of wood.
2. These two sets of projections for 2020 contrast a sustainable system of logging natural forests with tree plantations. The latter results in less erosion and deforestation. It uses far less land but more capital, labor, and other inputs.

TABLE 2.10. DIRECT USE OF PLASTIC BY SECTOR AND RESIN IN THE UNITED STATES IN 1987

	All Resins	HDPE	LDPE	PVC	PP	PET	PS	PU	Other
a. Resin by weight (millions of pounds)									
Packaging, all sectors	14,425	4,102	5,366	578	1,253	1,417	1,564	50	95
Nonpackaging, all sectors	33,355	2,807	3,438	7,029	3,973	182	3,112	2,630	10,180
Construction	9,475	811	812	5,453	178	1	325	505	1,391
Electrical & electronic goods	2,992	144	161	302	255	119	550	187	1,276
Transportation equipment	3,244	216	0	239	484	42	124	590	1,549
Health-care services	1,453	143	307	244	247	2	235	60	216
Other sectors	16,191	1,494	2,158	791	2,810	18	1,879	1,289	5,750
Total	47,780	6,909	8,804	7,607	5,226	1,599	4,676	2,680	10,276
	100.0	14.5	18.4	15.9	10.9	3.3	9.8	5.6	21.5
b. Percent distribution by resin (percent by weight)									
Packaging, all sectors	30.2%	59.4%	60.9%	7.6%	24.0%	88.6%	33.4%	1.9%	0.9%
Nonpackaging, all sectors	69.8	40.6	39.1	92.4	76.0	11.4	66.6	98.1	99.1
Construction	19.8	11.7	9.2	71.7	3.4	0.1	6.9	18.9	13.5
Electrical & electronic goods	6.3	2.1	1.8	4.0	4.9	7.4	11.8	7.0	12.4
Transportation equipment	6.8	3.1	0.0	3.1	9.3	2.6	2.7	22.0	15.1
Health-care services	3.0	2.1	3.5	3.2	4.7	0.1	5.0	2.2	2.1
Other sectors	33.9	21.6	24.5	10.4	53.8	1.1	40.2	48.1	56.0
Total	100.0	100.0	100.0	100.0	100.0	100.0	100.0	100.0	100.0

Source: Duchin and Lange 1998.
Notes: 1. By making use of classification schemes for industries and for resins, the table provides a complete and systematic description of resin use.
2. The resins, in order of columns, are high-density polyethylene, low-density polyethylene, polyvinyl chloride, polypropylene, polyethylene terephthalate, polystyrene, and polyurethane.
3. Totals may not add due to rounding.

disposal of plastics and analyzed prospects for recycling plastic wastes in the United States. A database was developed to describe the use of seven resins in all sectors of the economy, both in a past year and under alternative scenarios about future recycling practices. Two of the major challenges were to establish the use of resins by application in the base year of 1987, which is shown in table 2.10, and to estimate the future capability to recycle different resins economically and absorb recycled resins in specific applications, shown in table 2.11.

Tables 2.7 through 2.11 have provided concrete examples of the kinds of quantitative work that lie behind the empirical analyses. The substantive content covers all aspects of production and consumption. The common element is the methodology. In all cases, an industrial classification is selected, input coefficients for each sector are developed for a recent year, and assumptions are made about the changes that can be expected in these coefficients under alternative technological scenarios. The changes need to be documented to indicate the kinds of evidence and reasoning on which they are based.

TABLE 2.11. ASSUMPTIONS ABOUT RECYCLED PLASTIC CONTENT BY RESIN AND APPLICATION IN 2005

Category	% Recycled Content	Other Changes
a. Packaging Use of Plastic		
HDPE and LDPE film	15	
PET food containers	50	
Non-PET food containers	25	
Containers for household cleaning supplies, pharmaceuticals, etc.	50	
PVC		replace by other resins
b. Nonpackaging Use of Plastic		
Construction	5	
Transportation equipment	10	
Electrical and electronic goods	15	
Textiles	5	
Toys, housewares, etc.	25	
Health-care services	0	

Source: Duchin and Lange 1998.
Note: The table shows that some industries, namely health care, have virtually no capacity to absorb recycled resins. Containers are at the other extreme, with 50% recycled content. Food containers need to be sorted separately to achieve this outcome.

The Leontief Paradox and Other Empirical Findings

The power of Leontief's input–output economics is its ability to represent technology and technological change with sufficient concreteness and accuracy to permit an analysis with real empirical content. The first compelling empirical result to be reported in the economic literature on the basis of input–output analysis was the work that came to be called the Leontief paradox. The United States in the post–World War II period was widely assumed to be the preeminent example of a developed economy that was richly endowed with capital, by contrast with developing countries that possessed little capital but more than enough labor. It followed, according to elementary economic logic, that the United States would be expected to export goods and services produced with capital-intensive technologies in exchange for imports that would have absorbed large amounts of labor if produced domestically. Using the first input–output table, which had been constructed for 1947, Leontief found the opposite to be true: Exports required more labor (relative to capital) than imports. Trade was being used in the United States to absorb labor and economize on capital (Leontief 1953).

I do not know of another empirical result in the economics literature that stimulated as much reaction as this one. Dozens of articles were written over a couple of decades to explain how Leontief's numerical results were in fact consistent with the familiar assumptions about industrialized countries and the logic of comparative advantage. Leontief's own explanation was that the average American worker is substantially more productive than an average worker in the countries with which we trade. If, say, the average American worker is three times as productive as other workers, then the effective supply of "standard labor" would be three times as great as a simple head count would suggest. Therefore, he argued, the United States is really rich in labor, not capital, and for this reason uses its excess labor to produce exports while importing scarce capital.

Using the database and scenarios about technological change that have been described earlier,[1] I repeated Leontief's computation for various years over the period from 1960 to 2000. For the early years in that period I found the same phenomenon that Leontief had uncovered for 1947 (Duchin 1990): Exports were more labor intensive (in terms of employee-hours) and less capital intensive than imports. But the factor intensities converge in the more recent years due to changes both in technologies and in the mix of goods and services that are exported and imported. The convergence is explained by the increasing similarity of production techniques, as developing countries industrialize, and the increasing similarity of demand with the transfer of lifestyle aspirations. By the year 2000 the capital and labor intensity of imports and exports are practically the same.[2]

Technological change in the postwar period has involved the substitution of capital for labor. For this reason, what Leontief found is logical: The country experiencing the most rapid rate of technological change will seek ways to slow down this potential displacement of workers. One way is to produce labor-intensive exports, and that is what the United States did for as long as it was able to impose this imbalance. The paradox disappears when we recognize that an adequate theory of trade needs to take the logic of technological change—as well as the logic of comparative advantage—directly into account.

While the role of input–output analysis in establishing the so-called paradox was dramatic, Leontief's chief concerns lay elsewhere. He had begun to reflect early in his career on the displacement of human workers by automation (he called it instrumentation in the days before computers). He believed it was urgent to develop new public policies for distributing income in a society where a shrinking proportion of adults would spend fewer and fewer hours in paid labor. While the Leontief paradox was established using a simple comparative static computation, he had to wait several decades for an input–output model and database that could be used to examine his concerns about labor in a systematic and quantitative way.

A few years after I joined Leontief's research institute at New York University in 1977, we found a program officer at the National Science Foundation who was interested in funding an inquiry about the effects of technological change on employment.[3] Leontief seized this opportunity to test his ideas and set me the challenge of developing a dynamic input–output model that could be useful for empirical analysis. Using that model, past input–output tables, and scenarios based on five case studies about future technological change (all described earlier), our team reached its conclusions. We found that the displacement of labor due to computer-based automation in the United States would be relatively slow in the closing years of the twentieth century and would be experienced more in the white-collar occupations than on the factory floor (Leontief and Duchin 1986). After reflecting on these results, Leontief concluded that the displacement of workers would proceed more slowly than he had feared, leaving time to make the necessary adjustments. I believe that this computation was for him the one that most clearly demonstrated the power of input–output economics. His own thinking was swayed by the results, although he remains concerned about the welfare of workers in a technological society.

Collaborations with Engineers

Structural economists have taken the initiative to organize the kinds of data and case studies described in the earlier sections of this chapter. Nonetheless, economists cannot be expected to have adequate expertise for making estimates and projections and for evaluating assumptions about present and future technologies in all areas of the economy. When an economist alone constructs a scenario about technological change, it invariably involves highly stylized assumptions. Since it is convenient to make assumptions about named variables, the economist is likely to assume a particular percentage improvement in labor intensity or fuel efficiency since these are familiar named variables. It requires an engineer specialized in power generation to suggest the prospects for changes in named technologies, for example a switch from a conventional coal burner to fluidized-bed combustion, and to provide a quantitative description of the associated input structure.

The potential benefits of bringing the systems approach of the economist to bear on the specialized knowledge of technology of the engineer are evident, and there are many cases where this has been done more or less successfully. The collaboration is not easy, however, as the two professions have different conceptions of what constitutes important questions, the level of detail appropriate for an inquiry about technology, and the degree of accuracy to be required in quantitative descriptions. Nonetheless, this sort of collaboration is highly developed relative to others to be discussed in the following chapters.

My colleagues and I have from the outset drawn on the technical literature and consulted with technical experts in conducting our case studies. Our first direct collaboration with engineers was for a study commissioned by the American Society for Mechanical Engineers (ASME). On the basis of their participation, we were able to obtain funding from the Engineering Directorate of the National Science Foundation.

ASME requested a framework for evaluating the relative costs of alternative technological options from the perspective of decision makers in individual industries. The assumption was that engineers could enhance their status within corporations if they had analytic tools for making better, cost-saving decisions. The study made use of the database and the alternative scenarios that had been developed for the research about the effects of automation on workers. It was anticipated that the engineers would subsequently develop the technical data for their own case studies and make use of this framework to compare the costs of alternative technological options.

We developed a new optimization model and using it reached a few powerful conclusions that are particularly relevant to the arguments made in this book. First, we learned that a number of the technologies adopted since the 1960s were not cost saving. Instead, their selection appeared to reflect more complex social and strategic realities such as the effects of environmental regulations, positioning for future advantages, and quality improvements. Second, changes experienced in some sectors—this was most emphatically true for computers—had decisive effects not only on their own cost structures, but also on the relative costs of alternative technological choices faced by other sectors. In particular, we found that the new technologies were cost saving for eight sectors (out of nearly one hundred) *only* if the computer sector made the shift from the old to the new input structure. These eight sectors are printing and publishing, engines and turbines, construction and mining machinery, metalworking machinery, general industrial machinery, communications equipment, aircraft, and insurance (Duchin and Lange 1995).

This work involved a focus on prices and costs, wage rates and rates of return on capital, that had not been typical of our earlier work. We made use of the same database to ask a different set of questions: to what extent did the technological options have differential effects on workers' earnings versus profits on capital? To what extent did they lower the cost of consumption goods relative to that of investment goods? We learned that over the past few decades, the shares of income earned by labor and capital in the United States have remained rather steady despite technological change, but the cost of investment goods has fallen faster than that of items of consumption. According to our calculations, the purchasing power of an average employee's compensation (measured in terms of its command over consumption goods) hardly changed between 1967 and 1977 and is projected to increase by about 3 percent between 1977 and 2000. By contrast, the command of the average industry's profits over investment goods rose 17 percent in the first period and another 27 percent in the later one (Duchin and Lange 1992b). These kinds of questions are revisited in substantially more detail in the remainder of this book.

NOTES

1. That study of the effects of automation on workers is discussed in more detail in the text that follows.

2. This conclusion does not imply comparable material standards of living.

3. Dr. Eileen Collins provided us with substantial support for this project, even though it was out of step with the concerns and methods of the economics profession. This funding made it possible to build a database that was used in numerous studies of technological change that were carried out over the course of a decade.

Chapter 3
Technology, Lifestyle, and the Classification of Households

Many people have become aware that decisions that seem sound from an economic point of view, as narrowly defined, may have adverse social and especially environmental consequences and that decisions with more benign effects are not necessarily more costly in the long run. In contemplating the major social challenges, it is natural for people to consider their own responsibility in creating and resolving them. Economists tend to view the populace as a collection of passive actors responding predictably to changes in prices and incomes. An alternative is to regard them as the active agents of sustainable development, citizens who can and do deliberate before making decisions and who can anticipate the consequences for themselves of decisions made by others. One of the most important decisions they make is the choice of household lifestyle.

Households differ in their choice of lodgings—from large homes with extensive grounds to crowded apartments in high-rise buildings—and even those with similar incomes make different choices about the contents of their homes and where they shop, what they eat and how frequently they eat outside the home, their degree of mobility and modes of transportation, what they read and do for recreation, and so on. These various choices are not independent of each other, because value systems and financial means affect them

49

all. The set of choices made by a particular household is not unique because most cultural practices are widely shared (and the number of distinctly different lifestyle behaviors is limited). Many households will have essentially similar patterns of behaviors regarding food, housing, and so forth. I call each of these patterns a lifestyle and am interested in describing lifestyles and exploring the prospects for changes in lifestyles.

I described in chapter 2 the mathematical models of structural economics as deterministic rather than probabilistic. Yet I have just stressed the important role of households in making choices among alternative lifestyles, just as producers decide among alternative technologies. I furthermore recognize a substantial role for chance. There may appear to be a contradiction between choice and chance on the one side, and a deterministic model on the other.

Either a deterministic model or a probabilistic model can be constructed in the attempt to represent any particular set of events. (Of course, some events are so poorly understood that it is pointless to try to model them at all.) Most phenomena combine chance or choice with structure, but they differ in the relative importance of the two (e.g., roulette versus tic-tac-toe). My claim has been that once lifestyles and technologies are specified, the system relating them to quantities of output, material use, labor, pollution, investment, prices, and incomes is extremely well represented by a deterministic model.[1] The choice of lifestyles and technologies is part of a scenario; it is not fixed—in either a deterministic or a probabilistic way—by the rest of the system in the framework of structural economics.

Usually researchers using a specific kind of mathematical model interact mainly with others who use only the same kind of model. Concerns about sustainable development have had the salutary effect of increasing the professional contacts among researchers who work with different mathematical models of the global economic system. It has also promoted collaboration between them and a wide range of experts who understand individual parts of the system such as energy technologies, the water cycle, or the ecology of forests. The challenge of envisaging a sustainable future pushes all of these frameworks to their limits and calls forth both collaboration and possible new divisions of labor. Structural economics treats household lifestyles in a way that bridges the concerns of different kinds of analysts and facilitates incorporation of those concerns into a formal, analytic framework.

My basic claim is that two concepts, lifestyle and technology, are centrally important for all approaches to achieving sustainable development. Furthermore, they can be readily represented in both conceptual and analytic models of the economic system. Many of the models and databases of individual economies or the world economy include a representation of inter-industry exchanges. With some expansion and generalization of this input–output portion, it is possible to describe changes in lifestyle and technology in concrete detail. These changes can take place in the presence or absence of economic growth, and their analysis requires a framework that does not impose assumptions about growth.

Technology and technological change can be described in terms of methods for the extraction of fuels, materials, and biomass and their transformation into useful products and wastes. A number of studies of technological change were described in chapter 2, and the economics literature is full of many other examples. Lifestyle has been subjected to far less systematic investigation than technology, and the classification of households as a necessary prelude to the description of their lifestyles is explored here in some detail. A concrete way to effectively incorporate lifestyles into models of economic systems is described, and some new ideas about the representation of household activities are offered. The final section considers the content of specific scenarios.

Lifestyle and Technology As Organizing Concepts

Ehrlich and Holdren (1974) identified the main factors responsible for environmental degradation as population increase, affluence, and technology, providing three potentially important "handles" for operationalizing the concept of sustainable development. Overpopulation and overconsumption have both been identified as chief culprits. Indeed, world population is still growing, and many people in all societies aspire to American consumption patterns and copy them as soon as their means permit. Democratic governments could not deliver on international agreements limiting fertility or consumption, as these are the results of personal decisions made in specific cultural contexts. Only households are in a position to act on alternative lifestyle objectives. An immediate challenge, then, is to understand the considerations of households in making such decisions.

Economists are experts about decisions regarding prices and

quantities of items whose production and sale is mediated by market mechanisms. Their purview extends to roles for governments, not only in fiscal and monetary matters but also in regulating private-sector activities and providing certain kinds of social services. But households, the locus where most decisions about work, consumption, fertility, health care, and education are made, and where ethical values and civic attitudes are formed, have been largely ignored because of the economist's emphasis on people only as individuals and individuals only as consumers. By shifting the focus of description and analysis from individual consumers to communities of households, we can examine the lifestyle choices, including but not limited to consumption behavior and fertility, that characterize each of them.

Technology is the third fundamental determinant of the impact that a society has on its natural environment. The word *technology* seems to be well defined—compared, say, to *lifestyle*—in part because specialists like engineers and economists regularly use it. Both rich and poor countries, and many international organizations, are concerned with the transfer of technology. Too little attention, however, has been paid to the "transfer of lifestyle." I suggest that the two concepts are of parallel importance and of similar levels of abstraction.

A technology specifies the required inputs and the ways in which they will be transformed during the production process. Households and government agencies may make decisions influencing technology, but mostly these choices are in the domain of private firms. Firms producing similar outputs will tend to make similar technological decisions, just as households of similar sociodemographic characteristics will make similar lifestyle decisions.

Every society is composed of different kinds of households and different kinds of firms. In the United States today, for example, there are over 100 million households and a few million firms. In principle, they can be classified into relatively homogeneous household categories and industrial sectors, respectively. The firms have indeed been systematically classified according to the elaborately structured and heavily utilized Standard Industrial Classifications, described in chapter 2. Each industry, defined in terms of its common inputs and outputs, has its dominant technologies, and the choice among alternative technologies is affected by new alternatives, changes in prices and regulations, and longer-term, strategic considerations. There is no comparable classification scheme for households—even though there are so many more of them. An appropriate classification scheme could be devised that would likewise group households that share a characteristic lifestyle. Lifestyles change when new options arise or when options that were unrecognized become apparent, and the changes are congruent with the members' cultural, ethical, and civic values and are possibly reinforced by changes in prices and government regulations. Scenarios could be built to reflect potential changes in lifestyles. In this way, lifestyle and technology can serve as organizing concepts for building and analyzing scenarios about sustainable development.

Structural Change versus Growth and Contraction

In our times it is deeply ingrained to consider economic growth as natural and healthy by contrast with stagnation and depression. When the population of a country is expanding, as has been the case almost continually in most countries since the beginning of the Industrial Revolution, the economy also needs to grow simply to maintain the material standard of living of the average individual. Once the size of the population levels off, as it has in many developed countries, an objective of economic growth as it is usually conceived assumes increased consumption on the part of the average individual.

The commitment of the developed economies to growth is reinforced by memories of substantial unemployment and a lack of investment opportunities during the Great Depression and by the recent experiences of uncomfortably high unemployment at a time of only modest growth in population. Developing countries see economic growth as the vehicle for finally delivering the benefits of modern science and technology in the form of the rich countries' lifestyles—a transfer of technology to achieve a transfer of lifestyles. The widely disseminated recommendations prepared for the United Nations by the Brundtland Commission reflect this view of growth; they are based on the explicit assumption that suitable technological and organizational decisions will make it possible to achieve growth in all countries and simultaneously reduce pressures on the environment. However, our own detailed analysis (Duchin and Lange 1994) suggests that while this prospect may sound reassuring, it is unlikely to be achievable (see the discussion in chapter 1). Some economists are beginning to examine prospects for avoiding stagnation and achieving modernity in ways that do not rely on assumptions about growth, as the latter is conventionally defined and measured.

Many economies have failed to achieve economic growth and have even contracted in recent decades. There are, of course, celebrated historical examples of dramatic economic contractions as once flourishing civilizations have disappeared. Some observers are convinced that the modern consumer society is heading for involuntary changes in lifestyle if we do not opt for voluntary ones.

There is, in fact, a tradition of economists who subscribe to J.S. Mill's conviction that once population levels off in relatively affluent societies, people might prefer other forms of satisfaction to ever increasing consumption of purchased goods and services (Mishan 1969; Hirsch 1976; Scitovsky 1976), especially as they become increasingly aware of the pressures that different kinds of lifestyles place on the environment of "spaceship earth" (Boulding 1966; see also Daly 1977). Scenarios about the sustainable future of the global system should include assumptions about voluntary changes in lifestyle and reductions in overall consumption for at least some categories of households.

It is important to formulate and analyze scenarios based on alternative assumptions about technologies and lifestyles without prejudging as materially or politically infeasible, and therefore excluding, those that may involve contraction of GNP. I suggest that even individuals who will remain committed to growth as a social objective will find substantive interest in the formulation and analysis of such scenarios. These analyses may also point the way to improvements (over GNP) in the conception and measurement of well-being.

Since the mid-century contributions of J.M. Keynes, governments have had substantial experience with economic policies for smoothing out cyclical ups and downs experienced in growing economies, and there is a large literature about mathematical modeling of the implications of these kinds of policies. If plausible scenarios could result in reductions in GNP, new kinds of policies may be needed to counter downturns around a long-term trend of GNP that may be flat rather than rising. Models for evaluating such policies require a dynamic structure that does not automatically assume that the economy is expanding.

It is true that if purchases of goods and services fall, voluntarily or involuntarily, production will also fall and factors of production may be underutilized. This means that some resources will remain in the ground and less wastes will be generated, outcomes that can hardly be considered problematic from a social point of view. There would clearly be a potential for unemployment, but policies aimed at reducing the length of the work week might prove successful at distributing income in spite of a smaller number of person-hours worked. In the absence of growth, there would be far less expansion of the capital stock, and therefore also of domestic investment opportunities; at the same time, the level of profits available for investment would also cease to expand. While these outcomes regarding labor and capital may not be considered desirable for specific individuals or arguably for society as a whole, it is important to recognize that some of them are already being experienced. Labor is continually displaced by new technologies, and capital in developed countries is increasingly attracted by opportunities for the higher rates of return (associated with higher growth rates) of many developing countries—high enough to outweigh the various risks. Hardheaded realism requires us to acknowledge that growth in GNP is not the only reality or objective for an economic system.

Some measures leading to a contraction of factor inputs, such as improved energy efficiency, may be undertaken voluntarily; others, like the loss of investment opportunities, may occur despite social preferences. Scenarios about the future are able to take into account a wide range of prospects, including those associated with substantial changes in consumption patterns, without prejudging their implications. But for this potential to be realized, the frameworks that are used to build and analyze scenarios need to be flexible enough to accommodate alternative assumptions and outcomes. This section has put growth into perspective because entrenched ideas about its desirability and inevitability have deflected attention from the most important arenas of structural change: technology and lifestyle. When it comes to a formal analytic framework, some models will require a systematic methodological reformulation to break the implicit link between GNP and well-being and open up the framework for the more direct representation of the factors related to the quality of people's lives.

The Structural Table of the Economy

Neoclassical economists generally take two approaches to representing the operations of an economic system: general equilibrium and macroeconomic models. The models of structural economics differ in that they are explicitly conceived to represent technologies and technological changes through the incorporation of input–output tables. The input–output table provides a description of the average technology in use in each sector and thus a basis for building scenarios about technological change and technological alternatives. Neoclassical models generally also include an input–output table, which is valued for its ability to provide a sectoral level of detail and consistency, but the "production functions," governing the relations of outputs to inputs, do not take the pattern of use of individual goods and services directly into account.

Structural economics, as noted previously and detailed in chapter 4, is a conceptual framework for analyzing the relations among the economy, society, and the physical environment. A schematic *structural table* illustrating these relationships in terms of industrial sectors, occupations and households, and resources and wastes, is shown as figure 3.1. Figure 3.2 provides a small hypothetical example of classifications and numerical figures. Cells in the structural table are filled with numbers that quantify flows (of agricultural products, workers, carbon dioxide, etc.) from one place to another. The numbers in such a table constitute a part of the database to be analyzed using a mathematical model of the economy.

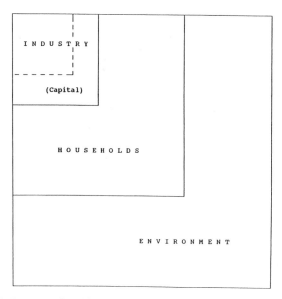

Figure 3.1. A Structural Table of an Economy

		Industry			Households		Environment	
							Carbon Dioxide	Degraded Water
		Agriculture	Manufacturing	Services	Rural	Urban	(tons)	(cubic feet)
Industry	Agriculture (tons)	10	20	10	50	120	20	50
	Manufacturing (machines)	20	10	50	25	50	30	10
	Services (services)	5	25	15	15	15	5	8
Households	Production (workers)	200	50	50				
	Office (workers)	10	20	40				
	Professional (workers)	20	30	50				
Environment	Fuels (BTUs)	10	40	10	15	20		
	Water (cubic feet)	80	20	10	5	5		

Figure 3.2. Hypothetical Example of Classifications and Numerical Values in a Structural Table

The square portion in the upper left of the structural table shows the inter-industry exchanges that are usually associated with an input–output table. In figure 3.2, there are three industries, and their output is measured in tons, number of machines, and number of services, respectively: 10 tons of agricultural output are used within the agricultural sector, 20 tons are delivered to manufacturing establishments, and 10 tons to service-sector establishments.

The industry portion of the table is bordered by a representation of household activities (a backward "L" of several rows and columns). The figures in the household rows show the amounts of labor used by each sector; the columns show the purchases by different categories of households of goods and services from industry. The classification used in figure 3.2 includes three categories of workers and two kinds of households. In this example, most professionals work in the service sectors and urban households purchase twice as many machines as rural households. The industry and household portions of the structural table are similar to parts of what is called a social accounting matrix (discussed below and in detail in chapter 5).

The description of industrial and household activities is bordered in the structural table by a representation of environmental inputs and outputs. In this portion of the table (the large, backward "L"), the rows show the quantities of different resources absorbed by the various industries and households (fuels and water in figure 3.2), and the columns depict the pollutants generated by industrial and household activities (carbon dioxide and degraded water). In the example, manufacturing establishments discharge 10 cubic feet of degraded water, while agriculture is associated with five times as much.

Technology, Natural Resource Accounting, and Material Balances

Technology is a powerful organizing concept because it provides a concrete focus for both qualitative and quantitative descriptions of the linkage between economic activities and some important aspects of the natural world. The technologies used in a society strongly influence and reflect its level of material well-being. They also govern requirements for inputs like materials, fuels, biomass, and water and effects on the environment like wastes and soil degradation. Fortunately, important aspects of a technology lend themselves to systematic quantitative description: namely, the assorted inputs and outputs associated with the production of a particular good or service. The analysis of this kind of information was discussed in chapter 2. The structural table illustrates the use of classifications to organize the information into a database. The approach is also applicable to households.

Once an industrial classification scheme is chosen for a structural table, the figures in the column corresponding to each industry describe its technology, and those in the row show the distribution of its sales. Reading down the column, one sees the inputs of goods and services (the last rows of the schematic industry table in figure 3.2 show capital inputs), the labor inputs, and the resource inputs, while the corresponding row shows the deliveries of the industry's output. The last portion of the row shows the amounts of wastes that are generated in the course of production for this industry.

The environmental portion of a structural table provides a framework for absorbing the kinds of information used in two important areas of research, the analysis of material balances and natural resource accounting, and has the important added advantage of integrating them with the associated production and consumption activities. Take, for example, the material balances for toxic chemicals estimated by Ayres and Ayres (1994); a structural table could show the net consumption of, say, ammonia-based chemicals by sector (a row) and the sectoral emission losses (in the corresponding column for ammonia-based chemicals). Transforming the free-form flow charts usually used in tracking material balances into the rows and columns of a structural table, starting with cases where there is enough information for at least a crude quantification (based, for example, on the pioneering work of Ayres and Ayres), can have a number of advantages. One of these is the association of the use and disposal of particular quantities of individual materials not only with specific industries but also with specific, alternative technologies.

The environmental portion of a structural table can also absorb the kinds of information, whether in physical units (preferably) or monetary ones, that is usually contained in natural resource accounts. The Norwegian natural resource accounts, for example, tabulate oxides of sulfur and of nitrogen (measured in millions of tons) emitted in individual sectors and the use of fishery and forest products (Central Bureau of Statistics of Norway 1992). The emissions would be represented as columns of output in the environmental portion of the matrix, and the fish and forest products as rows of environmental inputs. Other columns could correspond to the kinds of wastes included in the Dutch natural resource accounts (de Haan, Keuning, and Bosch 1993): greenhouse gases, depletion of ozone, acidification, eutrophication, and solid waste.

I will not take up the fundamental problem of the classification of resources and pollutants. The industry and commodity classifications customarily used in national accounting procedures span all business activities. A suitable household classification scheme likewise needs to span virtually all types of workers and households in a society. The industrial and worker classifications of figure 3.2 are readily disaggregated to much greater levels of detail, and the challenge of a detailed household classification is taken up later in this chapter. One of the most formidable tasks still facing structural economics (and other analytic fields dealing with sustainable development) is the construction of a moderately detailed, comprehensive classification for resources and wastes. Such a classification needs to be simultaneously suited for distinguishing technologies and for capturing the most important aspects of resource use and environmental degradation. Until now, both material balances and natural resource accounting have provided only very partial coverage of resource use and waste generation (this is also the case in figure 3.1), in part because of the absence of an adequate classification scheme (see Lange and Duchin 1994). However, for any given classification scheme, the structural table framework makes it possible to provide an integrated representation of technologies in terms of inputs of goods and services, resource inputs, and the wastes generated using specific technologies to produce a specific good or service.

The simple layout of a structural table enables it to play a useful symbolic function, conveying the embeddedness of the economy in the society, and of both within the environment. However, the information is basically descriptive. This kind of table is of limited use for the analysis of scenarios because it does not represent the relationship between workers and households (i.e., the mix of workers in each kind of household) and between resources and pollution (e.g., carbon emissions associated with each unit of fuel use). In subsequent chapters I describe input–output economics as an analytic framework for studying inter-industrial relations. Then I offer a framework for integrating an industrial with a household analysis. The true integration of the industrial, household, and environmental analysis has not yet been achieved.

Lifestyle, Social Accounting Matrices, and the Classification of Households

Lifestyle can be a powerful organizing concept for describing the structure of an economy and for building scenarios about alternative options, because it provides a concrete focus for qualitative and quantitative descriptions of the linkage between economic activities and some important aspects of cultural and social life. The mix of lifestyles in a society directly and indirectly influences and reflects what is produced, how much is produced, and how it is produced. The lifestyle of a household directly influences and reflects its members' participation in the labor force in various capacities, their consumption practices, fertility, use of leisure, and so on. Some important characteristics of distinct lifestyles lend themselves to systematic quantitative description with which economists have a great deal of experience: namely, the goods and services consumed and the kinds of work performed in the marketplace by members of the average household of each type.

An explicit focus on households, which has so far been absent from work about the restructuring of economies in response to environmental pressures (exceptions are Parikh et al. 1991 and Biesiot and Moll 1995) and from models of an entire economy, not to mention the global economy, can provide a conceptually powerful way to bring social and demographic phenomena, and the practices of everyday life, into the analysis of structural change. The pioneer in the systematic quantitative description of social systems was Richard Stone, who recognized the fundamental distinction between the relatively easy task of collecting lists of demographic and social statistics and indicators, on the one hand, and their integration into a structural framework, on the other (chapter 5 includes a discussion of Stone's work). Stone arranged accounting data describing demographic characteristics, migration behavior, education, and health in an input–output format and analyzed the tables using mathematical models. There were two major shortcomings to this work, however: first, it was not integrated with economic data and models; and second, individuals were grouped on the basis of one-dimensional criteria like age categories.

One of Stone's legacies is the social accounting matrix (often called a SAM), which describes the money flows in an economy over a given accounting period. It extends an input–output flow table (social accounting matrices use relatively aggregated input–output tables that are quantified in money units) by explicitly showing money flows to, from, and among institutions; these institutions include different categories of households. The households are grouped largely on the basis of similar incomes, but other consider-ations that are sometimes taken into account include urban or rural location and whether the designated head of the household is employed in agriculture or owns land.

Keuning and de Ruijter have pointed out the inadequacy of the common practice of using income categories only and stress the importance of conveying "the institutional reality of the geographi-cal area under study" (Keuning and de Ruijter 1988, p. 72). They identify several classification criteria including the requirement that each institution have a basis in groups that are recognizable for pol-icy purposes and that exhibit relatively stable characteristics.

In practice, the use of criteria other than occupation or income to classify institutions in social accounts has been very limited. Some of the early efforts included only two or three categories of households, and it is rare to have as many as the ten categories found in the official accounts for Indonesia. Most social accounting matri-ces have been compiled for developing countries where the criteria for classifying households almost always include a geographic char-acteristic or two, usually the distinctions between rural and urban location and ownership of small, medium, and large parcels of land.

A number of countries compile social accounting matrices as part of their national accounts; these include Indonesia, Thailand, Botswana, a few Latin American countries, and the Netherlands. Social accounts are used to analyze the effects of government poli-cies not only on growth but also on the distribution of income among the different categories of households (and the other institu-tions). The preferred analytic frameworks in this tradition are either the computation of so-called multipliers or the incorporation of the social accounting data into a general equilibrium framework. The social accounting matrices and the studies based on them are limited by the rudimentary classification of households, a focus on income flows only, and the lack of a dynamic conceptual framework for projecting the transformations over time in the practices of each household category and shifts in the population among household categories. In this book I substantially expand and generalize the information about households in a social accounting matrix for inclusion in the structural table and carry out a more generalized structural analysis based on input–output models.

In compiling the figures that make up a social accounting matrix, one has to select a concrete classification scheme for the households. This challenge has been sidestepped in the discussion until now on the implicit assumption that, given a set of objects, one can always come up with a classification. One of J. L. Borges's nonfiction essays provides a cautionary tale, however, that illustrates that innumerable classifications are possible for a given set of objects, but many may make little sense. To dramatize the inevitable "ambiguities, redundancies, and deficiencies" of any scheme, the reader is presented with John Wilkins's seventeenth-century classification of stones into ordinary, intermediate, precious, transparent, and insoluble, as well as the division of animals, attributed to an obscure Chinese encyclopedia, into those that belong to the emperor, those that have been embalmed, those that are trained, and eleven other categories (Borges 1964, p 103).

Despite their ultimate arbitrariness, however, many instances of effective classifications exist. The Standard Industrial Classification and Standard Occupational Classification used by national bureaus of statistics are good examples. The community of national accountants also has a recommended approach to classifying households although it is far less used than the others. This is illustrated in figure 3.3, which shows a symmetric, top-down tree structure. All households are divided into urban and rural, and each of these main branches is subdivided into those earning their principal income in one of three ways: from property-type income and pensions or other transfers, from salaries, or from self-employment. Households of salaried workers are further distinguished as agricultural or nonagricultural, and the latter are subdivided into three skill classes employed in one of four kinds of establishments. Self-employed agricultural households are distinguished by the amount of land they work, and self-employed nonagricultural households by whether they have employees and whether their business is formal or informal. The resulting structure has forty-two categories (agricultural ones being suppressed in the urban areas), but no social accounting matrix has made use of all these categories. Often the three skill levels for describing the so-called reference individual in a household are replaced by categories for high, medium, and low household incomes.

This tree structure is called top-down because it is deduced from general considerations that are assumed to hold for any society rather than being based on the characteristics of households in a specific society. It is in principle ensured that all households are covered because each branching point is meant to encompass all possibilities. Not all trees are symmetric; the symmetry of this one is intended to assure an even-handed treatment of different types of households, facilitating comparisons, for example, between sources of income in urban and rural households. Unfortunately, the tendency to homogenize the categories in this way also conceals many social contrasts. Examples of nonsymmetric trees are the Standard Industrial Classification and the taxonomies associated with the division of the natural world into the great kingdoms of bacteria, protoctists, animals, plants, and fungi (Margulis and Schwartz 1982).

A New Classification for Households

The classification system used in most social accounting matrices represents a vast improvement over categorizing households on the basis of a single variable such as income. I have realized for some time the need for a new household classification scheme in which multiple household characteristics are used simultaneously to define household categories. Unduly influenced by the dominant concept of a top-down, symmetric tree structure, however, I believed that distinguishing households by not only income but also geographic location, type of housing, number of members, and characteristics of all members (rather than only a "head," or reference individual, which is implicitly assumed in figure 3.3) would require hundreds if not thousands of categories (Duchin 1988). It was a major discovery to realize that a bottom-up approach to household classification can reveal other, more fruitful concepts of structure.

Market researchers in the United States have developed alternative systems for describing over 100 million American households in terms of about forty categories. Their systems were developed for

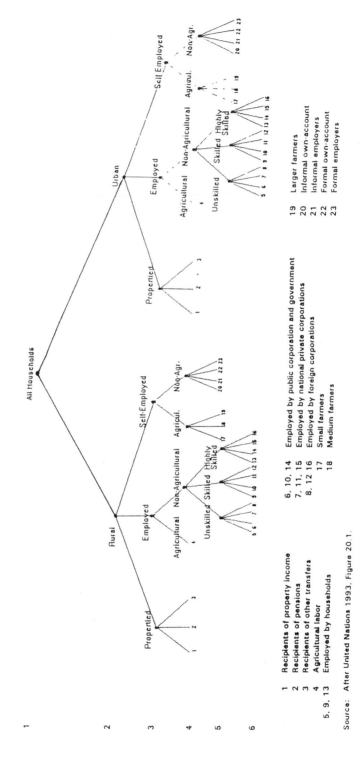

Level

1

2

3

4

5

6

Properticd

Rural

Employed

Agricultural Non-Agricultural

Unskilled Skilled Highly
Skilled

All Households

Self-Employed

Agricul. Non-Agr.

Urban

Properticd

Employed Self Employed

Agricultural Non-Agricultural Agricul. Non-Agr.

Unskilled Skilled Highly
Skilled

1   Recipients of property income   6, 10, 14   Employed by public corporation and government
2   Recipients of pensions   7, 11, 15   Employed by national private corporations
3   Recipients of other transfers   8, 12, 16   Employed by foreign corporations
4   Agricultural labor   17   Small farmers
5, 9, 13 Employed by households   18   Medium farmers

19   Larger farmers
20   Informal own-account
21   Informal employers
22   Formal own-account
23   Formal employers

Source: After United Nations 1993, Figure 20.1.

Figure 3.3. Top-Down Approach to the Classification of Households: 6-Level Tree

marketing and advertising and are used extensively today for those purposes. The underlying concepts are sufficiently powerful that their classifications can serve us well as a starting point for a more general approach to distinguishing different lifestyles. The guiding idea is to describe each household in terms of a set of variables and then use statistical techniques to cluster the households in terms of their similarities on those variables. It helps if the similarities of households in each cluster are sufficiently intuitively evident that each cluster can be given a suggestive name. Then there needs to be an unambiguous rule for assigning an individual household—one that was or was not in the original database—to one and only one cluster.

The creator of geodemographic lifestyle clusters, and the founder of the first firm to commercialize so-called micro-marketing services based on them, was Jonathan Robbin, who is widely quoted as saying, "Tell me someone's zip code, and I can predict what they eat, drink, drive—even think" (Weiss 1988).[2] After the United States Post Office partitioned the country into 36,000 areas, each associated with a unique five-digit "zip" code, to help automate the handling of mail, Robbin observed that people who live in close enough proximity to share a zip code tend to have similar lifestyles. He built a substantial database about household practices in each of these small areas; the database included detailed information from the Census of Households, automobile purchase lists, credit card information, voting records, social values from surveys carried out at the Stanford Research Institute, and a host of specialized, private surveys. On the basis of extensive analysis of hundreds of variables, he discovered that thirty-four variables accounted for almost 90 percent of the variation among neighborhoods. These variables described a household's social rank, mobility, ethnicity, position in the family life cycle, and style of housing. Each zip code was rated on the thirty-four factors simultaneously as a basis for assigning it to one of forty distinctive clusters, and an individual household was assigned to a cluster on the basis of its zip code. The basic idea is that a given neighborhood will be relatively homogeneous in lifestyle, and neighborhoods that are separated geographically may be virtually identical in lifestyle and thus fall into the same cluster. Robbin created a name for each cluster by examining its weighting on each variable. The resulting household classification scheme, which is widely used by American corporations to customize their messages for niche markets, is shown in table 3.1. This is the kind of household classification envisaged for the structural table.

TABLE 3.1. HOUSEHOLD CLASSIFICATIONS AND CHARACTERISTICS FOR THE UNITED STATES IN 1987

ZQ	Cluster	Description	% U.S. Households	Median Income	Median Home Value	% College Graduates
1	Blue Blood Estates	America's wealthiest neighborhoods; includes suburban homes and one in ten millionaires	1.1	$70,307	$200,000	50.7
2	Money & Brains	Posh big-city enclaves of townhouses, condos, and apartments	0.9	45,798	150,755	45.5
3	Furs & Station Wagons	New money in metropolitan bedroom suburbs	3.2	50,086	132,725	38.1
4	Urban Gold Coast	Upscale urban high-rise districts	0.5	36,838	200,000	50.5
5	Pools & Patios	Older, upper-middle-class, suburban communities	3.4	35,895	99,702	28.2
6	Two More Rungs	Comfortable multi-ethnic suburbs	0.7	31,263	117,012	28.3
7	Young Influentials	Yuppie, fringe-city condo and apartment developments	2.9	30,398	106,332	36.0
8	Young Suburbia	Child-rearing, outlying suburbs	5.3	38,582	93,281	23.8
9	God's Country	Upscale frontier boomtowns	2.7	36,728	99,418	25.8
10	Blue-Chip Blues	The wealthiest blue-collar suburbs	6.0	32,218	72,563	13.1
11	Bohemian Mix	Inner-city bohemian enclaves à la Greenwich Village	1.1	21,916	110,668	38.8
12	Levittown, USA	Aging, post–World War II tract subdivisions	3.1	28,742	70,728	15.7
13	Gray Power	Upper-middle-class retirement communities	2.9	25,259	83,630	18.3
14	Black Enterprise	Predominantly black, middle- and upper-middle-class neighborhoods	0.8	33,149	68,713	16.0
15	New Beginnings	Fringe-city areas of singles complexes, garden apartments, and trim bungalows	4.3	24,847	75,354	19.3
16	Blue-Collar Nursery	Middle-class, child-rearing towns	2.2	30,077	67,281	10.2
17	New Homesteaders	Exurban boomtowns of young, mid-scale families	4.2	25,909	67,221	15.9
18	New Melting Pot	New immigrant neighborhoods, primarily in the nation's port cities	0.9	22,142	113,616	19.1
19	Towns & Gowns	America's college towns	1.2	17,862	60,891	27.5
20	Rank & File	Older, blue-collar, industrial suburbs	1.4	26,283	59,363	9.2
21	Middle America	Mid-scale, mid-size towns	3.2	24,431	55,605	10.7
22	Old Yankee Rows	Working-class rowhouse districts	1.6	24,808	76,406	11.0

66

No.	Cluster	Description				
23	Coalburg & Corntown	Small towns based on light industry and farming	2.0	23,994	51,604	10.4
24	Shotguns & Pickups	Crossroads villages serving the nation's lumber and breadbasket needs	1.9	24,291	53,222	9.1
25	Golden Ponds	Rustic cottage communities located near the coasts, in the mountains or alongside lakes	5.2	20,140	51,537	12.8
26	Agri-business	Small towns surrounded by large-scale farms and ranches	2.1	21,363	49,012	11.5
27	Emergent Minorities	Predominantly black, working-class, city neighborhoods	1.7	22,029	45,187	10.7
28	Single City Blues	Downscale, urban singles districts	3.3	17,926	62,351	18.6
29	Mines & Mills	Struggling steeltowns and mining villages	2.8	21,537	46,325	8.7
30	Back-Country Folks	Remote, downscale, farm towns	3.4	19,843	41,030	8.1
31	Norma Rae–ville	Lower-middle-class milltowns and industrial suburbs, primarily in the South	2.3	18,559	36,556	9.6
32	Smalltown Downtown	Inner-city districts of small industrial cities	2.5	17,206	42,225	10.0
33	Grain Belt	The nation's most sparsely populated rural communities	1.3	21,698	45,852	8.4
34	Heavy Industry	Lower-working-class districts in the nation's older industrial cities	2.8	18,325	39,537	6.5
35	Share Croppers	Primarily southern hamlets devoted to farming and light industry	4.0	16,854	33,917	7.1
36	Downtown Dixie-Style	Aging, predominantly black neighborhoods, typically in southern cities	3.4	15,204	35,301	10.7
37	Hispanic Mix	America's Hispanic barrios	1.9	16,270	49,533	6.8
38	Tobacco Roads	Predominantly black farm communities throughout the South	1.2	13,227	27,143	7.3
39	Hard Scrabble	The nation's poorest rural settlements	1.5	12,874	27,651	6.5
40	Public Assistance	America's inner-city ghettos	3.1	10,804	28,340	6.3
	National median			$24,269	$64,182	16.2

Source: Weiss, 1988, pp. 4, 5, 12, 13.

Notes: 1. The ZQ (Zip Quality) index, based on income, home value, education, and occupational status, measures socioeconomic rank.

2. The source document does not report the year for which the data apply or the price unit. The household percentages are based on 1987 data, but the values appear to be for 1986 in current prices. The table shows a median household income of $24,269; this compares with figures of $23,618 for 1985 and $24,897 for 1986, according to the U.S. Bureau of the Census, Statistical Abstract of the United States (1994), table no. 707.

3. The upper census limit for home values is $200,000+; the figures for Blue Blood Estates and Urban Gold Coast are estimates.

The median income for each household cluster is shown in table 3.1. It can be seen that seven of the forty clusters have a median income within 5 percent of the national median, but the descriptions of these clusters suggest substantial differences in lifestyles; this diversity is confirmed in the table by the wide range of home values and college graduation rates among these clusters.

This bottom-up classification of U.S. households has about the same number of categories as the top-down classification described in figure 3.3. It would be hard to argue that the top-down system provides a better basis for describing lifestyles or analyzing scenarios about changes in lifestyle. Nonetheless, there is substantial arbitrariness surrounding the definition of the bottom-up clusters that will need to be reduced in the course of developing guidelines for standardizing the classification of households in a given society. Attention should be given to the variables used to characterize households, the statistical significance and independence of clusters, and their nomenclature. It is my hope that social scientists will take up this invitation. Despite all the remaining challenges, this body of work by market researchers is an extraordinary contribution to the study of households because it has demonstrated the plausibility of classifying over 100 million households into forty distinct categories, each of which is relatively homogeneous with respect to many types of economic and civic behavior.

Cluster analysis is frequently used by social scientists to identify variables that are highly correlated. In fact, a cluster analysis was carried out for Indonesia on the basis of socioeconomic information. Drake (1989) tabulated information on forty-eight variables, such as literacy, the ability to speak the common language (Bahasa Indonesia), type of work, and access to electricity, from census and other data collected by the Central Bureau of Statistics of Indonesia. The unit of analysis is the province, and most data were converted to a per capita basis for each of the twenty-seven provinces. The province containing the dominant city of Jakarta was eliminated from the analysis because it had extreme values on many of the variables. A total of nine factors ended up accounting for 75–85 percent of the variation among provinces (without Jakarta). The "sociocultural" factor called urban/media, for example, identified the common characteristics of East Kalimantan, the more urban provinces of Sumatra, Riau, South Kalimantan, and Yogyakarta, which are all in the western part of the country, while the "interaction" factor called sea transportation/road density groups the Javanese provinces and Bali at one pole (high road density) and Irian Jaya, East Kalimantan, Riau, Maluku, and Central Kalimantan at the other (high sea transport). (The regions of Indonesia are discussed in chapter 7 and identified in the map of figure 7.1.)

The most striking characteristics of Robbin's approach, as contrasted with the more typical approach to clustering of Drake, are his choice of the household as the unit of analysis, his boldness in aiming for tens of thousands of observations (households within a zip code), his ability to assemble a relevant database at that level of detail, and his use of the resulting factors to create a partition among the observations such that each could reasonably be assigned to one and only one factor. Of course, this outcome could be achieved only because the commonalities that he had hypothesized were in fact confirmed by the statistical analysis.

Now that the feasibility of the enterprise has been established, the cluster approach could be applied to many other societies if household-level data were available. In fact, with at least one demonstrated clustering of households, crude classifications can possibly be created for other societies by individuals familiar with them, even without passing by the demanding step of statistical cluster analysis. Clearly, the named clusters for each society will be very different; the unmistakably American characteristics of the clusters in Table 3.1 make this evident. It will be a slow process to move toward a Standardized Household Classification using these principles, as they reveal and emphasize the uniqueness of each society.

In applications of the International Standardized Industrial Classification scheme each country uses a customized version that features particular detail in the sectors in which it specializes. Societies naturally differ even more widely in their household than their industrial classifications, but this does not mean that each one requires a completely unique classification. I suspect that there are many categories of households that are found in different societies. In all societies, people progress through predictable cycles, marked by changes in lifestyle that may include establishing their first household after leaving that of their parents (if they do so), having children, children leaving home, retirement from active economic life, and taking in parents. There are many commonalities in urban lifestyles that distinguish them, across societies, from suburban and rural lifestyles. After experience has been accumulated in the development of bottom-up clusters for perhaps a dozen different societies, it will no doubt prove fruitful to attempt to compare and contrast them and identify common and unique household classifications for different societies. In this trial-and-error way, an appropriate degree of standardization across societies can be expected to emerge to provide some guidance for the admittedly somewhat arbitrary process of defining clusters in any given case. I suspect that the eventual outcome will take the form of a nonsymmetric tree as the bottom-up clusters are increasingly organized by top-down considerations.

Scenarios about Technology and Lifestyle

Having established the central roles of technology and lifestyle in human activities and sketched the ways in which descriptions of them could be represented in a structural table, we now turn to specific elements of alternative scenarios. Technological alternatives involve different ways of using energy, materials, water, land, biomass, and other resources. Options that conserve inputs, and those that make use of wastes or generate less of them, will tend to be interesting from both an environmental and an economic point of view. More generally, however, technologies will differ by the substitution of larger amounts of one set of inputs for smaller amounts of another. These options are more complicated to formulate and to evaluate. Based on my experience with scenarios about energy conservation, the recycling of materials, and the widespread adoption of the best of the current technologies (Duchin and Lange 1994), I have concluded that bolder efforts than these are needed if pollution globally is to be reduced in the foreseeable future.

A number of bolder technological scenarios have already been articulated. They are highly speculative in the sense that many decades would be required for their realization. People are understandably reluctant to take action in these cases, even in the absence of major technological obstacles, because of the substantial uncertainty that all the other required pieces will fall into place. In the area of energy use, an example is the use of photovoltaic cells to create hydrogen fuel, in the place of fossil fuels, hydroelectric power, and nuclear power (Rogner 1993; Nakicenovic 1994). Such a scenario would require changes in the input structures of sectors that use energy as well as those that produce it. Extensive analysis of the potential benefits of moving in that direction could tip the balance in terms of creating a critical mass of interest or discouraging it.

Another area that involves technological innovation is the large-scale cultivation of trees and other forms of biomass to provide a sink for carbon, improve soils, slow the harvesting of natural forests, and substitute for fuels and industrial materials of mineral origin (Morris and Ahmed 1992). These kinds of scenarios would require new agricultural and processing activities and necessitate changes in the input structures of some sectors switching to products of biological origin. Here the competition over land for growing food, on the one hand, and for urbanization, on the other, might be the most important focus of analysis.

Yet another area involves closing the loops in industrial processes by recovering products of economic value in what formerly was a waste stream. Scenarios would involve changes in the input structures of the industries affected, such as those that process foods or produce chemicals, and the effective use in the same or other industries of the reclaimed by-products. One could investigate in this way the scale of accomplishment such an initiative could hope to achieve as a basis for both funding and marketing the initiative.

The most promising domains for substantial environmental improvements due to technological change also require changes in lifestyle. Perhaps the clearest example is a dramatic reduction of reliance on private automobiles, which could be made possible and desirable only through the increased availability of nonmotorized and public transport and mixed-use community design that satisfies people's requirements with far less personal displacement (Engwicht 1993; Plate 1994; Durning 1996). This kind of scenario would involve changes in the product mix of the sectors that produce motor vehicles and in the operations of those that provide transport services as well as in the practices of households. An important first step would be qualitative descriptions of the kinds of lifestyles that could be accommodated in this way.

The volume of municipal solid waste and the composition and condition of the waste stream, which affect the success of composting or recycling parts of it, depend on the lifestyles of the households that the community comprises. Changes in personal habits that would reduce the volume and change the composition are directly related to patterns of consumption, which, in turn, reflect more general lifestyle choices.

Unlike the case of technology, there is little systematic knowledge about current lifestyles and differences in lifestyles. As a basis for examining the association between solid waste and American lifestyles, for example, it would be useful to start by extracting from the Current Population Surveys a description of consumption and work patterns for the forty household categories shown in table 3.1 (by matching zip codes). A description of the lifestyle of each household category would involve the ways in which it carries out the activities that are characteristic of this society. These include food preparation, furnishing and cleaning the home, personal care, recreation, work outside the home, leisure, and so on; a comprehensive list is shown in table 3.2. In the case of household disposal of plastics, for example, it turns out that a few activities account for the overwhelming share of most resins, mainly food preparation, and that there are systematic differences among the use and disposal practices of different categories of households (Duchin 1994).

The classification of household activities shown in table 3.2 is no doubt relevant for other countries besides the United States. For developing countries, many other activities would need to be distinguished, especially for households living outside of urban areas. An important, until now unexplored, line of investigation is what could be called a household process analysis or activity analysis. The idea is to describe in detail how a particular activity, say food preparation, is carried out in different categories of households in a given society or in different societies, while maintaining the discipline of using similar definitions, classifications, and units in the different cases. This undertaking is entirely analogous to the process analyses that are commonly carried out of individual aspects of industrial production, such as an analysis of the generation as distinct from the distribution of electricity.

TABLE 3.2. HOUSEHOLD ACTIVITIES

1. Food
2. Care of old and young
3. Health care
4. Personal care
5. Education
6. Household administration
7. Clothing (garments and cleaning)
8. Recreation and entertainment
9. Vacations
10. Housing (systems and maintenance)
11. Household furnishings
12. Household cleaning
13. Transportation
14. Home work for pay
15. Home work for community
16. Work outside home
17. Idleness

The basic motivation for studying the prospects for lifestyle changes in the rich countries is to explore ways to reduce resource use and pollution without sacrificing quality of life. In developing countries, the priority is to explore the lifestyle changes in entire communities that, largely unanticipated and unintended, accompany the entry of increased numbers of individuals into paid employment outside the home. The implications of the adoption by a small and influential elite in the developing countries of lifestyle changes pioneered in the rich countries and the emulation of them by other categories of first urban and subsequently rural households are also important to understand.

NOTES

1. The wage rates and other so-called factor costs also need to be specified.

2. The following description of the first commercial system, PRIZM, is from Weiss 1988. Today there are eight competing products of this kind in the United States (Mitchell 1995) and similar products in other countries.

Chapter 4

The Conceptual Framework of Structural Economics

Structural economics aims to describe and explain many of the salient features of technological, social, and environmental changes and their interactions within an economic system. The latter includes all activities related to the transformation of energy, materials, and other parts of the natural system, like soils and water, to serve human purposes. The emphasis on structure implies an interest in the state of the economic system during a particular interval of time, rather than only or mainly in rates of change. The state of an economy is described systematically and with a substantial amount of detail.

Many of the development economists active in the 1950s took what they called a structuralist approach to development policy (Chenery 1975). While they by and large accepted the relevance of neoclassical assumptions for developed economies, they felt that developing economies were characterized by "structural rigidities" requiring flexible policies that could not be analyzed within a neo-classical framework. Chenery recognized the advantages of the input–output system, but in advocating its absorption into a general equilibrium framework, he failed to anticipate the many advances that would be made in a structural approach.

Structural economics offers a framework for the empirical

description and quantitative analysis of changes from one state to another that have taken place in the past. But its principal use is for the evaluation of alternative scenarios about future paths for the economy. In fact, a major part of its ambition is to stimulate new thinking about promising scenarios for the future. This is accomplished in stages, by demonstrating the usefulness of what can be learned through the evaluation of scenarios that reflect current thinking and, in the process, pinpointing the insufficiencies in these scenarios as a basis for improving them.

Structural economics shares many characteristics of other contemporary approaches to studying real economies in that it focuses on production and consumption activities and evaluates trade-offs among alternative ways of proceeding. The main difference is that within structural economics these activities are seen as inseparable from the larger social systems in which they take place, and the latter in turn are understood to be an integral part of the material world. Social and material considerations are accorded sufficient importance that many familiar but unrealistic assumptions about the autonomy of strictly economic forces are eschewed. Relinquishing these assumptions has consequences that go beyond increased empirical relevance.

Neoclassical economists assume that competitive selection through increased efficiency at the firm level is the sole driving force for economic change; they offer this microeconomic theory of the firm as the foundation for macroeconomic relationships (see the discussion in Gowdy, forthcoming). Structural economists have to replace these succinct, and therefore convenient but overly restrictive, formal assumptions with assumptions that can allow a more open-ended inquiry. Meeting this challenge requires a broader theoretical formulation as well as more realistic empirical content. The need for substantive knowledge outside of the specialized domain of economics opens wide the doors to both the difficulties and the opportunities of interdisciplinary collaboration.

In all fields of scientific inquiry, tensions exist among the kinds of questions that one wants to ask, the state of knowledge and understanding, and the framework for formal analysis. For one thing, the questions change from time to time. Answering new questions adequately requires knowledge and understanding that is more extensive than, and perhaps different from, what is explored in the literature and codified in textbooks. New questions may reflect a change in perspective emphasizing different variables, different aspects of the relations presumed to hold among them, and changed units of analysis.

A formal mathematical framework that can yield numerical solutions is generally a substantial simplification of the common body of understanding. It provides unequaled power for deducing consequences of assumptions but constrains analysis in many ways, not least by building in assumptions that, mainly out of habit, cease to be questioned, and in the process discouraging lines of inquiry for which it is not well suited. The first objective of this chapter is to review the kinds of questions that structural economics intends to address. Next, its roots in input–output economics, and the expanded input–output framework that has been developed mainly over the last twenty years, are discussed, and the principal examples of the application of structural economics to analyzing scenarios about sustainable development are described. The final section is about the future of structural economics. Following the excursion of chapter 5 into social accounting, an important stimulus for extending the structural framework into the domain of households, chapter 6 provides a description of the formal, mathematical framework for this particular extension of Structural Economics.

Scope of Inquiry

In the modern world it is generally assumed that the objective of economic policy is to improve the material standard of living. For this reason, interest in personal consumption is of long standing among economists. Many aspects of household behavior that are related to the obtention and use of goods and services have been studied in great detail by other social scientists as well. Consumption can be viewed as the motor propelling an economy, in that producers fabricate those items that consumers want to buy. Until now, however, economists have devoted far more attention to production than to consumption (while the opposite has been true for other social scientists). The focus on production entails analysis of technological choice because methods that economize on costly inputs can increase profitability directly and indirectly enhance the comparative advantage of a firm, a sector, or even the economy as a whole.

Recently, environmental concerns have provided a new stimulus for interest in patterns of consumption and, by extension, in people's lifestyles. Most environmental degradation can be traced to the behavior of consumers, either directly, through activities like the disposal of garbage or the use of cars, or indirectly through the production activities undertaken to satisfy them. Clearly, changes surrounding consumption, no less than technological changes in the production process, would alter and could alleviate pressures on the environment.

Most developing countries have espoused modernization as a means to achieve affluence for a broader segment of the population. Growth is promoted by means such as the transfer of modern technologies, investment and credit, the cultivation of an entrepreneurial class, and the discouragement of traditional ways. Many of these economies are in fact becoming increasingly industrialized and urbanized, and their integration into the global economic system is reinforced by an internationally oriented middle class that aspires to the lifestyles of the affluent in the rich countries. Transfers of modern technologies and lifestyles reinforce each other.

What is not generally realized in the rich countries is that most households in the developing world operate largely outside of the "formal" economy, and in many instances the process of modernization increases their numbers and puts additional pressures on their ability to adapt. De Soto (1989) provides a pathbreaking analysis of the informal sector based on work in Peru, and Chickering and Saladine (1991) collected a set of applications of de Soto's methods to countries in Asia and the Middle East. It could be argued that the assistance provided by institutions modeled after the Grameen Bank,[1] in the form of small, self-administered loans for small-scale, often traditional economic activities, has been more valuable for more people than the far larger sums dispensed for vast, modern projects by the World Bank. The operation of the informal economies and the adoption of "appropriate" rather than "high" technology are important components of strategies for sustainable development that have been insufficiently studied by economists until now. See Schumacher (1973), Mollison (1988), and Todd (1991) for pioneering work on appropriate technologies and Timmer (1975) for rare insight from an economist as to the reasons inappropriate choices are common.

The most severe environmental problems in the developing countries, notably water pollution and soil erosion, are still those associated with lifestyles of poverty rather than affluence. Modernization and urbanization also have characteristic environmental consequences, such as the clearing of forests and the generation of toxic wastes and atmospheric pollutants. The relative importance of different pressures naturally varies in each case.

Structural economics is a framework for formulating scenarios about sustainable development, mainly (but not exclusively) in terms of technological and lifestyle options. The basic question being asked is: What would be the major economic, social, and environmental implications if specific changes in technology and lifestyle took place? The economic implications have to do with changes in costs, prices, incomes, consumption, taxes, and terms of trade; social implications, with the mix of jobs or the relative importance of different types of households and the private or public provision of public services; and environmental implications involve volumes of material and energy use and wastes generated.

Economists who are concerned exclusively with competitive markets have made theoretical and methodological commitments to taking the individual firm and the individual consumer as the basic units of analysis. Given the types of questions it intends to address, structural economics is concerned with lifestyles of households rather than the consumption of individuals and with strategic investment decisions about technological alternatives rather than the market shares of individual firms.

Even at the individual level, consumption behavior is tightly linked with employment, in that earned income has to cover outlays for purchased goods and services. It is also related to other people's consumption and employment. If many individuals stop buying and using cars, auto workers (and, by a domino effect, other kinds of workers like those in petroleum refineries) would soon be without jobs and income; if they buy more cars, the opposite dynamic is initiated. Most people live in households that include more than one consumer and often more than one paid worker. At least a portion of each income is pooled, based in part on custom and in part on negotiations among the members of the household, to pay for shared goods like the residence itself and often an automobile—or, in developing countries, a motorbike—and to provide support for children and other financially dependent members.

A minimal description of the lifestyle of a household needs to reflect both employment and consumption practices. Employment takes the form of different types of paid or unpaid work, in terms of specific occupations; and consumption involves the purchase and use of various goods and services. Lifestyle choices and outcomes are influenced by cultural background, income, moral values, and the social pressures to which the household members are sensitive. For household categories to serve as a sound unit of analysis, the millions of households in a particular society must be partitioned into a few dozen, or at most a few hundred, so that all those in the same grouping have similar lifestyles. The classification presented in chapter 3 suggests that it is possible to meet this challenge.

Structural economics is concerned with the characteristics of production sectors, the ensembles of establishments producing similar products by similar means, more than with the competition among individual firms within a sector. The major considerations for grouping establishments in the same sector are a similar mix of inputs, including the employment and remuneration of different types of workers, the use of resources and the environmental effects of production, overall efficiency or productivity and the prospects for improving it, and the economic implications of alternative choices of technology. While a society may have thousands or even millions of business establishments, these can be classified into a few dozen (or at most several hundred) sectors that are relatively homogenous; this is done on a regular basis when Standard Industrial Classifications are utilized. It may be appropriate to create separate sectors when there is a substantial difference in quality and technology for products that serve similar functions. This could be the case, for example, for consumer goods produced in informal household enterprises (microenterprises) using simple technologies as well as their capital-intensive counterparts in registered factories using more modern techniques.

The household category and production sector as the units of analysis have a social significance lacking in a more atomistic choice of units. The number of actors has been reduced by several orders of magnitude, making it possible to describe the actual situation and the future prospects for each social unit at a depth of quantitative and qualitative detail that would not otherwise be possible. It is true that, as a consequence of the choice of unit, structural economics will not be able to analyze relations among individual persons or firms. This is not an impediment for the kinds of scenarios that are envisaged.

Economic process for a neoclassical economist is defined in terms of market-clearing competition among individual actors during the course of which new, equilibrium prices are established. A typical dynamic conception generalizes this notion of equilibrium and is also concerned with rates of growth, especially of macroeconomic aggregates. Structural economics relies on a representation of the interdependency among the parts of the economic system that is much less restrictive than "general equilibrium." There are many fewer, and weaker, behavioral assumptions built into the theory or model. Consequently, more assumptions need to be made in the analysis of particular scenarios, and outcomes involve more sorts of results that need to be interpreted. A study usually requires a team of analysts and often is able to reveal layers of empirical content.

Input–Output Economics

Structural economics is an expansion of input–output economics, which was created to deepen the empirical content of economic analysis (Leontief 1936, 1937). During his long career, Leontief has taken a number of pioneering positions that are further developed in structural economics. He achieves an intimate relationship among verbal theory, empirical information, and the mathematical language used in drawing quantitative conclusions by providing a framework that can be used to evaluate alternative scenarios. In his conception of the importance of structure, he stresses the central role of "an adequately defined classification of industries" that "constitutes the cornerstone of effective input–output analysis" (Leontief 1952, 8). Structural economics takes up the challenge of extending the framework to include an adequate classification of households and using it to analyze scenarios about sustainable development.

Input–output economics has influenced practices in statistical offices and government agencies around the world. Input–output tables that describe the structure of the economy during a given year in the recent past are collected on a periodic basis by government statistical offices in over a hundred countries around the world, where they are utilized in applied analyses. However, despite the award to Leontief of the Nobel Prize in economics for 1973, input–output economics has failed to maintain the interest (past the 1960s) of academic theorists, who regard it as a simplistic form of general equilibrium analysis. Curiously, many input–output economists have accepted this indictment. The standard charge was the use of "fixed coefficients," meaning that parameters that in principle should be variable were instead treated as constant.

In recent years only the simplest input–output studies have actually used parameters that do not change; on the contrary, much of the research effort in input–output economics is devoted to the projection of the parameters that correspond to alternative scenarios. The failure of academic economists to take note of the changed practices reveals the deeper objection to "fixed" coefficients. It is not that the coefficients do not change but more specifically that physical structures do not respond automatically to changes in prices, as they do in a neoclassical conception of rational behavior. Elasticities of substitution are not built into the conceptual framework of input–output economics. Substitution behavior on the part of consumers or even producers is not considered to be a straightforward reaction to prices. Instead of ubiquitous substitutions among atomistic constituents on the margin, input–output economists deal with discrete and explicit changes in structures.

The layout of a standard input–output table is shown in figure 4.1 as a rectangular matrix with three non-zero portions. The table quantifies the transactions among industries, such as rice production or specific kinds of services; factor inputs to production like labor or capital; and deliveries of outputs to final users, such as for consumption or export. Table 4.1 shows a ten-sector input–output table for Indonesia in 1985 using actual figures in money values. This reduced and simplified version has a single column aggregating all final deliveries and a single row showing value added, or the money value of all primary inputs. A table in money values at current prices has the feature that row totals equal column totals; this is seen in table 4.1, where, for example, the value of all inputs to the mining sector total 16,727 billion rupiahs, the same as the total value of all deliveries of the output of this sector. Input–output

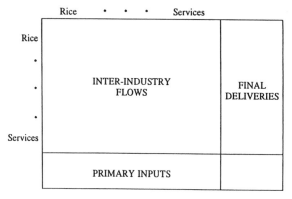

Figure 4.1. Schematic Input–Output Table

TABLE 4.1. TEN-SECTOR INPUT–OUTPUT TABLE FOR INDONESIA IN 1985 (BILLIONS OF RUPIAHS)

	1	2	3	4	5	6	7	8	9	10	Final Deliveries	Total
1 Agriculture, forestry and fisheries	2,894	1	11,214	0	436	1	1,065	3	0	80	12,852	28,546
2 Mining	4	640	6,340	101	727	0	0	0	0	0	8,915	16,727
3 Manufacturing	1,931	389	10,224	772	6,925	323	1,194	1,525	178	1,845	22,587	47,893
4 Utilities	23	5	272	287	11	107	150	51	43	214	639	1,802
5 Construction	107	106	113	50	31	88	65	180	437	112	16,568	17,857
6 Trade	581	57	2,419	110	2,274	66	402	202	25	349	7,328	13,813
7 Restaurants and hotels	17	93	214	2	69	171	26	95	79	50	4,978	5,794
8 Transportation and communication	226	133	969	48	729	311	163	871	154	197	6,401	10,202
9 Business services	232	550	600	14	410	642	214	258	608	313	4,157	8,098
10 Services	130	180	299	22	21	139	61	1,170	169	279	13,221	15,691
Value added	22,401	14,573	15,229	396	6,224	11,965	2,454	5,747	6,405	12,252		
Total	28,546	16,727	47,893	1,802	17,857	13,813	5,794	10,202	8,098	15,691		

Source: BPS 1989, table 9.
Note: Totals may not add due to rounding.

tables generally distinguish several dozen if not several hundred sectors and at least a handful of factor inputs and final deliveries.

The passage from a descriptive table to a framework for analysis relies on the important observation that each sector has a characteristic mix of inputs per unit of output. Table 4.2 shows the inputs per unit of output corresponding to the input–output table for Indonesia in 1985. It is obtained by dividing each figure in table 4.1 by the corresponding column total. Inspection of the columns of coefficients shows, for example, that manufacturing makes intensive use of primary materials. The column of coefficients for manufacturing represents what is called its input structure. This structure would be altered in the event of technological change. It would also change with a shift in the mix of products that are fabricated. In fact, it would be useful for the purposes of analysis to disaggregate the manufacturing sector to separately represent, say, food processing, textiles and apparel, and petroleum refining.

Five objects, a matrix and four vectors, can now be distinguished. Call the coefficient matrix (like the one in table 4.2) $\mathbf{A}$, the vector of final demand y, total output x, value added v, and prices p. $\mathbf{I}$ is the identity matrix. The two fundamental equations of input–output economics are as follows:

(1) $x - \mathbf{A}x = y$
Equation 1 can also be written as $(\mathbf{I} - \mathbf{A})x = y$, or $x = (\mathbf{I} - \mathbf{A})^{-1}y$.

(2) $p - \mathbf{A}'p = v$
Equation 2 can also be written as $(\mathbf{I} - \mathbf{A}')p = v$, or $p = (\mathbf{I} - \mathbf{A}')^{-1}v$.

Of the many thousands of input–output analyses that have been carried out over the past several decades, the overwhelming majority involve applying equation 1 to data derived from an official input–output table, that is, one prepared by a government agency.

Equation 1 states that the portion of output (x) that is not used in the course of production ($\mathbf{A}x$ is the amount that is used in production) is left for final deliveries (y). It provides a way of calculating changes in the production requirements (x) if there are changes in consumption (that is, in final demand, y) or in input structures $(\mathbf{A})$. The inverse matrix, $(\mathbf{I} - \mathbf{A})^{-1}$, is of considerable economic interest because it captures both direct and indirect input requirements. It has been called the Leontief inverse, and the one corresponding to the numerical example is shown in table 4.3. To see its significance, observe that no mining inputs are sold to any of the service sectors.

TABLE 4.2. COEFFICIENT MATRIX FOR INDONESIA IN 1985 (RUPIAHS OF INPUT PER RUPIAH OF OUTPUT)

		1	2	3	4	5	6	7	8	9	10
1	Agriculture, forestry and fisheries	0.1014	0.0001	0.2341	0	0.0244	0.0001	0.1838	0.0003	0	0.0051
2	Mining	0.0001	0.0383	0.1324	0.0560	0.0407	0	0	0	0	0
3	Manufacturing	0.0676	0.0233	0.2135	0.4284	0.3878	0.0234	0.2061	0.1495	0.0220	0.1176
4	Utilities	0.0008	0.0003	0.0057	0.1593	0.0006	0.0077	0.0259	0.0050	0.0053	0.0136
5	Construction	0.0037	0.0063	0.0024	0.0277	0.0017	0.0064	0.0112	0.0176	0.0540	0.0071
6	Trade	0.0204	0.0034	0.0505	0.0610	0.1273	0.0048	0.0694	0.0198	0.0031	0.0222
7	Restaurants and hotels	0.0006	0.0056	0.0045	0.0011	0.0039	0.0124	0.0045	0.0093	0.0098	0.0032
8	Transportation and communication	0.0079	0.0080	0.0202	0.0266	0.0408	0.0225	0.0281	0.0854	0.0190	0.0126
9	Business services	0.0081	0.0329	0.0125	0.0078	0.0230	0.0465	0.0369	0.0351	0.0751	0.0199
10	Services	0.0046	0.0108	0.0062	0.0122	0.0012	0.0101	0.0105	0.1147	0.0209	0.0178

Source: Table 4.1.

This is indicated by the entries of 0 in row 2, columns 6 through 10, in table 4.2. Yet the service sectors naturally do make use indirectly of minerals, such as the metals in buildings. The Leontief inverse shows that delivery of a billion rupiahs' worth of restaurant and hotel services requires as much as 49 million rupiahs' worth of mining outputs, indicated by the entry 0.049 in row 2, column 7, of table 4.3.

The price model (equation 2) was developed early in the history of input–output economics. It states that the price of a unit of output (p) is equal to the cost, or quantity times price, of inputs ($\mathbf{A}'p$) plus value-added (v). Thus the price relationships depend upon the same matrix, $\mathbf{A}$ (or actually $\mathbf{A}'$) as the quantity relationships. For given changes in $\mathbf{A}$ (or v), the equation can be used to calculate the changes in relative prices. If the construction sector were able to economize on material inputs (a change in input structure in $\mathbf{A}$), both its own unit price and the unit prices of all sectors using its output would fall. Likewise, a change in factor inputs or a value-added tax in a given sector (represented as changes in v) would affect all prices directly or indirectly.

A discussion of units will demonstrate the value of the price model while also revealing why it is not utilized more frequently. If output is measured in physical units, say bushels of grain and tons of iron and of steel, then these are the units of the x vector that is the solution to equation 1. A sample element of the $\mathbf{A}$ matrix would be tons of iron required to make a ton of steel. Then the units of the price vector, which is the solution to equation 2, will be money values such as dollars per bushel of grain, per ton of iron, and per ton of steel.

Most analysts, however, use a database where output is measured in money units, such as dollars' worth, rather than physical units like bushels. A sample entry of the $\mathbf{A}$ matrix would be dollars' worth of iron required to make one dollar's worth of steel. In this case, all prices determined by equation 2 will be 1.0, meaning that it will cost exactly one dollar to make a dollar's worth of output. This solution is tautological and therefore not very interesting.

It is not generally recognized that even in this case the price model is valuable for carrying out experiments. In the event that technological changes are incorporated into the $\mathbf{A}$ matrix, new solutions will be obtained for x and p. Suppose that the resulting prices for grain, iron, and steel are now 1.01, 0.85, and 0.93. This means that the technological changes have had the effect of raising the price of a bushel of grain by 1 percent while lowering the price of a ton of

Table 4.3. Leontief Inverse for Indonesia in 1985 (rupiahs of input per rupiah of final deliveries)

	1	2	3	4	5	6	7	8	9	10
1 Agriculture, forestry and fisheries	1.142	0.014	0.350	0.190	0.171	0.018	0.295	0.073	0.025	0.054
2 Mining	0.016	1.046	0.185	0.170	0.118	0.009	0.049	0.038	0.014	0.027
3 Manufacturing	0.109	0.045	1.333	0.717	0.544	0.056	0.337	0.263	0.081	0.181
4 Utilities	0.002	0.002	0.011	1.197	0.007	0.011	0.036	0.012	0.009	0.019
5 Construction	0.006	0.009	0.009	0.041	1.010	0.011	0.019	0.025	0.060	0.011
6 Trade	0.030	0.009	0.079	0.122	0.164	1.012	0.100	0.045	0.018	0.037
7 Restaurants and hotels	0.002	0.007	0.009	0.008	0.010	0.014	1.009	0.013	0.012	0.005
8 Transportation and communication	0.014	0.012	0.038	0.060	0.065	0.029	0.047	1.106	0.029	0.021
9 Business services	0.015	0.040	0.034	0.038	0.050	0.054	0.057	0.054	1.088	0.029
10 Services	0.008	0.014	0.018	0.031	0.017	0.016	0.023	0.133	0.028	1.024

Source: Table 4.2.

iron by 15 percent and the price of a ton of steel by 7 percent. Thus the effects on relative prices can be estimated using the price equation even if the unit prices are not explicitly represented.

An input–output analysis does not depend on the existence of an official table based on accounting information about purchases and sales that have taken place in the past. A coefficient matrix can be built directly, in physical or mixed units rather than in money units only, on the basis of technical information about input structures coming from a wide variety of sources. (Alternatively, a given matrix in money units can be converted to mixed units; for example, the unit for petroleum can be changed from dollars to barrels if the price per barrel is known.) The same kinds of data sources can be used to build alternative scenarios about the future using a flow table for a base year as the point of departure. Thus, for example, one could develop assumptions about changes in input structures corresponding to new technologies for recycling steel or paper and then use equations (1) and (2) to quantify the effects on output volumes (including tons of coal and kilowatt hours of electricity) and on relative prices.

The input–output model is readily used to assess the implications for output of changes in the pattern of household consumption or other categories of final deliveries (y). If employment requirements per unit of output are known, these are readily assembled into a row vector and multiplied by the solution vector (x) to determine labor requirements associated with the scenario.

The basic model already has several key features that are shared by all input–output models. The physical model provides a direct link to the natural world. From measuring electricity output in kilowatt hours, it is a small step to a physical conception of factor inputs, such as labor requirements in persons, or emissions of carbon, sulfur, and nitrogen in tons per kilowatt hour. In the corresponding price model, such characteristics as pollutants may, but do not have to, have money values associated with them.

The inter-industry portion of an input–output table could in principle be built in terms of separate business establishments. But, following Leontief, input–output economists have been concerned with the characteristics of an entire sector rather than the differential profitability of individual firms, or the division of market share among them. Input–output analysis spans microeconomics and macroeconomics by covering the entire economy at an intermediate level of detail.

An Expanded Input–Output Framework

Equations 1 and 2 constitute what has been called the open, static input–output model. It is static in that it describes the state of an economy during a single accounting period (generally a given year). A comparative static analysis of changes in state from one year to another can be carried out, but the dynamics of change cannot be traced. The basic model is called open because many important assumptions need to be made outside of the framework rather than being deducible within it (in which case it would be closed for those assumptions). In particular, all information about final deliveries and factor prices is exogenous. The progressive closure of the model is achieved as one exogenous variable after the next becomes endogenous. Most of the extensions of the conceptual framework of the input–output model involve its closure: for investment (dynamic model), for the choice of technology, and for international trade (world model). The other major extension is the development of systematic methods for absorbing new kinds of information from unconventional sources into the input–output database. Conceptual advances that have made possible broader or deeper empirical investigations are described in the following paragraphs, and applications are described in the next section. The conceptual and practical closure of the model for households is the subject of chapter 5.

A dynamic input–output model, in both physical and price versions, was sketched by Leontief (1953, 1970). This formulation attracted substantial interest from economists; the generalization of investment dynamics from a two-sector to a multisectoral context made for a model with intriguing mathematical properties, and a number of refinements were made to Leontief's conception. In all cases, however, the solution was expressed in terms of the eigen-values and eigen-vectors of a single matrix of technical coefficients (one incorporating both current account and capital requirements). The mathematical equation involving this matrix imposed two critical assumptions: Technology did not change over the entire time horizon of the analysis, and all sectors grew at the same rate. Because of these strong restrictions, only stylized empirical applications were possible—essentially, the calculation of the highly unstable, so-called balanced growth rate. Eventually, Leontief's model was modified by incorporating an additional variable, the production capacity of each sector (Duchin and Szyld 1985). The new formulation, by allowing operation below (or temporarily above) capacity, made it possible for sectors to grow at different rates or even to contract. In this framework, it was straightforward to allow changes in structure to reflect technological changes as well as the accumulation of stocks of physical capital.

The new dynamic model was first used to analyze a phenomenon that had concerned Leontief for over fifty years: the pace at which workers would be displaced by machinery and the implications for their material standard of living (Leontief and Duchin 1986; Duchin and Lange 1992b). The model has been implemented for Italy (Costa 1988, 1992; Leontief and Costa 1996), Germany (Edler 1990; Edler et al. 1990), and Indonesia (Duchin, Hamilton, and Lange 1993; Duchin and Lange 1993).

The static input–output system bears a family resemblance to a linear programming problem except that the former is generally not used to maximize an objective function. The input–output analyst investigates the implications of alternative scenarios one by one instead of relying on a formal criterion for selecting among them. However, the optimization framework has proved fruitful within a static input–output framework for choosing among alternative technologies, or input structures, those that minimize the costs of production of a single sector or of the economy as a whole. For the closure of the static physical model for the choice of technology, see Carter (1970) and Leontief (1986) and for a physical and price formulation of the optimization problem, Duchin (1988) and Duchin and Lange (1995).

Leontief used the occasion of his Nobel lecture in 1973 to describe an input–output model of the world economy, requiring the closure of the input–output model for international trade (Leontief 1973). This formulation has been used and extended for over two decades in several large-scale, empirical inquiries (Leontief, Carter, and Petri 1977; Leontief, Mariscal, and Sohn 1983; Leontief, Koo, Nasar, and Sohn 1983; Leontief and Duchin 1983; Duchin and Lange 1994).

Analysts posing questions that go beyond the conventional confines of economics have found a structural approach well suited to describing various aspects of economic activities. Input–output models have appealed to ecological economists, including Nicholas Georgescu-Roegen, who made a mathematical contribution in this area (1951), and Herman Daly, who used the input–output formalism to illustrate the interdependence between human activities and the natural world (1968).

An important generalization of the input–output framework was made by Robert Ayres and his colleagues for the explicit representation of material balances (Ayres and Kneese 1969; Ayres 1978). Ayres has also produced figures quantifying flows through the economy for several materials (notably, Ayres and Ayres 1994; Ayres and Ayres 1996), but they have yet to be utilized in an empirical analysis of production and consumption. Two studies of the use and disposal of plastics make use of industry sources of information about material balances for individual resins (Duchin 1994; Duchin and Lange 1998).

Bruce Hannon and his colleagues made equally important extensions for the representation of energy balances (e.g., Herendeen and Bullard 1975) and have analyzed a variety of alternative scenarios— for example, an evaluation of the energy savings that might be associated with the use of buses rather than cars (Hannon and Puleo 1975). Hannon and colleagues have recently proposed extensions of the input–output framework for describing relationships within ecological systems (Hannon, Costanza, and Ulanowicz 1991).

The representation of material and energy inputs to production overlaps with the developing practices of natural resource accounting (e.g., Central Bureau of Statistics of Norway 1992; de Haan, Keuning, and Bosch 1993; Lange and Duchin 1994). The integration of these entirely new kinds of information within an economic framework requires applying a common set of concepts, classifications, and definitions to data that come from various sources. An important, ambitious example is de Haan and Keuning 1996. Mathematical relationships that incorporate this information within a structural framework have been developed in a number of recent studies (e.g., Lange and Duchin 1994).

The so-called input–output case study methodology was developed at the Institute for Economic Analysis at New York University to facilitate the utilization of a great deal of fragmentary information to construct scenarios and to represent them in the database. It provides a systematic way to organize quantitative information, using standard classifications and units, as well as qualitative information, which is often helpful for interpreting results (Duchin and Lange 1994, 195–98; see also Duchin, Hamilton, and Lange 1993; Idenburg 1993). These guidelines make it possible for individuals with subject expertise to produce empirical case studies that can satisfy the requirements of formal analysis. The methods also substantially improve consistency across case studies.

Structural economics incorporates the extensions to input–output economics that have been described above. The generalization from an input–output table to a structural table was shown in schematic form in figures 3.1 and 3.2, where the square inter-industry portion of the table is shown in the upper lefthand corner in terms of any number of sectors. The single exogenous column of investment requirements of an input–output table (figure 4.1) is expanded to rows and columns describing capital requirements per unit increase in capacity by capital-using and capital-producing sectors (figure 3.1). The single column for household consumption (among final deliveries) and the single row for labor inputs (as value added) (figure 4.1) are expanded to accommodate consumption patterns for various categories of households and inputs of different kinds of labor. Resource use is explicitly included in terms of multiple types of inputs such as materials, energy, water, land, biomass, and so on; and a variety of wastes are also shown.

Such a table can be filled in with actual figures (as in the example of figure 3.2) and converted to a matrix of coefficients, or the coefficient matrix can be estimated directly. Various mathematical formulations for the closure of the input–output model and the manipulation of the structural table can be found in the references cited in this section and will not be repeated here. Conventional closures for industrial and household activities are described in detail in chapter 5, and the new one that I propose is presented in chapter 6.

Applications to Sustainable Development

Structural economics provides a firm basis for evaluating scenarios about sustainable development through a concrete and relatively detailed representation of economic activities and the interdependencies between them and the environment. The conceptual and analytic frameworks are fully operational and at the same time are intended to be extended and refined as questions evolve and experience is accumulated.

The analysis begins by determining the kinds of questions that will be addressed and the type of mathematical model that will be used or developed (e.g., price or physical model, static or dynamic model). Then classifications for industries, households, and resources are established, in view of the questions to be addressed.

A numerical table is developed that, on the basis of these classifications, quantifies inter-industry and household transactions, use of resources, and generation of pollutants in one or more historical years. These become the base years for the analysis. Even when official input–output tables are available and used as the point of departure, supplementary information is almost always required to complete them.

The next step is to build one or more scenarios around each of the questions to be explored. A scenario has two components: First, it specifies the content of an experiment—for example, assumptions about intensifying rice production and improving the diet. Second, that content must be expressed in the variables and parameters that serve as the language of the model. If the scenarios are well defined, executing the computations should be straightforward once the assumptions have been quantified. Interpreting the results generally requires drawing on a wider understanding of the context of the scenario than that which is expressed in the formal model. Two examples will demonstrate the process.

In preparing our evaluation of the feasibility of the Brundtland Report (discussed in chapter 1), my colleagues and I used an existing input–output model and database of the world economy. The construction of the scenario was accomplished in several stages.

The Brundtland Report makes moderate assumptions about future growth of population, sets ambitious economic targets, and calls for actions to reduce pressures on the environment. The authors suggest that these objectives can be achieved by using cleaner, more efficient technologies in factories, offices, and homes around the globe. Our scenario translated the intent of the Brundtland Report into optimistic assumptions about the adoption in all regions of the world economy of specific technologies that reduce requirements for energy and materials in industry and households. The decision was made to limit the investigation to three pollutants, chosen for a balance between relevance to the initial question and simplification of data collection and scenario construction. The assumptions were quantified on the basis of eleven case studies and were incorporated in the database as changes in parameters measuring inputs per unit of output or of material use or personal consumption. The "What would happen if . . . ?" question was: Would pollution (represented as endogenous variables) decrease as assumed in the Brundtland Report?

Another study involved development scenarios for Indonesia that could create not only rapid economic growth over the next several decades but also adequate employment for new workers and for those who are under current conditions underemployed or unemployed. One component of these scenarios was to modernize agricultural technology over the next two decades in order for Indonesia to remain self-sufficient in food while upgrading the nutritional quality and variety of the diet for a growing population and taking some of the most fertile land out of food production in the course of urbanization (Duchin, Hamilton, and Lange 1993). The scenario assumed changes in diet (i.e., in selected consumption parameters) and in input structures for the agricultural sectors to reflect optimistic assumptions of agricultural experts about the yields of new technologies. A dynamic model and database of the Indonesian economy were used to determine how much labor, land, and water would be required (these were endogenous variables) to support these assumptions.

Developing the data for a scenario generally involves a set of case studies. Each study is designed to cover several related areas of expertise so that it can draw on a coherent body of technical literature and specialists. For the investigation of the Brundtland Report, case studies were carried out for electric power generation, cement, construction, pulp and paper, chemicals, motor vehicles, processing and fabrication of metals, and the use of energy in industry and households. Case studies for Indonesia, focused on the use of land, water, and energy, were carried out for households, forestry, rice, other food crops, estate crops, livestock, pulp and paper, cement, chemicals, food processing, textiles and apparel, and basic iron and steel.

I have already reported that the kinds of technological assumptions made in the Brundtland Report are cost saving overall, but they result in increased, not decreased, pressures on the environment over the next twenty-five years as they prove inadequate to offset the growth in population and wealth. Even the most optimistic assumptions about the adoption of advanced agricultural technologies could not meet the expectations of the Indonesian government under the conditions that were specified; the analysis suggested that food would need to be imported. The modernization scenarios involved a total number of jobs that could match the anticipated supply of labor, but the analysis provided no basis for evaluating whether the experience and training of the potential workers was matched to the likely job requirements. The desire to address this question was the initial impetus for an inquiry into the changing lifestyles of Indonesian households.

The Future of Structural Economics

Input–output analysis has been used extensively over the past half century. Most applications have applied the basic, static physical equation to new sets of data. This simple framework has proven valuable in demonstrating the meaning of economic inter-dependency and in providing practical insights into the operations of their economies to large numbers of analysts around the world.

Nonetheless, this relatively mechanical use of a single equation has obscured the theoretical content of input–output economics and its roots in classical political economy. The ambition of structural economics is to utilize its powerful conception of interdependency in an increasingly broad context.

Cost-benefit analysis, one of the most practical areas of economics, is used to quantify the trade-offs among alternative ways of proceeding. Because it is intended for evaluating small projects that make a marginal contribution to an economy, it is freed from some of the assumptions of a general equilibrium framework but is steeped in the neoclassical concept of rationality through measures like consumer's surplus. The projects generally have substantial social and environmental implications, and new valuation categories—including so-called existence values, option values, and precautionary values—and techniques for assigning money values to them have been developed.

Substantial generalization of the cost-benefit approach beyond money valuations is needed to apply it to alternative scenarios for sustainable development. It is an ambition of structural economics to provide this generalization.

Scenario development has received surprisingly little attention among economists, even within the framework of cost-benefit analysis. Scenarios have a relatively short history of use in the social sciences and usually take a simple form in which only one or a few variables are assigned a high, medium, or low value. Detailed scenarios are not needed in a general equilibrium framework because most changes are due to automatic adjustments rather than exogenous assumptions. In the applied, partial equilibrium world of cost-benefit analysis, project options do have to be specified, but they are usually supplied to the analyst and the assumptions are interpreted and quantified in stylized ways. For these reasons, the development of content-rich scenarios for analytic evaluation is largely uncharted territory. Structural economics can contribute substantial experience in this area.

Valuation, on the other hand, is heavily trodden terrain. It is central to the neoclassical framework, in which money prices serve as the common denominator for reconciling values of all sorts. Individual money values that are determined analytically, rather than in markets, are combined with market values not only in cost-benefit studies but also in the compilation of various index numbers like "green GNP."

With the move from the evaluation of individual resources or characteristics, individual projects, and individual index numbers to evaluation of alternative scenarios for sustainable development, the temptation to reduce all values to money values for tactical purposes (i.e., to capture and maintain the attention of busy decision makers and the presumably unsophisticated public) is substantially reduced. If the scenarios are of sufficiently compelling interest, stakeholders will be frustrated by the absurd prospect of obscuring the social, environmental, and economic implications of a given course of action by reducing them to a single, more or less arbitrary number. An understanding of the outcomes requires at very least a set of numbers, only some of which are in money terms, and the advantages of this multidimensionality are further amplified by incorporating important but often unquantifiable characteristics of outcomes, such as preserving wetlands or maintaining the social relations within a community.

NOTES

1. The pioneering institution that provides credit to the very poor in rural Bangladesh through borrower groups that administer their own loans (see Huq and Sultan 1991).

Chapter 5

The Social Accounting Approach and Its Application to Indonesia

The Objectives of Social Accounting

National Accounts are integrated tables of economic and financial data compiled periodically by national and international statistical agencies. The accounts describe various aspects of the production and consumption of goods and services using concepts related to the gross domestic product (GDP). Today, many countries include input–output tables as part of their National Accounts.

The incorporation of a detailed representation of households into the description and analysis of production activities was instigated by Nobel laureate Richard Stone as an extension of input–output data and analysis. Stone envisioned what he called social accounts for "the systematic quantitative description of social systems, particularly in their economic aspect" (Stone 1986). A set of interlocking accounts for each nation would distinguish economic transactions according to the actors involved, the latter identified by their social and demographic characteristics. Stone made many pioneering recommendations for improving and extending the United Nations' System of National Accounts. The two most important extensions will be discussed here, sociodemographic accounts and social accounting.

Stone observed that many nations have extensive collections of social and demographic statistics, and he sought to develop principles for clarifying the relationships among disparate indicators and for integrating those kinds of information with economic data. In the accounting system he envisaged, people in a given society would be classified into "states." The disaggregation of a small, initial set of states would be accomplished by adding characteristics in a tree-like fashion (see the discussion surrounding figure 3.3 in Chapter 3). He offered sex and age groups as an example of a simple set of states; they would be further broken down by the principal activity of the individuals in a group (going to school, employed, etc.) and, further, by their health status (Stone 1986, 465). The unit of analysis is the individual person, who in the course of a year will change states in some transitions that can be logically anticipated, like aging, and others that are culturally determined, like continuing in school or entering the work force. Based on these ideas, he developed a framework for demographic accounts and used them to describe migration and the use of education and health-care services (Stone 1971). In particular, he developed a database and model for educational planning that tracks the population of the United Kingdom, classified by age and school attendance, as individuals move from one age category and schooling status to another, from birth until they leave the system by migration or death (Stone 1970). In principle, these accounts could be linked with accounts describing economic transactions, and an integrated analysis could evaluate the amount of spending on education of each type that would be required within the society in a given year.

The reliance on physical units (numbers of persons) in this body of work is noteworthy. So is the notion of linking the entire demographic framework with a description and analysis of a larger piece of the socioeconomic system to determine economic implications, rather than simply applying inevitably arbitrary prices to the physical units (the latter being the usual approach in, say, natural resource accounting). Unfortunately, Stone never achieved the integration, and this part of his work has not been actively pursued. The physical and value relationships described in chapter 6 and implemented in chapter 8, by making use of the quantity–price duality inherent in input–output models, attempt to pick up where Stone left off.

Stone also introduced the idea of expanding an input–output

table by disaggregating the single category of "households" (used to distinguish personal consumption from other final deliveries) into several categories on the basis of social and demographic criteria. With this extension, it is possible to describe the distribution of income among household categories and, on the basis of scenario analysis, to compute changes in the distribution of income. In addition, the establishment of household categories makes it possible to link information about income with other kinds of information that may be measured in a variety of units, provided that the latter are expressed in terms of the same household categories. Stone and his associates built the first social accounting matrix in the early 1960s for Great Britain.

Growth is seen as the principal national objective by many economists and other development professionals. However, persistent poverty and a widening gap in well-being between the poorest and richest have often been observed in the fastest-growing economies, and this reality has led to calls for "growth with equity." Just as the national accounts are designed to measure growth, the social accounting matrix as conceived by Stone provides a direct description of the distribution of income. As Keuning and de Ruijter (1988, 71) have pointed out, social accounting responds to the "dissatisfaction with the existing practice of national accounting, particularly its exclusive emphasis on measuring economic growth. After it had become apparent that economic growth per se is no guarantee for an increase in living standards of all population groups (not to mention a sufficient condition for the eradication of poverty), more information on distributional issues was called for." Following the pioneering application of Pyatt and Thorbecke (1976), social accounts have been constructed and used widely in the developing countries.

Current directions in social accounting include the expanded involvement of those who use the information in the accounts, particularly modelers who analyze scenarios, in developing the conventions governing data collection and preparation. This has been the case in my own collaboration with national accountants in the Dominican Republic and with Jan van Tongeren and others of the United Nations Statistical Office (Duchin and Nauphal 1996). See Pyatt (1991), Hanson and Robinson (1991), and other contributions in the same special issue of *Economic Systems Research* for a perspective on social accounting data requirements for general equilibrium models. See especially Keuning (1991) for the views of a national accountant who accords priority to variables that can actually be measured in contrast to the more abstract conceptions of the other contributors.

Social Accounting Matrices and Analysis

A social accounting matrix is a square table of numbers that includes the information in a rectangular input–output table and augments it in several ways. The square submatrix of inter-industry exchanges is in principle the same in the input–output table and the social accounting matrix, except that it is generally an order of magnitude more detailed in the former.[1] The social accounting matrix expands upon the representation of consumption (in the final demand columns of the input–output table) and factor payments (in the value-added rows of the input–output table) by making explicit the relationships between the two. The social accounting matrix is square because it allocates both rows and columns to *activities* (which correspond to industries), *factors* (which earn factor payments, or value added), and *institutions* (which own factors and pay for final deliveries). Unlike the input–output table, it records the delivery of factor payments to institutions and transfers of income among institutions. This additional information takes on special interest because factors and institutions, notably labor and households, respectively, are more disaggregated than they are in the standard input–output table.

All social accounting matrices share these common features. Nonetheless, the lack of comparability among actual numerical examples is much greater than that among input–output tables. One reason is that, while activities are classified using standardized industrial classifications, there are no commonly accepted classification systems for factors and institutions. Furthermore, the social accounting matrix absorbs information from a larger assortment of primary sources, so a greater diversity of conventions and definitions can naturally be expected.

The square social accounting matrix is built from four categories of transactions, which are shown schematically in figure 5.1 (numbered 1 through 4). The portion for the production activities (A) contains the same figures as the basic input–output flow table; a given row of A shows the payments to one sector from all production activities, and the corresponding column shows the payments of the sector to all activities. (This part of the social accounting matrix, and of the input–output table, is often given in two parts called use and make tables, but we have no need to descend to this level of detail.) The factor inputs include labor (often disaggregated by occupation or skill level) and various forms of property-type income; the payments to each factor from each activity are shown in the factor portion of the table (F). The institutional portion (C) shows money outlays for purchases by households and other institutions from production sectors. While the figures in these three submatrices are the same in the input–output table and the social accounting matrix, they are viewed somewhat differently by the two sets of analysts. For the input–output analyst, the column corresponding to an activity reflects its input structure or technology: the physical mix of inputs, at given prices, required for production. For the social accounting analyst, the same column records the money payments from the sector to its suppliers.

The transactions intermediating between the income earned by factors and that spent by institutions appear in the portions of the table labeled W and T. The ownership of factors by institutions, as

			EXPENDITURES			
RECEIPTS		1 Production Activities	2 Factors of Production	3 Institutions	4 Other Expenditures	Total
1	Production Activities	A		C	X	X
2	Factors of Production	F			X	X
3	Institutions		W	T	X	X
4	Other	X	X	X	X	X
	Total	X	X	X	X	X

Figure 5.1. Structure of a Social Accounting Matrix
Source: Adapted Social Accounting Matrix.
Note: Submatrices A, F, C, W, and T are discussed in test. Blank submatrices contain zeros. X indicates other nonzero submatrices.

reflected by the distribution of factor earnings to them, is shown in
W; the institutions may include households of different types, government agencies, and various categories of corporations. Transfers
of income among institutions, such as payment of taxes or receipt of
government services or remittances from a worker in the city to rel-
atives in the countryside, are shown in T. "Other Expenditures" is a
residual category and is discussed in more detail in chapters 6 and 7.
Sample social accounting matrices for the United States in 1982 and
for Indonesia in 1980 are shown in tables 5.1 and 5.2, respectively;
they are presented in their original forms. The table for the United
States distinguishes three activities, three factors, three categories of
households, and three additional institutions. There is a single category for labor, and households are classified according to whether
their principal source of income is from transfer payments, employment, or rents.

The social accounting matrix for Indonesia is rearranged in table
5.3 according to the format of figure 5.1. Table 5.3 (like table 5.2)
distinguishes two activities (agriculture; manufacturing and services), four factors of production (agricultural labor, nonagricultural labor, agricultural capital, and nonagricultural capital), two categories of households (rural and urban), and five other institutions.
The main principle of classification is whether or not the income
flow is associated with agricultural activities.

Table 5.3 shows that, not surprisingly, rural households earn
most of the labor income (5,052 billion Rp out of 5,356) and capital
income (6,121 billion Rp out of 7,327) associated with agriculture, a
small amount of the labor income earned in manufacturing and services (1,237 billion Rp out of 13,178), and none of the capital
income earned outside of agriculture. Urban households, by contrast, receive most of the labor income earned in the production of
manufactured goods and services and most of the associated capital
income. The transfer of income among households is shown in the
intersection of rows 7 and 8 and columns 7 and 8 (corresponding to
T in figure 5.1): only a small portion of income appears to be redis-
tributed, and this is mainly among urban households. The corresponding coefficient matrix is shown in table 5.4.

The simplest analysis based on a social accounting matrix is the
computation of the matrix of so-called multipliers. By analogy with
other economic multipliers, these quantify the effects of exogenous
changes as they ripple through the income-generating system. It is
customary to consider monetized transactions attributable to insti-

TABLE 5.1. SOCIAL ACCOUNTING MATRIX FOR THE UNITED STATES IN 1982 (BILLIONS OF DOLLARS)

| | Supplier | | | Value Added | | | Households | | | | | | Row |
| | 1 | 2 | 3 | 4 | 5 | 6 | 7 | 8 | 9 | 10 | 11 | 12 | |
Receipts	Farming	Industry	Services	Labor	Capital	Enterprise	Transfer	Labor	Rentier[a]	Government	Capital	Rest of World	Totals
Suppliers													
1 Farming	42.1	86.1	4.3				4.2	12.4	2.4	8.6	-0.5	19.6	179.0
2 Industry	44.4	1094.6	389.2				96.2	354.8	76.6	173.9	439.4	192.2	2861.1
3 Services	31.6	458.0	658.5				291.5	978.6	234.3	459.2	8.5	150.1	3270.2
Value added													
4 Labor	13.0	640.2	1253.8										1907.0
5 Capital	41.3	230.6	728.3										1000.2
6 Enterprise					1000.2					47.5			1047.8
Households													
7 Transfer										396.3			396.3
8 Labor				1637.5									1637.5
9 Rentier[a]						581.5							581.5
10 Government	3.1	66.7	189.0	269.5		63.1	4.5	206.3	203.1				1000.7
11 Capital account						403.2		85.6	63.8	-110.8			
12 Rest of world	3.5	285.0	47.2						1.3	26.1	-1.0		
Column totals	179.0	2861.1	3270.1	1907.0	1000.2	1047.8	396.3	1637.5	581.6	1000.7	446.3	361.9	

[a] Rentier: having income from property or investment.
Source: Hanson and Robinson (1991), table 4.

TABLE 5.2. SOCIAL ACCOUNTING MATRIX FOR INDONESIA IN 1980 (BILLIONS OF RUPIAHS; [A] AGRICULTURE, [N] NONAGRICULTURE)

Categories of Income		Factors — Labor A	Labor N	Capital A	Capital N	Institutions — Household Groups A	Household Groups N	Production Activities A	Production Activities N	Government	Capital Account A	Capital Account N	Rest of the World A	Rest of the World N	Total Incomes
Factors															
Labor	A							5,357							5,357
	N							589	12,590						13,179
Capital	A							7,327							7,327
	N								22,649						22,649
Institutions															
Household groups	A	5,053	1,237	6,121		81	90			235			86		12,903
	N	304	11,941		21,339	89	1,771			560				156	36,160
Production activities	A					7,537	6,615	6,988	2,134	14	296		2,712		26,299
	N				123	3,140	7,454	5,167	13,640	3,909	874	7,976		15,284	57,444
Government						261	8,257	389	92	1,174					10,296
Capital account	A					977	242			590			-415		1,394
	N					343	10,498			2,523				-2,864	10,500
Rest of the world	A			1,206		471		482			224				2,383
	N				1,187		1,236		6,337	1,291		2,525			12,576
Total expenditures		5,357	13,178	7,327	22,649	12,899	36,163	26,299	57,442	10,296	1,394	10,501	2,383	12,576	

Source: Morrison and Thorbecke 1990, table 2.

TABLE 5.3. REARRANGED SOCIAL ACCOUNTING MATRIX FOR INDONESIA IN 1980 (BILLIONS OF RUPIAHS)

	Production Sectors		Factors of Production				Households		Other Institutions	Total
	1	2	3	4	5	6	7	8	9	10
Production Sectors										
1 Agriculture	6,988	2,134	0	0	0	0	7,537	6,615	3,022	26,296
2 Manufacturing and services	5,166	13,640	0	0	0	0	3,140	7,454	28,042	57,442
Factors of Production										
3 Agricultural labor	5,357	0	0	0	0	0	0	0	0	5,357
4 Nonagricultural labor	588	12,590	0	0	0	0	0	0	0	13,178
5 Agricultural capital	7,327	0	0	0	0	0	0	0	0	7,327
6 Nonagricultural capital	0	22,649	0	0	0	0	0	0	0	22,649
Households										
7 Rural	0	0	5,052	1,237	6,121	0	81	90	321	12,902
8 Urban	0	0	304	11,941	0	21,339	92	1,771	716	36,163
Other Institutions										
9 Government, capital account, rest of the world	871	6,429	0	0	1,206	1,310	2,052	20,233	5,048	37,149
10 Total	26,296	57,442	5,356	13,178	7,327	22,649	12,902	36,163	37,149	

Source: Table 5.2.

Note: Totals may not add due to rounding.

TABLE 5.4. COEFFICIENT MATRIX FOR THE SOCIAL ACCOUNTING MATRIX FOR INDONESIA IN 1980 (RUPIAHS OF INPUT PER RUPIAH OF OUTPUT)

	1	2	3	4	5	6	7	8
1 Agriculture	0.266	0.037	0	0	0	0	0.584	0.183
2 Manufacturing & services	0.196	0.237	0	0	0	0	0.243	0.206
3 Agricultural labor	0.204	0	0	0	0	0	0	0
4 Nonagricultural labor	0.022	0.219	0	0	0	0	0	0
5 Agricultural capital	0.279	0	0	0	0	0	0	0
6 Nonagricultural capital	0	0.394	0	0	0	0	0	0
7 Rural households	0	0	0.943	0.094	0.835	0	0.006	0.002
8 Urban households	0	0	0.057	0.906	0	0.942	0.007	0.049

Source: Table 5.3.
Note: Columns do not sum to 1.00 because receipts of institutions other than households are not included.

tutions other than households as exogenous, while the activities, factors, and households constitute the endogenous system. The first three blocks of rows and columns in figure 5.1 make up the endogenous portion of the flow table. If we call this submatrix of coefficients M (representing table 5.4), then the inverse of $I - M$ is the matrix of multipliers. (I is the identity matrix. See Chapter 6 for more detail on the manipulation of the $I - M$ matrix.) Multipliers for Indonesia are shown in table 5.5, which is a generalization of the Leontief inverse described in chapter 3.

The significance of the multipliers is revealed by a comparison of tables 5.4 and 5.5. The first column of table 5.4 shows that to produce an extra million rupiahs' worth of agricultural goods, farmers would require 266,000 Rp of seeds and seedlings (from agriculture), 196,000 Rp of manufactured goods and services, and so on. But table 5.5 shows that an exogenous increase of a million Rp in final demand for agricultural goods would require the production of as much as 2.5 million Rp of agricultural goods and 1.2 million Rp of manufactured goods and services, and generate 1.1 million Rp of income for rural and 0.8 million Rp for urban households. These multipliers are much larger than the direct coefficients because they take all indirect requirements into account. For example, the first multiplier cited covers not only the needs for producing agricultural output but also the food needed to feed the workers to produce the

TABLE 5.5. MULITPIERS FOR THE SOCIAL ACCOUNTING MATRIX FOR INDONESIA IN 1980 (RUPIAHS OF INPUT PER RUPIAH OF FINAL DELIVERIES)

	1	2	3	4	5	6	7	8
1 Agriculture	2.51	.63	1.57	0.72	1.36	0.59	1.63	0.62
2 Manufacturing & services	1.22	1.88	1.15	0.69	0.99	0.61	1.18	0.64
3 Agricultural labor	0.51	0.13	1.32	0.15	0.28	0.12	0.33	0.13
4 Nonagricultural labor	0.32	0.43	0.29	1.17	0.25	0.15	0.29	0.16
5 Agricultural capital	0.70	0.18	0.44	0.20	1.38	0.16	0.46	0.17
6 Nonagricultural capital	0.48	0.74	0.45	0.27	0.39	1.24	0.47	0.25
7 Rural households	1.11	0.31	1.65	0.42	1.45	0.27	1.73	0.28
8 Urban households	0.82	1.15	0.81	1.40	0.65	1.38	0.77	1.46

Source: Table 5.3.

manufactured goods to grow the seeds to produce the additional agricultural products. Comparison of the last two columns of multipliers shows that an infusion of an additional million Rp to urban households stimulates the domestic economy far less than a comparable infusion to rural households. Table 5.2 shows the reason: well over half of urban income "leaks" out, mainly to investment and to the government.

Assessing the implications of changes in the consumption pattern of one kind of household for the incomes of other households is a major motivation for preparing the Indonesian accounts (BPS 1991, 7). Interestingly, this kind of application has also been carried out for analyzing the interdependency of household activities at the village level (Subramanian and Sadoulet 1990).

Analysis based on social accounting multipliers generally assumes that the coefficients governing inter-industry inputs, factor inputs, and income distribution remain constant under alternative assumptions about exogenous changes. By contrast, the household consumption coefficients are sometimes modified to reflect marginal changes in expenditure patterns (see, for example, a study of the Mexican economy by Adelman and Taylor, 1990). In the last study, however, the factor inputs are not distinguished from the institutions that own them. A comparison of table 5.6 with table 5.4 shows the difference between describing the labor and capital inputs to activities in the Indonesian economy in terms of either factors or the households that provide them. The latter shortcut effectively

TABLE 5.6. SIMPLIFIED COEFFICIENT MATRIX FOR INDONESIA IN 1980

		1	2	3	4
1	Agriculture	0.266	0.037	0.584	0.183
2	Manufacturing & services	0.196	0.237	0.243	0.206
3	Rural households	0.427	0.021	0.006	0.002
4	Urban households	0.032	0.570	0.007	0.049

Source: Table 5.3.

reduces the data requirements and the size of the matrix that must be handled (here from 8 × 8 to 4 × 4). The practice, however, produces different results when used in the analysis of scenarios that involve changes in coefficients (see the proof in Appelbaum, Duchin, and Szyld 1995). Other examples of this abridged treatment of factors include Robinson and Roland-Holst (1988) for the United States and Civardi and Lenti (1988) for Italy.

Applications to Indonesia

Official social accounting matrices have been constructed for Indonesia by the Indonesian Central Bureau of Statistics, or Biro Pusat Statistik (BPS), for 1975, 1980, 1985, and 1990. A detailed examination of several applications involving the matrices will reveal the nature of these analyses while also providing an empirical description of some aspects of the social structure of Indonesian society.

The Indonesian economy grew rapidly during the 1970s, based largely on the infusion of revenues from petroleum exports. Following the precipitous decline in the price of petroleum by the early 1980s, strenuous attempts were made to adjust to the drastically changed conditions and, in particular, diversify exports away from oil. These efforts were largely successful at the level of the economy as a whole. The social accounts have been used to measure and monitor the distribution of income before and after the period of windfall profit from petroleum and as a basis for calculating the potential implications of various policy responses for the earnings of different categories of households.

The official social accounting matrix for Indonesia consists of a set of accounts that, at their most detailed, include information for twenty-two activities, twenty-three factors of production, and twelve categories of institutions. The classifications are described in

Appendix B, where the matrix for Indonesia in 1985 is also provided. Categories of labor are distinguished by urban or rural location of the place of work, four broadly defined types of occupations, and whether the worker is paid a money wage. Five nonlabor factors of production are included in the accounts.

Rural or urban location and primary dependence on agriculture or a livelihood outside of agriculture are the most fundamental distinctions among households in Indonesia and many other developing countries (Keuning 1989b) and provide the basis for the household classification adopted for the social accounting matrix. Within agricultural households, land ownership is considered the most important consideration, and the three categories include those owning or operating small farms (defined as under half a hectare), medium farms (less than a hectare), and larger farms (over a hectare). For households earning most of their income outside of agriculture, the type of occupation is considered the most important determinant of the standard of living. The geographic region in which a household is located, in particular the specific island, figures in some of the analyses but is not part of the official accounts. Other supplementary data about households, such as quantities of nutrients in the diet, are included in the most recent publications containing the social accounts. While substantial additional information about households is collected by BPS and published in other places (e.g., SUPAS 1985; SUSENAS 1987), the failure to use the same household categories makes matching the information in the accounts impractical.

Some of the major studies using the social accounts for Indonesia are identified and briefly described in table 5.7. The listing is not exhaustive; these particular studies were selected because they reflect the range of issues that have been addressed with the social accounts and the principal methods used to analyze them. The authors of these analyses are Erik Thorbecke and Steven Keuning, innovators in the construction and analysis of social accounts especially but not exclusively in Indonesia, and Tirta Hidayat, who was a student of Thorbecke at Cornell University.

The first study provides a simple description of the figures in a social accounting matrix and is important for demonstrating the value of the database even in the absence of mathematical analysis; this is the approach that will be taken in chapter 7. The second study is a comparative static analysis of the changing distribution of income in the period of rapid growth between 1975 and 1980. The

TABLE 5.7. APPLICATIONS OF SOCIAL ACCOUNTING MATRICES IN INDONESIA

Objective	Method	Results
Analyze origin of profits (Keuning 1985).	Descriptive analysis of 1975 SAM	Most foreign and substantial public capital income was generated by petroleum. Food production and retail trade generated most of the unincorporated capital income. Private, national incorporated capital income originated mainly in whole-sale trade, selected manufacturing activities, and construction.
Analyze sources and distribution of benefits from productivity growth (Keuning 1993b).	Comparison of changes in SAMs between 1975 and 1980	Real per capita incomes rose between 1975 and 1980, but income inequality among households did not decrease.
Analyze impact of reduced government spending on income distribution (Keuning and Thorbecke 1989).	Static multiplier	Selective budget reductions protected the incomes of the poorer households more than proportional reductions across all expenditure categories would have.
Evaluate regional interdependence and policies to improve interregional equity between Java and the other islands (Hidayat 1991).	Static multiplier	Regional development grants had little impact on inter-regional income distribution, but the latter improved with the expansion of nonoil exports.
Design "satellite" social accounts that could be linked to SAMs (Keuning 1989a, 1989b, 1994).		
Demonstrate suitability of SAMs for models of world trade (Thorbecke 1989).	Comparison of social accounting methods with input-output analysis and general equilibrium analysis	
Analysis of stabilization and structural adjustment policies (Thorbecke 1992).	SAM combined with a general equilibrium model	Internal and external equilibrium were restored at some cost to growth but with more equal distribution of income.

next two studies are both multiplier analyses. The first investigates the effects of changes in government spending on the distribution of income; the latter adds a regional dimension to the multiplier framework. The next set of articles identifies limitations of social accounting methods for analyzing development options and recommends kinds of information that could supplement the formal framework. The last two articles provide one perspective about broadening the analytic framework. My alternative proposal for doing that is presented in the following chapters.

The first study identified in table 5.7 describes the origin and distribution of profits in Indonesia in 1975; it is based on information contained in the social accounting matrix for that year supplemented by a detailed labor force survey (Keuning 1985). Only 21 percent of earned income consisted of money wages and salaries. The remaining 79 percent was operating surplus, and over half of it was received by unincorporated businesses, mainly in small-scale agricultural production and retail trade. The operating surplus on petroleum exceeded that in food crops and was paid mainly to foreign owners and also to the government. This constituted most of foreign capital income and a substantial share of public capital income. Only 12 percent of the operating surplus was earned by domestic private corporations, and it originated mainly in wholesale trade, construction, and the production of paper, paper products, basic metals, metal products, and machinery.

Estimates (called *imputations*) are made for salaries implicitly earned by entrepreneurs and unpaid family workers, and they are deducted from the operating surplus of unincorporated businesses. These imputed earnings amounted to almost as much as money wages, leaving only about 60 percent (rather than 79 percent) of total income as a true return on capital, or profit. Unlike the earlier social accounting matrices, the one for 1985 benefits from Keuning's work and explicitly distinguishes imputed salaries.

As for the use of profits, a large share of total operating surplus went into retained earnings which constituted a significant part of the country's savings in 1975, and about 25 percent of foreign profits were remitted overseas. Total corporate savings made up over half of the nation's total savings, but the actual uses of the funds could not be traced. The author recommended according high priority to a flow-of-funds analysis in order to establish the links between savings and investment.

The next study (Keuning 1993b) describes the transformation of the Indonesian economy between 1975 and 1980, focusing in particular on the relationship between changes in productivity and income distribution. Using the social accounting matrices for 1975 and 1980 and detailed employment data, Keuning found that real per capita incomes rose substantially over the period, but income inequality among households did not narrow because urban wages, higher to start with, grew faster than rural wages. The average wage rate for females relative to males, however, increased from .49 to .60.

In the 1980s the government of Indonesia substantially reduced its budget in response to a steep drop in the price of oil, the main source of foreign exchange at the time. Keuning and Thorbecke (1989) disaggregated the institutions in the social accounting matrix for 1980 to distinguish different types of government activities. Using the matrix of multipliers, they were able to conclude that while all households suffered a loss of real income, the selective nature of the reduction in government spending succeeded in protecting the incomes of the poorest households.

The concentration of industry and government programs on Java is associated with considerable differences in per capita income between it and the other islands. Hidayat (1991) examined the structure of regional interdependence and the potential for government policies to achieve a more equal regional distribution of income. Starting from the official social accounting matrix for 1985, he created a matrix with two regions, Java and all other islands combined, in terms of nine activities, twelve factors of production, and twenty-three institutions. He then computed the matrix of multipliers for the two-region social accounting matrix and used various techniques to analyze its structure. Each multiplier measures the effects on income in one region of changes in exogenous outlays in the same or the other region, taking into account the effects transmitted by interregional trade.

Hidayat found that the interregional effects of exogenous changes are much smaller than intraregional ones, although an exogenous change in spending in the outer islands had a larger effect on incomes in Java than the other way around. He also found that regional development grants from the government of Indonesia between 1983 and 1987 appeared to be too small to have a measurable impact on equalizing incomes between the two regions, although the expansion of nonoil exports in the 1980s did significantly narrow the income discrepancy.

The more equal distribution of income is only one among many criteria for social progress. The government of Indonesia is also concerned with direct measures of the quality of housing, nutritional status, literacy, access to social services like education, health care, and an operational justice system (see BPS 1991). For the first time the social accounts for 1985 are accompanied by tables estimating average per capita intake of calories, protein, fat, and carbohydrates obtained from seventeen types of food for ten types of households. The distinctive feature of these tables, benefiting again from the influence of Keuning, is that they use the same classifications as the familiar accounts but report variables other than income flows, using physical rather than money units.

Keuning (1989a, 1989b, and 1994) has been an effective proponent of maintaining the analytic structure of social accounting while incorporating new kinds of information in "satellite" accounts, measured in physical units, that would describe—besides the intake of nutrients—household composition, demographic characteristics, housing situation, health conditions, access to education, numbers of people, stocks of capital, and foreign debt using the same classifications as the original social accounting matrix.

Thus the sociodemographic information would be linked to the income flows through common classifications for activities, factors of production, and institutions. In an early effort to construct supplementary accounts for the 1975 social accounting matrix, the ten categories of households appearing in that matrix were disaggregated, with agricultural households distinguished by fourteen categories of land ownership and both urban and rural nonagricultural households distinguished by fourteen occupational categories. Keuning's intention was for each household category to be described by per capita income, caloric intake, years of schooling, leisure time, access to specific durable goods, land owned, quality of dwelling, and access to piped water. To demonstrate the feasibility, Keuning (1989b, 137) estimated per capita calorie intake for ten categories of households. These figures were later incorporated into the official 1985 social accounts.

The purpose of maintaining and updating satellite accounts is primarily to monitor social well-being. Keuning points out the importance of organizing the data in "a fully consistent, *analytical* framework, analogous to Input–Output tables and SAMs" (Keuning 1994, 18; author's emphasis), but as for analysis, he acknowledged that the methods remained to be worked out. Furthermore, while many of the data listed above are available, they are still not structured in the kind of organizing framework proposed by Keuning.

Evaluation

The articles reviewed in this section are all based on a simple manipulation of the social accounting matrix in which it is treated like an input–output table. The endogenous portion is specified and converted from a flow table to a coefficient matrix, $\mathbf{M}$. Then one computes the generalized Leontief inverse, $(\mathbf{I} - \mathbf{M})^{-1}$; it is called the matrix of multipliers. The analysis consists of interpreting the multipliers or multiplying them by hypothetical changes in the exogenous variables to obtain new levels of income by activity, factor, and institution. Most of the articles make some reference to extending the analytic framework in one of two ways. First is the replacement of the "average" coefficients that figure into the multipliers by "marginal elasticities." Second is the incorporation of the social accounting information into a computable general equilibrium (CGE) model that can make endogenous an equilibrating role for prices and the relations between savings and investment (dynamics) and between imports and exports. These directions are most explicit in the work of Thorbecke, who states: "It has become conventional to use computable general equilibrium models for this purpose. As long as these models are not too ambitious and too large (i.e., in terms of attempting to explain too many variables endogenously), they may be helpful in explaining the interrelationship among different economies in a disaggregated and consistent manner" (Thorbecke 1992, 14–15; see also Thorbecke 1989). He goes on to say, "It is important to explore . . . a feasible and defensible middle road between a full-fledged CGE approach to world trade modelling and the more limiting SAM multiplier approach. Note that I exclude the even simpler IO Leontief approach as being far inferior to the SAM methodology excluding as it does some of the crucial links within a socioeconomic [system]" (Thorbecke 1989, 16).

In these remarks, Thorbecke fails to recognize that "SAM methodology" is simply the mathematics of the open static input–

output model applied to a social accounting matrix. He also appears to be unaware that structural economics has many options for extending that analytic framework, depending on the questions that one wants to ask. The work reported in the following chapters provides an alternative to the approaches advocated by Thorbecke.

Indonesia is a vast, rapidly modernizing country with enormous social and economic diversity. The social accounting studies that have been reviewed describe the generation and distribution of income in Indonesia but do not provide a sense of the cultural mix and the social transformations that have been accompanying, and will continue to accompany, rapid economic development. The major limitations are the classification of households, the focus on income flows only, and the lack of a dynamic conceptualization about the principal social transformations that are taking place.

Development and modernization are accompanied by substantial, often dramatic, social and cultural changes as nomadic hunters and gatherers become sedentary agriculturalists, large households (for example, communities occupying a common "longhouse") are replaced by smaller ones in separate living units, women who had previously worked in the household and the community become wage earners employed in factories, and children receive formal schooling and stay in school for an increasingly long period of years. These kinds of changes have predictable economic implications: household purchasing power grows, consumption is increasingly oriented to market transactions, and traditional institutional arrangements that functioned within the household and the community may be completely undermined well before their functions are assumed by marketed services. The migration from rural to urban areas or from one region to another has profound effects not only on work and consumption patterns of households and quality of life but also on what infrastructure needs to be provided by the government. The studies that have been described shed little light on these realities.

The kind of information system proposed by Keuning (see "Applications to Indonesia" earlier in this chapter) can describe some of these changes, and his set of indicators could be expanded to include even more information. The fundamental challenge, however, is to provide a conceptual structure for this social information that makes it possible to pass, as Richard Stone envisaged, from a collection of separate indicators to an interrelated set of variables and parameters that can be useful for analyzing the social changes accompanying economic development. Some steps in this direction are taken in the next two chapters.

NOTES

1. *Input–output table* and a *social accounting matrix* are the terms that are customarily used. The term *input–output matrix* is reserved for the coefficients derived from an input–output table.

Chapter 6
The Analytic Framework

The input–output model of interdependency serves as the core of the new analytic framework. However, an input–output model needs to be substantially extended for the analysis of development strategies, and I call the result of this extension a structural model to reflect its greater generality. The key feature of a structural model for the purposes of this book is that it "closes" the input–output model for households; that is, both the consumption and employment of different categories of households are endogenously determined rather than needing to be specified as exogenous. To achieve this closure, assumptions are made about the conceptual links among household activities and the links between these and other economic activities. Other extensions to the basic input–output model are discussed in chapter 4.

The closure of a static input–output model for households is based on the same kinds of assumptions and computations that are associated with a so-called multiplier analysis of the social account-ing matrix. While there are many common elements shared by the input–output and social accounting traditions, they have developed largely independently, resulting in distinctive expectations about what can be taken for granted and what requires explanation and in differences in the conventions governing the preparation of data and mathematical notation. There are also systematic differences in the questions that are addressed in an analysis and in the approach to interpreting results. This chapter begins with a description of the basic input–output model and its closure for households, indicating along the way the relationship of this model to the multiplier approach to analyzing the social accounting matrix. I then proceed to generalize the input–output model in directions that have already proven fruitful in other areas of input–output economics, namely the explicit representation of the duality between the quantity model and the price model. Price and quantity relations are represented separately while maintaining certain aspects of their interdependence. In particular, physical changes as specified by a scenario are automatically reflected both in changed quantities and in changed costs and price. On the other hand, changes in prices do not have an automatic feedback on physical relationships. This last feature is one of the fundamental characteristics of a structural approach as contrasted with neoclassical models, since the latter assume a feedback from changes in prices to changes in physical quantities that is governed by elasticity parameters. In structural analyses, far more importance is accorded to the long-term, strategic considerations that provide the content of alternative scenarios in determining fundamental choices among technological and lifestyle alternatives than to marginal variations in the prices of individual goods and services.

Distinguishing the Analytic Objects

An empirical analysis involves data and a mathematical model for analyzing them. Surprisingly, the two are often confused. This misunderstanding is due to the fact that the data used in analysis have often been subjected to at least simple mathematical manipulations, like averaging, and this manipulation can be mistaken for a model. It is also true that the solution of a linear model implicitly involves the computation of a matrix inverse; this inverse is often called a data object rather than being recognized as part of the solution to an underlying model. In the interest of clarity, I propose the following distinctions: The primary data for a structural economic analysis are contained in *tables* of figures representing stocks and flows. A table is converted to a *matrix* of parameters through a simple manipulation such as the division of all entries in a column by a common figure to arrive at inputs (i.e., stocks or flows) per unit of output. A matrix of parameters can also be constructed directly rather than being deduced from an existing flow table. While tables are generally built from accounting data, directly estimated matrices are based on measurements or expert judgments in particular substantive areas. Flow tables and matrices, whatever the source of the figures in the table and whether the matrix is calculated from a table or directly estimated, are the basic data objects for a structural analysis.

A matrix inverse $(\mathbf{I} - \mathbf{M})^{-1}$ (used in both input–output analysis and the multiplier analysis of social accounting matrices) is derived in the solution of a mathematical equation (i.e., the solution of $(\mathbf{I} - \mathbf{M})x = y$ for x). When an inverse is analyzed, the associated mathematical equation should be made explicit. This will be done below.

Another confusion has to do with the degree and nature of the "closure" of the input–output model. A completely closed linear model, of the form $(\mathbf{I} - \mathbf{M})x = 0$, does not yield a unique solution; the associated matrix, $(\mathbf{I} - \mathbf{M})$, is singular and cannot be inverted. To obtain a solution for x, some variables (i.e., some components of the vector x) have to be treated as exogenous and therefore moved to the now nonzero right-hand side of the equation, or their values must be determined by a more general mathematical model. From a formal point of view, any one or more variables can be treated as exogenous. From a substantive point of view, however, it is clear that some are a better choice than others. A proper representation of investment requires a nonlinear dynamic formulation because of the lag between the time when capital goods are ordered and produced and the time when capacity is effectively expanded. Likewise, a useful endogenous representation of international trade requires a comparison of cost structures across potential trade partners. Investment, imports, and exports are best treated as exogenous in a linear model; the resulting framework is a static, one-region model that does in general yield a numerical solution.

The closure for households and other institutions, by contrast, can in principle be accommodated in the linear framework. The underlying assumption is that as the employment prospects and other opportunities to earn income of a particular category of households rise or fall, their consumption patterns and the relative importance of other outlays of income will change in predictable ways. Furthermore, it is assumed possible to anticipate systematically the kinds of changes that would take place in these relationships and to reflect them in a scenario through quantitative assumptions. In a social accounting analysis, changing relationships are sometimes represented by replacing the consumption coefficients, which are averages for a given household category, with estimates of *marginal* propensities to consume. The logic is focused on small changes in consumption patterns in response to small changes in income and prices. A structural scenario reflects a focus on larger-grained changes, whose most important effects, it is believed, will overwhelm such marginal movements. Discrete changes in the lifestyles of these households are described in terms of new, average coefficients rather than marginal changes from old ones. The closure for other institutions, like government, involves different but related considerations.

The construction of structural scenarios about changes in lifestyle and other institutional practices is at an early stage. The challenge is similar to that already faced in building scenarios for analysis with the basic linear, static input–output model of production. If the demand for a product increases, what assumptions should be made about the production technology? The neoclassical approach would highlight the use of marginally more or less capital and labor and possibly other inputs, as governed by elasticities of substitution, in response to changes in relative prices. There would be no mention of the nature of the technological changes. A structural approach would focus on the technical content of the scenario, say an emphasis on recycling, in which case the response of the steel industry might be a shift to electric arc technology with the attendant implications for the coefficients governing the use of iron, scrap, and electricity. The coefficients may change independent of changes in the relative prices of these inputs.

Most economists working in the social accounting tradition consider it their ultimate objective to provide closure for the linear model by placing it within a computable general equilibrium, or CGE, model with its accompanying sets of elasticities. A structural approach, by contrast, seeks to achieve closure through the development of detailed scenarios and a dynamic input–output model of the world economy.

Revisiting the Social Accounting Matrix

A social accounting matrix is a flow table that records the amounts of income generated and received in the different parts of an economy. It is useful to organize it in terms of three kinds of units: activities, factors, and institutions. As in an input–output framework, activities (or sectors or industries) use the inputs of other activities and of factors, and they deliver their outputs to institutions. But the social accounting matrix further specifies the income flows from factors to institutions and the money transfers among institutions that are only implicit in the input–output table. From the perspective of extending the input–output framework, it is natural to represent the structural table that includes both industries and households with the inter-activity or inter-industry transactions in the upper left, with the factor inputs below and the institutional receipts to the right as in an input–output table. (There is no standard social accounting practice in this regard: to see this, compare tables 5.1 and 5.2.) Then the additional rows and columns corresponding to factors and institutions fall readily into place, with the rows and columns for investment and trade forming a border to the rest of the table. In the case that until now has been customary, where all entries are in money values, the matrix is formed by dividing every element by the corresponding column total. A schematic matrix is shown in figure 6.1 (an elaboration of figure 5.1). Five types of submatrices are distinguished in this figure: the inter-activity relationships (A), labor and other factor inputs to activities (F_1 and F_2, respectively), consumption by households and other institutions (C_1 and C_2, respectively), factor ownership by institutions (W_{11}, W_{12}, W_{21}, and W_{22}), and transfer payments among institutions (T_{11}, T_{12}, T_{21}, and T_{22}). The representation is completed by savings and investments (shown in row and column K) and by transactions with the rest of the world in the form of imports and exports (in row and column R).

The entries in a social accounting matrix are in money units (dollars for the United States), and the total of all entries in a row equals the total for the corresponding column. The entries are transformed to coefficients for use in computation by dividing each one by the corresponding column or row total.

The mathematical equation most frequently used for manipulating a social accounting matrix is made explicit in matrix form in figure 6.2; it shows an equation of the form $(\mathbf{I} - \mathbf{M})x = 0$, where $\mathbf{M}$ is derived from the matrix in figure 6.1. The vector of column totals includes sectoral output (x), factor earnings (f_1 and f_2), institutional income (d_1 and d_2), the value of savings (c, assumed equal to investment), and the value of imports (r, assumed equal to exports). Since the right-hand side of the equation is zero, $x = \mathbf{M}x$. (In the last equality, x is defined to represent the entire solution vector. I have also used x to represent that portion of the solution vector cor-

| | | Factors | | Institutions | | | |
	Activities	Labor	Other Factors	Households	Other Institutions	K	R
Activities	A			C_1	C_2	investment	exports
Labor	F_1						
Other Factors	F_2						
Households		W_{11}	W_{12}	T_{11}	T_{12}		
Other Institutions		W_{21}	W_{22}	T_{21}	T_{22}		
K				savings	savings		
R	imports						

Figure 6.1. Schematic Social Accounting Matrix
Note: See text. Shaded areas show locations of nonzero entries.

responding to sectoral output. I apologize for the possible confusion.) That this equality holds is evident from the definition of the coefficients.

A system of this form cannot be solved for x. It is true that in the base case, a vector x that satisfies the equation is known. However, if elements of $\mathbf{M}$ are changed to represent the assumptions of a scenario, the new system cannot be solved for a unique, new value of x.

One way to resolve the dilemma is to make some variables—like the nonhousehold institutions, savings and investment, and trade—exogenous. The resulting model, achieved by aggregating the corresponding columns as flows, moving them to the right-hand side, and dropping the corresponding rows, is shown in figure 6.3. Now the matrix can be inverted, and a unique solution can in general be obtained. Figure 6.3 utilizes notation common to input–output modeling, in that x is the vector of sectoral output and y is final deliveries (now excluding household consumption); this notation is reversed in the social accounting tradition.

	A	F	F	I	I	K	R			
A	$I-A$			$-C_1$	$-C_2$	$-K_A^c$	$-R_A^c$	x		0
F	$-F_1$	I						f_1		0
F	$-F_2$		I				$-R_F^c$	f_2		0
I		$-W_{11}$	$-W_{12}$	$I-T_{11}$	$-T_{12}$			d_1	$=$	0
I		$-W_{21}$	$-W_{22}$	$I-T_{21}$	$I-T_{22}$		$-R_I^c$	d_2		0
K				$-K_I^r$		I		c		0
R	$-R_A^r$	$-R_F^r$		$-R_I^r$			I	r		0

Figure 6.2. Basic Mathematics of Social Accounting
Notes: 1. Notation as in Figure 6.1 (see text) with savings/investment and trade parameters (in columns labeled K and R, respectively), output vector, and right-hand-side vector of 0's. 2. The submatrices R and K are identified by subscripts and superscripts. For example, R_A^r are the rows of import coefficients, and R_A^c are the columns of export coefficients.

Multiplier Analysis of Social Accounting Matrices

The standard analysis of a social accounting matrix consists of specifying the matrix and the right-hand-side vector shown in figure 6.3 and solving the equation for two objects: the left-hand-side vector and the matrix inverse. In the typical comparative static analysis, a scenario will consist of a change in the right-hand-side vector (called an injection if positive and a leakage if negative) and possibly a change in the household consumption coefficients (to reflect marginal rather than average income elasticities). Results are deduced from an element-by-element comparison of the left-hand-side vectors resulting from two computations and a comparison of multipliers, that is, of specific blocks of the inverse. The entire inverse, its constituent blocks, and even individual entries in the inverse can be considered as multipliers: They measure how changes in the right-hand-side variables—often called *exogenous shocks*—ripple through the economy. Both the mathematics that are presented in the social accounting literature and the interpretation of results often focus on a formal decomposition of the multiplier matrix. The shortcoming of this approach is that it isolates the formally separable causes of what are in fact simultaneous effects. Several such studies about the Indonesian economy are described in chapter 5.

Input–Output Model with Closure for Households

The ordering of rows and columns of the structural matrix, the notation, and the explicit form of the matrix equation in figure 6.3 were developed as a static input–output model closed for households. For a given matrix and right-hand side, of course, the solution vector and inverse are the same as those that would be obtained in a social accounting analysis. But the scenarios of interest to me are about neither exogenous shocks nor marginal changes reflected in elasticities. Instead, I am concerned with prospective changes in technologies and in lifestyles, and I interpret the results of different scenarios with respect to these different assumptions rather than through a formal decomposition.

Technological changes in a particular activity are represented by changes in the coefficients in the corresponding columns of the activity and factor matrices (A and F in figures 6.1, 6.2, and 6.3), considered from a technological point of view as a single unit. Simple scenarios can be specified as a kind of sensitivity analysis: for example, what would be the consequences if all inputs for making

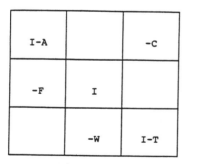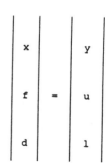

x   sectoral output
f   incomes paid to workers
d   household incomes

y   other final demand (besides household consumption)
u   other factor payments (besides workers' incomes)
l   other household income (besides labor earnings and intra-household transfers)

Figure 6.3. The Input–Output Model Closed for Households

steel, or producing rice, were reduced by 10 percent? In empirical studies, however, scenarios are constructed on the basis of substantive assumptions about specific technological changes: for example, the adoption of electric arc technology in steelmaking or a more efficient irrigation system for rice. In these cases, coefficient changes are based on case studies of technological alternatives and typically involve assumptions about the use of specific materials and forms of energy, and different categories of labor and capital goods. (The last are represented in only an abridged way in a static model.) Because of the importance accorded to distinguishing different types of paid and unpaid labor, and technological changes such as substitutions among materials, activities are represented in considerably more detail in most input–output studies than in social accounting studies.

Changes in the lifestyle of a particular category of household are represented in the corresponding columns of the consumption, factor ownership, and transfer matrices (C, W, and T in figures 6.1, 6.2, and 6.3). The assumptions should be based on a case study for that type of household and can be expected to involve the types of paid and unpaid work that are done, the relative importance of other, nonlabor sources of income, the pattern of consumption, and the delivery of money to, and receipts from, other kinds of households. It becomes important that households be classified in a way that facilitates the simultaneous consideration of these characteristics. A classification according to income deciles, for example, is adequate for a formal manipulation of household activities and a description of income disparities. However, it is a weak starting point for building scenarios about changes in lifestyles because there would be too much variation in lifestyle (despite the similarity in income) within a given category.

Structural Model of Quantities and Prices with Closure for Households

One of the major strengths of the input–output framework is the explicit representation of the duality between quantity relations and price relations. Empirical analyses based on the solutions to both quantity and price models have been carried out, with both static and dynamic as well as optimization frameworks. The latter approach has proven useful for identifying cost-saving technological options and their implications for the price structure and the material standard of living (Duchin and Lange 1992b, 1995).

The significance of distinguishing quantities from prices in the input–output model is often not fully appreciated because of the practice of economists—followed even by most input–output analysts—of using only data that are measured in money values. Before presenting the dual quantity and price models for the input–output model closed for households, I will consider first the simpler example of the basic input–output model as represented in the quantity, price, and income equations (see Duchin 1988 on the income equation):

(1) $(\mathbf{I} - \mathbf{A})x = y$
(2) $(\mathbf{I} - \mathbf{A}')p = v$
(3) $p'y = v'x$

In the first case to be considered, variables and parameters are calculated from a standard flow table measured in current prices. Despite the fact that it is therefore expressed in terms of money values, equation 1 is a quantity model in that the unit of measure is the volume of output, valued in constant, base-year prices. That is, if one assumes changes in $\mathbf{A}$ and computes new values for x, the percentage changes in x correspond to volume changes since prices remain unchanged.

It is the purpose of equation 2 to determine changes in prices. In the case where variables and parameters are calculated from a balanced flow table measured in current prices, the calculated prices (i.e., the components of the vector p) are equal to 1: that is, it will cost one dollar to buy a dollar's worth of output. Because of this apparently trivial interpretation of p, only equation 1 is used in the vast majority of input–output analyses, and it alone is the basis for the multiplier analysis of the social accounting tradition. But this is unfortunate because equation (2) provides, with little additional effort, information that cannot be obtained from equation 1. If one assumes changes in $\mathbf{A}$, it is equation 2 that reveals the effects on unit prices.

Thus, if technological changes are reflected in changed coefficients in the $\mathbf{A}$ matrix, the dual formulation makes it possible to calculate changes in output quantities (1) and prices (2). Both will be modified in such a way that the income equation (3), which is more interesting in the case of the dynamic formulation, still holds. The calculated quantities are index numbers in that they are measured in terms of the unchanged—and unknown—base-year prices. The computed prices are also index numbers, or deflators.

Now consider the general case where outputs are measured not in money values but in physical units such as tons, bushels, and kilowatt-hours. Then the solution of equation 2 will be the prices per ton, per bushel, and per kilowatt-hour. (Assume, in this simple example, that factor payments, v, are an aggregated measure in dollars of "value added" per ton, etc.) In scenario analysis, actual quantities are calculated in equation 1 and actual unit prices in equation 2, rather than only index numbers. These results obviously provide more information than the first case. However, additional information is required in the original database: the vector of physical outputs or, alternatively, the vector of actual unit prices in the base year. This is the general form of the dual model. It is a special case when the physical units are volumes valued in base-year prices and the unit prices are equal to 1.0.

The duality between quantity and price relations exhibited in both of these cases is readily extended to the input–output model closed for households. The parameters and the endogenous and exogenous variables for the formulation focused on workers and households are identified and defined in figure 6.4 in terms of n activities, m factors (categories of workers), and k institutions (categories of households). There are five sets of parameters as in figure 6.1. Industrial and factor inputs (A and F) are expressed in physical units (commodities and workers) per physical unit of output, and consumption is in physical units (commodities) per worker. The six endogenous variables measure the volume of commodity output (x), number of workers by occupation (f), number of workers by household categories (h), price per commodity (p), price per factor (v), and household earnings (d). The exogenous variables, also identified in figure 6.4, are final deliveries to institutions other than households (y), unemployed workers (u), household workers outside the labor force (l), non-labor factor payments (π), savings of workers (o), and savings of households (s).

The mathematical equations for the quantity, price, and income models closed for households are shown in figure 6.5. These models have two new and noteworthy features. First, writing the equations in explicit form calls due attention to the right-hand sides (i.e., the exogenous variables). In the social accounting framework, only the quantity model is solved, and only final deliveries (y) are treated as

Matrices of Parameters

A	nxn	inter-industry matrix: input per unit of output (x)
C	nxk	consumption per worker (h)
F	mxn	worker requirements per unit of output (x)
W	kxm	share of workers (over households)
T	kxk	transfers per unit of earnings (d)

Endogenous Variables

x	nx1	volume of commodities
f	mx1	numbers of workers (by occupation)
h	kx1	numbers of workers (by household category)
p	nx1	price per commodity
v	mx1	price per factor
d	kx1	household earnings (h)

Exogenous Variables

y	nx1	final deliveries to institutions other than households
u	mx1	unemployed workers
l	kx1	household workers outside of labor force
π	nx1	factor payments other than for labor
o	mx1	savings of workers
s	kx1	savings of households

n   activities
m   factors (workers)
k   institutions (households)

Figure 6.4. Parameters and Variables of the Input–Output Model Closed for Households

exogenous. The present formulation allows for a more general solution with the existence of unutilized factors (e.g., unemployment). Analogously, the price model allows for exogenous factor costs and savings that are not utilized in the current period. While some of these exogenous variables can be ignored in a numerical implementation, it is clear that the right-hand side must be nonzero—that is, they cannot all be ignored.

Second, the income equation opens up new territory that is ripe for further exploration. It shows the implication of the price

Quantity Model

I-A		-C		x		y	
-F	I			f	=	u	
	-W	I		h		l	

(1) $(\mathbf{I} - \mathbf{A})x = Ch + y$ or $x = (\mathbf{I} - \mathbf{A})^{-1}(Ch + y)$
(2) $f = Fx + u$
(3) $h = Wf + l$

Price Model

I-A′	-F′		p		π	
	I	-W′	v	=	o	
-C′		I-T′	d		s	

(1) $(\mathbf{I} - \mathbf{A}')p = F'v + \pi$ or $p = (\mathbf{I} - \mathbf{A}')^{-1}(F'v + \pi)$
(2) $v = W'd + o$
(3) $C'p = (\mathbf{I} - \mathbf{T}')d - s$ or $d = (\mathbf{I} - \mathbf{T}')^{-1}(C'p + s)$

Income Model

(1) $p'y + v'u + d'l = v'x + o'f + s'h + d'Th$

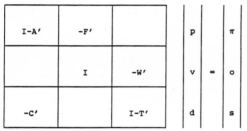

Derivation of Income Model:
    Write the quantity model as
$$\mathbf{M}x = y \tag{A}$$
where $\mathbf{M}$ is the matrix, x is the left-hand side
vector $\begin{pmatrix} x \\ f \\ h \end{pmatrix}$, and y is the right-hand side vector $\begin{pmatrix} y \\ u \\ l \end{pmatrix}$.

Call the matrix figuring in the value model $\mathbf{M}' - \mathbf{N}'$, where
$$\mathbf{N} = \begin{matrix} 0 & 0 & 0 \\ 0 & 0 & 0 \\ 0 & 0 & T \end{matrix}$$
Then the value model is $(\mathbf{M}' - \mathbf{N}')p = z$ or
$$\mathbf{M}'p = \mathbf{N}'p + z \tag{B}$$
where p and z are the left-hand side and right-hand side
vectors $\begin{pmatrix} p \\ v \\ d \end{pmatrix}$ and $\begin{pmatrix} \pi \\ o \\ s \end{pmatrix}$, respectively.

Premultiply (A) by p'. Transpose (B) and then postmultiply it by x.
Since $p'(\mathbf{I} - \mathbf{M})x$ is common to both expressions, this yields:
$$p'y = z'x + d'Th \tag{C}$$

The last term in (C) is obtained by multiplying out the matrix expression
involving $\mathbf{N}'p$, exploiting the sparsity of $\mathbf{N}$. Substituting in (C) for $p, y, z,$
and x yields the income model.

Figure 6.5. Input–Output Quantity, Price, and Income Models
Closed for Households

and quantity relations for assuring that the exogenous demands on the economy (like consumption of the unemployed) are actually paid for.

Chapter 8 reports the results of analyzing a scenario for the Indonesian economy using these quantity and price models and those exogenous variables that actually appear in the official social accounting matrix. All variables in the base year are measured in money values. Consequently, the solutions are measured in constant prices for the quantity model and price deflators for the price model. Numbers of workers and households in the base year are available, or are estimated, in physical units. This information is fully utilized in interpreting the results of the computations.

Chapter 7

The Households of Indonesia

The objective of this chapter is to describe how members of Indonesian households earn their livings as a basis for the subsequent formulation and analysis of scenarios about lifestyle changes associated with development. The first section offers a qualitative description of the households of Indonesia. It is followed by a set of statistical tables that illustrate many of the same points in a more concrete and systematic way. Next, a statistical description based on social accounting data illustrates the advantages of the household as the unit of analysis within a highly integrated accounting framework. The final section offers recommendations for revising the design of the social accounts so as to enhance their social content.

Diversity and Unification

Indonesia stands out among developing countries for its large population, natural wealth, unique and varied biomass, and strategic location at the eastern entrance to the Indian Ocean. Its leadership was effective at achieving substantial economic growth prior to the financial crisis of 1998. While its future course is uncertain, the country can be expected to command increasing attention on the international scene. For these reasons, and because of the marked diversity of the Indonesian people and the inevitable unevenness with which modernization has affected them, the Indonesian experience provides an exemplary case for developing methods to study the relationship of social change to economic and technological change.

In 1990 about 180 million people in 40 million households worked, raised their children, cared for their elderly, and carried out other tasks and ritual practices in Indonesia. Despite substantial pressures toward uniformity, the lifestyles of those households reflect material and cultural adaptations to a multitude of distinct environments. The geographic landscape of tropical rain forests and mangrove swamps, arid lowlands, and snow-capped mountains is crisscrossed by water. Indonesia consists of over thirteen thousand islands, of which over six thousand are named and nearly one thousand are inhabited (Mantra 1990, 1). The map of Indonesia in figure 7.1 identifies the five major islands (Java, Sumatra, Kalimantan, Sulawesi, and Irian Jaya) and the two most populated archipelagos (Nusa Tenggara and the Malukus).

Except for the Papuans who reside on the island of Irian Jaya, Indonesians have common racial origins, and most profess Islam. Nonetheless, the people of Indonesia represent over three hundred cultural traditions and still speak hundreds of distinct languages, not to mention innumerable dialects. Diverse, distinctive material structures include the extravagant roofs of the Toraja of Sulawesi and the tiered gables of Minangkabau architecture (Dawson and Gillow 1994).

The population of Indonesia includes nomadic hunters and gatherers and shifting (slash-and-burn) cultivators, found in greatest numbers on the large islands of Kalimantan, Sulawesi, and Irian Jaya. Some Indonesians are still animists, and ancestors are worshipped in many parts of the country even by peoples nominally converted to modern, monotheistic religions.

The government has exerted substantial pressures to assimilate these people, for example through the national project for the Management of Isolated Populations, and so have foreign missionaries, whose universalist religious doctrines serve as a powerful modernizing influence. Traditional practices that have been made illegal or are at least strongly discouraged include the taking of heads and cannibalism, public nakedness, ritual tattooing, ritualized communication with ancestors, certain kinds of festivals, and communal longhouses. In the late 1970s, there were only about 1,500,000 members of truly isolated populations (Tsing 1993, 92). By one informed estimate, however, fully 26 percent of the population in 1992 still iden-

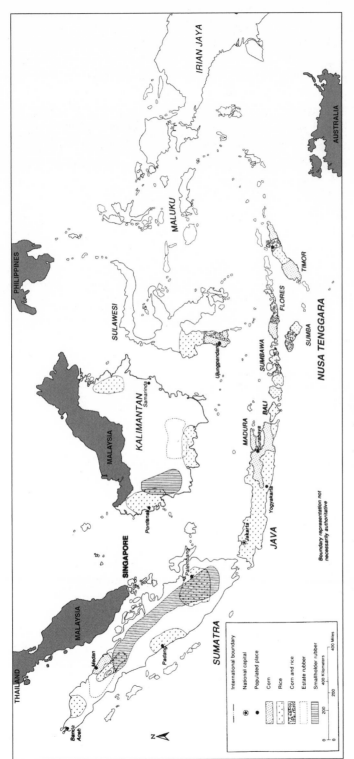

Figure 7.1. Map of Indonesia Showing the Major Agricultural Areas
Source: Frederick and Worden 1993, p. 170.

tified with one of the numerous small ethnic minorities, including the Toraja, Dayak, Weyewa, Tanimbarese, and Asmat, among many others (Kuipers 1993, 99).

The most effective pressure on the nomadic way of life is the claim by the government, and private owners or concessionaires, on the forests and other resources that provided the livelihoods of the tribal peoples. As the traditional ways of life become physically impossible and uniform national laws progressively replace the highly variable, local customary laws (*adat*), these people swell the ranks of settled subsistence farmers and agricultural laborers.

Tens of millions of village peasants, the bulk of the population, are mainly occupied with agricultural activities, livestock, and fishing; many of them work the irrigated rice fields in Java, Bali, and parts of southern Sumatra. While new ways have influenced their appearance, beliefs, and practices, their economies still rely in varying degrees on the property relations surrounding customary funeral feasts and marriage exchanges between "wife givers" and "wife takers," as well as the many distinctive rituals that punctuate other points in the life cycle. There are also smaller numbers of coastal traders and sailors (like the Bugis of Sulawesi), who play a distinctly important economic role in a nation of islands and have cultural roots reaching back many centuries.

H. Geertz (1963) distinguished the categories of wet-rice farmers, coastal Islamic traders, and interior swidden (slash-and-burn) farmers. Others (like Guinness 1994) have added new categories that reflect the emergence, in the last few decades, of a secular, urbanized, internationally oriented middle-class, including at its narrow apex a business and military elite that is found mainly in Jakarta. The latter have acquired substantial influence and share many of the privileges and habits of the middle and upper classes in rich countries, such as high-rise apartments and large homes with well-maintained gardens, cars, and access to computers. New village elites constitute a rural middle class influenced by urban consumer patterns.

As Kuipers (1993) has pointed out, "Hereditary ruling classes and traditional elites—reinforced by their positions in the Dutch colonial bureaucracy—no longer possess unchallenged access to political power and wealth. Indeed, they could not even claim to be an elite culture in the late twentieth century. The most powerful generals . . . and capitalists . . . of the post-independence period [are] newcomers to their positions . . ." (pp. 86–87). In the words of

Guinness (1994, 289), "In both town and village there is unmistakable evidence that the display of wealth in house, style, possession of a motor vehicle, and clothes and jewelry has become important in status claims, alongside more traditional markers such as patronage, ritual and landholding."

An important legacy of former President Sukarno is the single nation forged out of this mixture of independent peoples. President Suharto and the country's ruling classes remained committed to the creation of a modern, unified society focused strongly on economic development. The chief means have been a common language, education, the media, and administrative control—and occasional resorts to force.

The creation in the twentieth century of Bahasa Indonesia, a modified form of Malay that is now the single, official national language, was the most fundamental step toward unification. Today, the vast majority of the population and especially the young people can speak Bahasa Indonesia. However, according to relatively recent reports, only 12 percent of the total population uses the official language in their homes: 36 percent in urban areas and 5 percent in other places (Way 1984, 187). In their homes, another 40 percent speak Javanese, 15 percent Sundanese, and 5 percent Madurese; the remaining 28 percent include speakers of Batak, Minangkabau, Balinese, Buginese, and Banjarese, which jointly account for 10 percent of the total. These are rough estimates, but even in the mid-1980s the percentage reporting Bahasa Indonesia as their "primary language" was well under 5 percent (Kuipers 1993, 96).

Public education, conducted in Bahasa Indonesia, is built around a core of Pancasila, the name given to the official state philosophy of "unity in diversity," which is intended to prepare young people for life in their rapidly changing society. Thirty-six million students were enrolled in primary and secondary schools and almost 2 million in tertiary institutions in 1990 (Johnson, Gaylord, and Chamberland 1993, xi). These figures represent two-thirds of the population aged five to nine, 84 percent of those between ten and fourteen, over 40 percent of those fifteen to nineteen, and 10 percent of the twenty to twenty-four year olds (population by age from BPS 1992, 127). The curriculum in Islamic schools, however, which enrolled 1.2 million young people in 1987 (Guinness 1994, 298), is almost exclusively religious; memorizing the Koran in Arabic takes the place of Pancasila. Over nine thousand Indonesian students were studying at universities in the United States, compared to a handful in 1978 (Johnson, Gaylord, and Chamberland 1993, xi). Although education in literacy, skills, and attitudes appropriate to structured workplaces is clearly one of the key elements of the development strategy of Indonesia, foreign companies have repeatedly identified the lack of skilled or literate personnel as the major obstacle to doing business in Indonesia. While the government of Indonesia has imposed conditions that require the use and training of an Indonesian labor force, it is deemed necessary to make many exceptions, especially in jobs requiring managerial or technical expertise (Business International Asia/Pacific 1975, 127).

Government-controlled communications distributed by radio, television, and newspapers transmit the message of unification and modernization on a daily basis in Bahasa Indonesia. While there is a conscious effort to prevent the politicization of the population, the realities of the modern world relentlessly seep in through education, the media, and a dramatically expanded transportation network. Virtually everyone is affected by the need to earn a living in a landscape transformed by a pervasive government administrative structure promoting modernization and by economic growth, population growth, and the resulting complex patterns of migration.

Prior to 1960, there was practically no industry in Indonesia. The earliest activities were initiated by the arrival of foreign companies with the intention of extracting the country's natural resources. The foreign companies were later largely replaced by national companies as Indonesia became a substantial producer and exporter of forest products, plywood, petroleum, natural gas, rubber, tin, aluminum, coffee, and tea. An increasing portion of the labor force is involved in manufacturing, but it is still small (under 10 percent) compared to the number engaged in agriculture (well over half).

The growth of cities and industry, and the absence of an adequate economic base to provide livelihoods for workers outside urban areas, has been accompanied by a predictable rural-to-urban exodus. With about one-third of the population living in cities in 1990, Indonesia is the least urbanized among the "newly developing" societies in the region. Nonetheless, the trend is clearly reflected in official statistics that show the percentage of urban inhabitants at 15.5 percent in 1961, 17.3 percent in 1971, and 22.4 percent in 1980 (Rutz 1987, 31); it is expected to reach 52 percent by 2020 (Wirakartakusumah 1993, 18). Simultaneous with the move to the urban areas has been a substantial amount of voluntary out-migration and government-initiated "transmigration" from densely populated areas to the outer islands (the collective name given to the islands other than Java and Madura). Indonesians also practice "circular migration," meaning that many households have at least one member working in a distant location for at least part of the year.

By many measures Indonesia's pursuit of modernization and development since it gained its independence from the Dutch in 1949 has been successful. While the country was once a major importer of rice, self-sufficiency in providing a growing population with its staple food was achieved. In another impressive success, diversification efforts restored the high rates of growth of the 1960s and 1970s that were interrupted by economic crisis in the early 1980s because of the fall in the price of exported petroleum. It is likely that the country will try to continue on this path when it recovers from the financial crisis that began in 1997.

Rapidly modernizing economies experience two common dilemmas, and they are both pronounced in Indonesia. The first is the disappearance of indigenous cultures that have withstood the test of time and generally remain attractive to their adherents but are unable to hold their own against modern ways. The apparent backwardness of traditional peoples is embarrassing to the national elite, and the land and resources they use are desired for other purposes. But the tactics necessary to absorb them are problematic both ethically and practically, and there is the nagging feeling that the disappearance of these cultures is an irreversible loss, strikingly comparable to the loss of biological diversity through the destruction of the habitat of plants and animals. Some traditional peoples desire to enter the modern world, and even reluctant ones are traveling that road because they have no alternatives.

The second dilemma is that people are drawn into the market economy to varying degrees, and large numbers find themselves in having lost advantages of the old way of life and not yet achieved those of the new way. Still untouched by modernization are peoples like the isolated hill tribes whose homelands are sufficiently remote to assure minimal exchanges with the outside world even at the end of the twentieth century. At the other extreme are urban workers whose entire income is supplied by a regular paycheck and whose needs are met mainly through purchased goods and services.

Today in Indonesia most people are somewhere in between those extremes, and operating largely within what has been called the "informal sector" in both urban and rural locations. These people may earn some income through wages and make some purchases for money, but their survival is strongly dependent on informal networks of exchange of goods and services. They generally follow traditional practices at home, while publicly they "swear loyalty to the Indonesian state in school and church, or at the polls. In the early 1990s, one's identity as an Indonesian was still interwoven with one's familial, regional, and ethnic heritage" (Kuipers 1993, 72).

A nearly allegorical depiction of these tensions is provided by the phenomenon of inner and outer villages as a response to cultural confrontation. The most dramatic example is that of the Baduy of Banten, the "hidden people" in the western mountains of Java. Baduy inner villages strictly observe the traditional ways; in particular, the use of objects made by outsiders is prohibited. The outer villages serve as a buffer zone: their inhabitants participate in commerce and have accommodated to the modern world in various ways in order to shield the inner zone from such contacts. To complete the symbolism, white robes are worn in the inner villages, while the garments of the outer Baduy are dyed in deep hues of indigo (Homan et al. 1990, 38–45). A similar adaptation involving the protection of pious inner villages by outer ones was observed in Tana Towa in Sulawesi (Hanbury-Tenison 1975, 127). Many urban dwellers play a similar if less dramatic role mediating between the modern world and their native villages.

The transformation of the economy over the past several decades has unleashed many interrelated changes that have affected the lives of virtually all Indonesians, directly and indirectly. The process of modernization is always uneven in its effects, and this is especially true in a society that at the outset is as diverse as this one. The description of Indonesian households in this chapter is intended to launch a structured inquiry into the nature of these changes as a basis for analyzing alternative prospects for the future of the different segments of the population.

Descriptive Statistics about Indonesia

The work of anthropologists provides a rich and sensitive depiction of many aspects of people's lives. My objective is to build upon this qualitative description to develop a more complete and systematically organized quantitative description that can be used as a basis for analyzing scenarios about the future.

The investigation of social welfare in developing countries has a long history. The objective of such inquiries was generally to assess the distribution of wealth in order to improve the ability to control and tax the population. Probably the first social surveys in Indonesia were carried out under the Dutch colonial regime. Over the period from 1905 to 1920 the Dutch Commission for the Investigation of the Diminishing Welfare of the Indonesian Population published thirty volumes of survey-based data about village life in Java (Koentjaraningrat 1967, 13–14). More recently, surveys and analyses have been conducted by the government of Indonesia to determine whether the poorest households are sharing in the new prosperity and, if not, how they could be more effectively drawn into the modern economy.

The national statistical office, Biro Pusat Statistik or BPS, was created in Jakarta in the 1970s with technical and financial assistance from the Japanese. Data collection began during that decade and accelerated in the 1980s. Nonetheless, analysts have observed that it was not until the early 1990s that "for the first time genuinely detailed information on independent Indonesia—quantitative data—began to accumulate" (Frederick and Worden 1993, xliii).

BPS follows the guidelines and classifications recommended by international conventions, namely those of the United Nations' System of National Accounts (SNA). Social and economic data are recorded in decennial demographic, social, and economic censuses and in the large number of specialized surveys, principally SUSENAS (National Economic and Social Survey) and SUPAS (Inter-Census Population Survey). This enormous body of information is published in a variety of documents. The units for which data are collected and reported include the individual (in per capita statistics), the household, and the geopolitical district, such as the island or province. I now turn to this information to piece together a more formal, quantitative description of some of the attributes described in the last section.

The Indonesian economy has grown substantially over the last few decades. Population has increased at over 2 percent a year on the average since 1950 (see table 7.1). Enormous reductions in fertility have been achieved.[1] While they are offset by continuing declines in mortality,[2] the size of the population is far lower than most observers anticipated a few decades ago (Hull 1994).

The average annual real growth of gross domestic product was nearly 6 percent over the period between 1960 and 1997, despite the

TABLE 7.1. GROWTH OF THE ECONOMY AND POPULATION OF INDONESIA 1950–93

	Population		Gross Domestic Product			
			Prices			
			Billions of Rupiahs			
	Millions	Average Annual Rate of Growth	Current Prices	Constant Prices of 1990	Average Annual Rate of Real Growth	Millions of U.S. Dollars Current Prices
1950	83.4	—	—	—	—	—
1960	100.7	1.90%	0.4	37,128	—	5,311
1970	122.9	2.02	3,451.5	53,732	3.77%	9,457
1980	154.9	2.34	48,914.0	111,234	7.55	78,262
1990	187.7	1.94	195,597.0	195,597	5.81	106,209
1993	197.2	1.65	298,026.0	235,477	6.38	142,754
1950–1993		2.02				—
1960–1993		2.06			5.76	

Sources: Population data from U.S. Bureau of the Census; international data from website http://www.census.gov/ipc-bin/idbsprd; GDP data from Macroeconomic Division of United Nations Secretariat, provided in personal communication by D. Walker in 1996.

violent insurrection leading to a military takeover in 1965–66 and the crisis related to petroleum prices that culminated in the early 1980s. The magnitude of the inflation in the 1960s is evident in table 7.1 from a comparison of the values in current prices and constant prices reported for those years, and the devaluation of the currency is seen in comparing the values in current domestic prices with values in U.S. prices.

The uneven spatial distribution of the population is illustrated in table 7.2, which shows the population density by major island: Java, with 7 percent of the land area, is home to 60 percent of the people. One reason for this concentration is the high quality of the soils of volcanic origin on Java. The principal agricultural regions are indicated on the map of Indonesia in figure 7.1.

The main resources earning foreign exchange are petroleum, liquid natural gas, coal, bauxite, tin, nickel, copper, gold, logs and other forest products, palm oil, and rubber. These riches are concentrated in East Kalimantan, Sumatra (especially the provinces of Riau, Aceh, and South Sumatra), and Irian Jaya. Table 7.3, which shows the portions of regional gross domestic product originating in mining and agricultural sectors, provides a rough indication of the regional differences in resource endowments. There is a substantial literature on regional variation in Indonesia (Hill and Weidemann 1989).

TABLE 7.2. AREA AND POPULATION BY ISLAND IN INDONESIA IN 1990

	Area (sq km)	Population (millions)	Density (persons/sq km) 1971	Density (persons/sq km) 1990	Households (millions)	Household Size
Java	132,186	107.5	576	814	24.9	4.3
Sumatra	473,481	36.5	44	77	7.5	4.9
Nusa Tenggara	88,488	10.2	75	115	2.1	4.8
Kalimantan	539,460	9.1	10	17	1.9	4.7
Sulawesi	189,216	12.5	45	66	2.6	4.9
Maluku/Irian Jaya	496,486	3.5	4	7	0.7	5.1
Outer Islands	1,787,131	71.8	24	40	14.8	4.9
proportion	0.93	0.40			0.37	
Indonesia	1,919,317	179.3	62	93	39.7	4.5

Source: BPS 1992.

Structural Economics

TABLE 7.3. RELATIVE IMPORTANCE OF MINING AND AGRICULTURE BY ISLAND AND
PROVINCE IN INDONESIA IN 1979 (MILLIONS OF RUPIAHS IN 1975 PRICES)

Province	Mining		Agriculture	
	RGDP mining	% of total RGDP	RGDP agriculture	% of total RGDP
Java				
Jakarta	—	—	26.4	1.7
West Java	218.4	9.4	704.3	30.4
Central Java	5.2	0.3	598.3	39.4
Yogyakarta	0.5	0.3	63.7	36.7
East Java	6.6	0.3	868.2	36.3
Sumatra				
Aceh	310.7	61.1	115.9	22.8
North Sumatra	150.9	15.0	373.3	37.0
West Sumatra	0.6	0.2	92.9	37.0
Riau	1,409.4	84.4	61.0	3.7
Jambi	5.8	4.5	64.9	
South Sumatra	134.0	17.7	148.0	19.5
Bengkulu	0.5	1.0	23.9	46.0
Lampung	0.5	0.2	140.9	45.0
Kalimantan				
West Kalimantan	0.5	0.2	98.6	42.9
Central Kalimantan	0.4	0.3	49.7	46.6
South Kalimantan	0.6	0.3	76.9	38.0
East Kalimantan	654.0	62.8	85.7	8.2
Sulawesi				
North Sulawesi	2.2	1.1	82.9	40.6
Central Sulawesi	0.6	0.8	43.8	53.4
South Sulawesi	3.3	0.6	254.2	50.3
Southeast Sulawesi	8.8	15.1	23.8	41.0
Nusa Tenggara				
Bali	1.5	0.6	99.3	42.2
West Nusatenggara	3.9	3.0	68.6	52.0
East Nusatenggara	0.2	0.2	84.3	63.8
East Timor	n.a.	n.a.	n.a.	n.a.
Maluku and Irian Jaya				
Maluku	10.6	7.6	68.4	48.7
Irian Jaya	142.4	52.9	67.8	25.2

RGDP = regional gross domestic product
Source: Drake 1989, pp. 152–53.

Rates of illiteracy by age group in rural and urban areas are
shown in figure 7.2. Among ten- to fourteen-year-olds, literacy is
nearly universal in Indonesia today. The recent date of this achievement is indicated by the fact that over half of the people over fifty
living in rural areas today are illiterate. Even in urban areas, more
than 30 percent of the older population cannot read and write.

The material standard of living of most Indonesians is extremely modest by the criteria of the rich countries, especially in rural areas. Figure 7.3 shows the number of people at each level of consumption, from under 8,000 rupiahs per month (about $4 per person at the exchange rate in the early 1990s; see appendix C) to the relatively affluent living on 150,000 rupiahs ($75) or more. While more than twice as many people live in the countryside as in cities (121.9 million versus 57.4 million), the number of urban residents exceeds the number of rural ones at each level above 50,000 rupiahs ($25) per month. The highly affluent, such as professionals in Jakarta earning the equivalent of tens of thousands of dollars a year, are not visible on this graph (or in any of the official data sources cited in this chapter). It is not clear whether information about them has simply not been included or their numbers are insignificantly small. This question will be revisited in the context of household income later in the chapter.

Access to basic amenities such as piped water, electricity for lighting, modern cooking fuels, and modern toilets is shown in table 7.4. Residents of the outer islands, accounting for 40 percent of the total population, constitute 46 percent of those receiving piped water but only 27 percent of those using gas or electricity for cooking. The last row of the table shows that the overwhelming majority of Indonesian households cook with charcoal or kerosene, fewer than 20 percent have piped water or modern toilets, and fewer than half have access to electricity even for lighting.

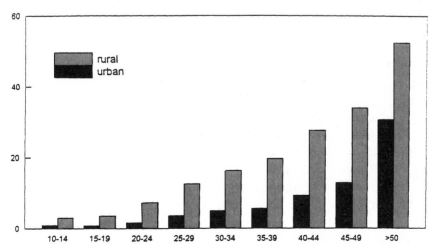

Figure 7.2. Illiteracy in Rural and Urban Areas by Age Group in Indonesia in 1990
Source: Based on BPS 1992, p. 131.

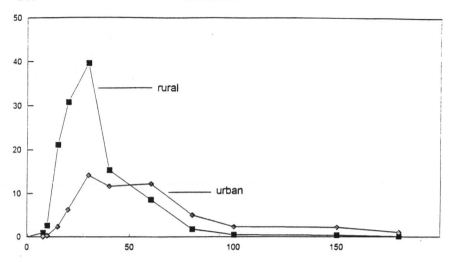

Figure 7.3. Monthly Rural and Urban per Capita Consumption in Indonesia in 1990
Source: Based on BPS 1992, pp. 540–53.
Note: Each symbol indicates the number of people within the following 10 ranges
(thousands of rupiahs per month): < 8, 8–10, 10–15, 15–20, 20–30, 30–40, 40–60,
60–80, 80–100, 100–150, > 150. The symbol is plotted at the upper end of the
range. Lines joining the symbols are added for visual clarity.

Ownership of modern equipment on the major islands is shown
in table 7.5. Residents of the outer islands account for about 40 percent of motorcycles, the principal means of private motorized transport. In the country as a whole, however, fewer than 15 percent of
all households own a motorcycle, and many fewer have a car.[3]

Personal cars and telephones are at the disposal of barely 2–3
percent of households, and fewer than 30 percent of such privileged
households are in the countryside. The television is about as widely
dispersed nationally as the motorcycle but with greater regional variation.

Most employed individuals are engaged in agriculture, especially
on the outer islands. Mining absorbs less than 1 percent of the
national labor force, and even on the islands richest in minerals it
does not exceed 1.5 percent. Java has a disproportionately large
share of the jobs in manufacturing and in modern services, like
finance, many of them concentrated in Jakarta. These figures are
shown in table 7.6.

Because of the relative fertility of the soil, Indonesian households can subsist on small land holdings. Sixty-nine percent of all

TABLE 7.4. PIPED WATER, ELECTRIC LIGHTING, MODERN COOKING FUELS, AND
MODERN TOILETS BY ISLAND IN INDONESIA IN 1989 (NUMBER OF HOUSEHOLDS)

	Piped Water	Electric Lighting	Modern Cooking Fuel	Modern Toilets
Java	3,047,923	11,570,158	618,132	4,265,952
Sumatra	752,760	2,820,327	139,328	1,411,834
Nusa Tenggara	365,492	766,746	18,413	289,753
Kalimantan	902,015	747,331	21,215	277,577
Sulawesi	469,199	938,717	50,231	477,142
Maluku/Irian Jaya	98,984	189,738	4,879	107,302
Outer islands	2,588,450	5,462,859	234,066	2,563,608
Proportion of total	0.46	0.32	0.27	0.38
Indonesia (total)	5,636,373	17,033,017	852,198	6,829,560
Share of all households	0.14	0.44	0.02	0.18

Source: BPS 1992, pp. 151–54.
Notes: 1. *Modern* means electricity or gas cooking fuel rather than firewood, charcoal, or
kerosene; private toilet with septic tank.
2. The outer islands include all except Java.

TABLE 7.5. OWNERSHIP OF CARS, MOTORCYCLES, TELEPHONES, AND TELEVISIONS
BY ISLAND IN INDONESIA IN 1990

	Cars	Motorcycles	Telephones	Television
Java	955,516	3,702,941	639,268	4,043,900
Sumatra	200,455	1,317,310	151,625	1,062,028
Nusa Tenggara	47,472	339,580	29,328	179,982
Kalimantan	52,601	339,954	27,240	325,234
Sulawesi	47,038	337,147	44,223	247,624
Maluku/Irian Jaya	10,128	46,034	14,855	71,703
Outer Islands	357,694	2,380,025	267,271	1,886,571
Proportion of total	0.27	0.39	0.29	0.32
Indonesia (total)	1,313,210	6,082,966	906,539	5,930,471
Share of all households	0.03	0.15	0.02	0.15

Source: BPS 1992.
Notes: 1. Data are for 1990 except telephones (1988) and televisions (1989).
2. Share of households owning each item assumes that all items are in households
and that no household owns more than one of each.

TABLE 7.6. WORKERS BY INDUSTRY AND BY ISLAND IN INDONESIA IN 1990

	1	2	3	4	5	6	7	8	9	10	
	Agriculture	Mining	Manufacturing	Electricity	Construction	Trade	Transportation and Communication	Finance and Business Services	Public Services	Other	Total
a. Workers (thousands)											
Java	22,080	285	5,843	89	1,496	8,111	1,657	367	6,002	85	46,015
Sumatra	10,363	128	719	24	292	1,482	357	56	1,448	19	14,888
Nusa Tenggara	3,309	24	426	7	117	518	88	21	430	4	4,944
Kalimantan	2,433	56	327	6	76	400	95	19	409	8	3,829
Sualwesi	3,258	27	332	5	60	474	96	11	596	8	4,867
Maluku/Irian Jaya	936	6	48	3	19	80	19	4	187	1	1,303
Outer islands	20,299	241	1,852	45	564	2,954	655	111	3,070	40	29,831
Indonesia	42,379	526	7,695	134	2,060	11,065	2,312	478	9,072	125	75,846
b. Island Distribution by Industry											
Java	0.52	0.54	0.76	0.66	0.73	0.73	0.72	0.77	0.66	0.68	0.61
Sumatra	0.24	0.24	0.09	0.18	0.14	0.13	0.15	0.12	0.16	0.15	0.20
Nusa Tenggara	0.08	0.05	0.06	0.05	0.06	0.05	0.04	0.04	0.05	0.03	0.07
Kalimantan	0.06	0.11	0.04	0.04	0.04	0.04	0.04	0.04	0.05	0.06	0.05
Sulawesi	0.08	0.05	0.04	0.04	0.03	0.04	0.04	0.02	0.07	0.06	0.06
Maluku/Irian Jaya	0.02	0.01	0.01	0.02	0.01	0.01	0.01	0.01	0.02	0.01	0.02
Outer islands	0.48	0.46	0.24	0.34	0.27	0.27	0.28	0.23	0.34	0.32	0.39
Indonesia	1.00	1.00	1.00	1.00	1.00	1.00	1.00	1.00	1.00	1.00	1.00
c. Industry Distribution by Island											
Java	0.48	0.01	0.13	0.00	0.03	0.18	0.04	0.01	0.13	0.00	1.00
Sumatra	0.70	0.01	0.05	0.00	0.02	0.10	0.02	0.00	0.10	0.00	1.00
Nusa Tenggara	0.67	0.00	0.09	0.00	0.02	0.10	0.02	0.00	0.09	0.00	1.00
Kalimantan	0.64	0.01	0.09	0.00	0.02	0.10	0.02	0.00	0.11	0.00	1.00
Sulawesi	0.67	0.01	0.07	0.00	0.01	0.10	0.02	0.00	0.12	0.00	1.00
Maluku/Irian Jaya	0.72	0.00	0.04	0.00	0.01	0.06	0.01	0.00	0.14	0.00	1.00
Outer Islands	0.56	0.01	0.10	0.00	0.03	0.15	0.03	0.01	0.12	0.00	1.00
Indonesia	0.56	0.01	0.10	0.00	0.03	0.15	0.03	0.01	0.12	0.00	1.00

Source: BPS 1992.

Note: Totals may not add due to rounding.

agricultural households operate farms of less than one hectare, although these account for only 28 percent of the land that is farmed (see table 7.7). In fact, 27 percent of the households live off of less than a quarter of a hectare. Only 6 percent of agricultural holdings are more than three hectares, but these constitute 28 percent of the land area that is farmed.

At the time of the last economic census in 1986, 5.2 million workers were employed in manufacturing in Indonesia (7.7 million in 1990, according to table 7.6). Despite their relatively small number, these workers collectively are of great importance because of their role in the transition from a peasant to an industrial society.

Over half of those employed in manufacturing activities worked out of their own or someone's else's residence in operations employing three or fewer persons. These microenterprises, accounting for as many as 93 percent of manufacturing establishments but only about 11 percent of the gross value of output, are highly labor intensive compared to the larger factories in Indonesia. Relevant figures are shown in table 7.8.

Only one-third of all manufacturing workers were in establishments with ten or more employees. These larger-scale operations accounted for only 1 percent of all manufacturing establishments but over 80 percent of the value of output. Output per worker was 15.3 million rupiahs in the larger establishments, 2.8 million in smaller ones with fewer than ten employees each, and 1.3 million in microenterprises. This situation is described in table 7.8, which also shows the substantial differences among manufacturing activities.

In 1986 all metal processing was carried out in thirty larger establishments with an average of 563 workers and 84 million rupi-

TABLE 7.7. FARMLAND AND NUMBER OF HOUSEHOLDS BY FARM SIZE IN INDONESIA IN 1983 (PERCENT DISTRIBUTION)

Hectares	Land	Households
< 0.25	4 %	27 %
0.25–0.5	8	20
0.50–1.0	16	22
1.0–2.0	27	17
2.0–3.0	18	7
> 3.0	28	6
Total	101	99

Source: Thorbecke and van der Pluijm 1993, pp. 69–72.

TABLE 7.8. NUMBER OF ESTABLISHMENTS, WORKERS, AND OUTPUT BY INDUSTRY AND SCALE IN INDONESIA IN 1986

a. Number of Establishments

Industry/Scale	Large/Med.	Small	Household	Total	Column Percentages				Row Percentages			
					Large/Med.	Small	Household	Total	Large/Med.	Small	Household	Total
Food	3,875	38,925	443,795	486,595	0.30	0.41	0.31	0.32	0.00	0.08	0.91	1.00
Textiles	2,852	15,068	149,124	167,044	0.22	0.16	0.11	0.11	0.02	0.09	0.89	1.00
Wood	1,160	14,393	467,071	482,624	0.09	0.15	0.33	0.32	0.00	0.03	0.97	1.00
Paper	602	2,348	7,130	10,080	0.05	0.02	0.00	0.00	0.06	0.23	0.71	1.00
Chemicals inc. petrol.	1,591	2,596	7,530	11,717	0.12	0.03	0.00	0.00	0.14	0.22	0.64	1.00
Minerals	1,208	13,582	105,789	120,579	0.09	0.14	0.07	0.08	0.01	0.11	0.88	1.00
Metals	30	0	0	30	0.00	0.00	0.00	0.00	1.00	0.00	0.00	1.00
Metal products	1,272	5,018	34,403	40,693	0.10	0.05	0.02	0.03	0.03	0.12	0.85	1.00
Other	175	2,604	201,794	204,573	0.01	0.03	0.14	0.13	0.00	0.01	0.99	1.00
Total	12,765	94,534	1,416,636	1,523,935	1.00	1.00	1.00	1.00	0.00	0.06	0.93	1.00

b. Number of Workers

Industry/Scale	Large/Med.	Small	Household	Total	Column Percentages				Row Percentages			
					Large/Med.	Small	Household	Total	Large/Med.	Small	Household	Total
Food	520,069	318,722	937,800	1,776,591	0.31	0.41	0.35	0.34	0.29	0.18	0.53	1.00
Textiles	389,072	132,718	238,956	760,746	0.23	0.17	0.09	0.15	0.51	0.17	0.31	1.00
Wood	181,452	106,080	805,394	1,092,926	0.11	0.14	0.30	0.21	0.17	0.10	0.74	1.00
Paper	62,531	21,476	14,880	98,887	0.04	0.03	0.00	0.02	0.63	0.22	0.15	1.00
Chemicals inc. petrol.	245,419	24,906	16,090	286,415	0.15	0.03	0.00	0.06	0.86	0.09	0.06	1.00
Minerals	80,980	106,063	248,799	435,842	0.05	0.14	0.09	0.08	0.19	0.24	0.57	1.00
Metals	16,894	0	0	16,894	0.00	0.00	0.00	0.00	1.00	0.00	0.00	1.00
Metal products	181,641	39,577	78,634	299,852	0.11	0.05	0.03	0.06	0.61	0.13	0.26	1.00
Other	13,377	20,602	373,711	407,690	0.00	0.03	0.14	0.08	0.03	0.05	0.92	1.00
Total	1,691,435	770,144	2,714,264	5,175,843	1.00	1.00	1.00	1.00	0.33	0.15	0.52	1.00

c. Value of Output (millions of rupiahs)

Industry/Scale	Large/Med.	Small	Household	Total	Large/Med.	Small	Household	Total	Large/Med.	Small	Household	Total
Food	7,511,173	1,044,243	1,547,957	10,103,373	0.29	0.48	0.44	0.32	0.74	0.10	0.15	1.00
Textiles	3,595,882	386,441	284,230	4,266,553	0.14	0.18	0.08	0.14	0.84	0.09	0.07	1.00
Wood	2,453,260	247,764	494,628	3,195,652	0.09	0.11	0.14	0.10	0.77	0.08	0.15	1.00
Paper	895,776	84,269	31,343	1,011,388	0.03	0.04	0.00	0.03	0.89	0.08	0.03	1.00
Chemicals inc. petrol.	4,648,445	113,076	24,646	4,786,167	0.18	0.05	0.00	0.15	0.97	0.02	0.00	1.00
Minerals	1,235,537	144,402	198,249	1,578,188	0.05	0.07	0.06	0.05	0.78	0.09	0.13	1.00
Metals	1,418,705	0	0	1,418,705	0.05	0.00	0.00	0.04	1.00	0.00	0.00	1.00
Metal products	4,008,379	108,542	113,874	4,230,795	0.15	0.05	0.03	0.13	0.95	0.03	0.03	1.00
Other	110,183	54,084	821,705	985,972	0.00	0.02	0.23	0.03	0.11	0.05	0.83	1.00
Total	25,877,340	2,182,821	3,516,632	31,576,793	1.00	1.00	1.00	1.00	0.82	0.07	0.11	1.00

d. Workers per Establishment

Industry/Scale	Large/Med.	Small	Household	Total
Food	134	8	2.1	3.7
Textiles	136	9	1.6	4.6
Wood	156	7	1.7	2.3
Paper	104	9	2.1	9.8
Chemicals inc. petrol.	154	10	2.1	24.4
Minerals	67	8	2.4	3.6
Metals	563	—	—	563.1
Metal products	143	8	2.3	7.4
Other	76	8	1.9	2.0
Total	133	8	1.9	3.4

e. Output per Worker (millions of rupiahs)

Industry/Scale	Large/Med.	Small	Household	Total
Food	14.4	3.3	1.7	5.7
Textiles	9.2	2.9	1.2	5.6
Wood	13.5	2.3	0.6	2.9
Paper	14.3	3.9	2.1	10.2
Chemicals inc. petrol.	18.9	4.5	1.5	16.7
Minerals	15.3	1.4	0.8	3.6
Metals	84.0	—	—	84.0
Metal products	22.1	2.7	1.4	14.1
Other	8.2	2.6	2.2	2.4
Total	15.3	2.8	1.3	6.1

Source: BPS 1992.
Note: Totals may not add due to rounding.

ahs of output per worker. At the other extreme, there were close to half a million establishments each for the processing of food and of wood. Well over 90 percent were microenterprises, with an average value of output per worker under 2 million rupiahs (under 1 million for wood). At the same time, there were five thousand larger food and wood processing establishments of about 150 workers each, with an output of about 14 million rupiahs per worker.

Even when they are classified as the same economic activity, the largest and smallest establishments generally turn out products of different qualities that are sold in different markets. Many of the microenterprises sell their output to other establishments or to households that are also within the informal economy.

Structural Description of the Indonesian Economy

The qualitative description of the Indonesian people that opened this chapter alerted us to the major challenges for development and guided the choice of the descriptive statistics that are reported in the figures and tables of the last section. The qualitative analysis plays an important role in helping us navigate the voluminous published and unpublished data.

Descriptive statistics derived from censuses and large-scale surveys are needed as a basis for making generalizations from the case studies of anthropologists to larger social units. In many ways they offer only a fragmentary framework, however. Not only does each data series use a different conceptual unit of analysis (namely, the individual, the household, or the province), but each unit is further categorized according to many different classifications. One series might show the per capita intake of nutrients with individuals classified by age group, while another indicates health status of the average individual classified not by age but by gender or province. Thus, the information in different tables cannot be reconciled or integrated; the tables function, instead, as sets of unrelated "indicators," each tracking only one of the various kinds of changes that are taking place.

In this section, we offer a third description of Indonesian households, this one based on the data in the official social accounting matrix for 1985. The integration offered by this approach requires more discipline in both the collection and the interpretation of the information. This discipline takes the form of standards and definitions that need to be discussed before the data are examined.

Despite the significance of the household as a social unit, it is much less frequently encountered in descriptive statistics than the individual, the implicit unit in per capita statistics. When people are grouped into households, virtually the only classification principle used by economists is one that distinguishes income categories. This situation is explained by the double focus on money values and on people as consumers. Surely demographers and anthropologists (and probably economists also) would make use of data organized according to other classifications if they existed. The ultimate reason that analysts use the individual as the unit of description is that there is no generally accepted classification for households.

An input–output table provides a practical framework for integrating information coming from different sources at a substantial level of detail. Structural economics extends the input–output framework by incorporating detailed information about households and about the environment in a systematic way (see chapters 4 and 6). The framework of social accounting (see chapter 5) provides some of the missing elements. In particular, it is based on household classifications that go beyond income categories, even though they do not yet satisfy all our criteria for an adequate classification (see chapter 3).

The first social accounting matrix of Indonesia was compiled by BPS for 1980 (published in 1987) and the second one, for 1985 (BPS 1991). These tables constitute the only database in which the households of Indonesia are systematically classified according to criteria other than income. Because of the intricate structure of the database, this uniform classification of households can provide the basis for an integrated analysis that links household activities to the other parts of the economy.

The Indonesian classification scheme follows the general SNA recommendations for social accounts and distinguishes ten categories of households and sixteen categories of workers. These two classifications are shown in table B.1 in appendix B.

The household categories include four in which household members live mainly from agriculture; one is landless, and the other three own land or have the use of it in exchange for a share of the harvest. Very small amounts of land are common; "larger farms" are households that own or operate as little as one hectare. There are three categories of urban and of nonagricultural rural households: low status, high status, and those called "nonlabor force and unclassified." Status is related directly to income, and the definition of "unclassified" is not clear.

As for employment, four kinds of paid and unpaid workers are distinguished: agricultural, production, service, and professional. Production work includes manual jobs in factories and operation of transportation equipment; service work includes clerical and sales jobs; and what I have called professional work (the category is far too inclusive to use in an industrialized society) is defined by BPS to include managerial and supervisory jobs, teachers, technicians, and the military.

The official social accounts are accompanied by so-called satellite accounts, many of which are measured in physical rather than money units but like the social accounts use the household classifications as the conceptual organizing device. This information includes the number of workers classified by household and occupational categories, and the intake of calories, protein, fat, and carbohydrates per capita per day by household category and seventeen categories of foods (BPS 1991).

Every area of data collection has its characteristic problems, and it is not my intention in this work to delve into technical details any further than is required to interpret the figures. For now I take these categories as given and see what can be learned from the data. Nonetheless, there are three issues that cannot be ignored because of the major effects they have, singly and jointly, on the statistical picture that will emerge.[4] The first has to do with the number of people and households in the country. Nomads and various sorts of homeless, including sailors, frequent migrants, and inhabitants of water based villages, are notoriously hard to include in a census. Usually, the intent is to include everyone and to make informed estimates for categories that are known to be undercounted, but no information about the possible inclusion of such estimates is available for Indonesia.[5]

The other two issues stem from the ambiguity surrounding the definitions of work and consumption, especially in a society with a large informal sector. Activities that qualify as work are intended to be included and assigned a money value in the accounts whether or not a salary is paid, and those that qualify as consumption are included and monetized even if no money payment is made for the goods and services. In practice, the determination first of what activities or items to count, and subsequently of what money values to "impute" to them, is not well defined.

All three of these problems are acute in Indonesia, and the prospects for systematic error are great, especially since decisions regarding these areas are not made in concert. The numbers of traditional peoples may be included in population estimates but their work or their consumption (or both) not taken into account since it is virtually invisible to the outside world. For the portion of the economy that operates on reciprocal exchange rather than monetized transactions, it could be that although certain activities are counted as labor, the fruits of that labor do not get imputed values as consumption (or vice versa). These problems must be kept in mind as the data are examined below.

Unfortunately, there is no explicit link between the social accounting database and demographic information, that is, no indication of how many households exist in each category, or how many people live in each kind of household. I have made my own estimates, which are shown in table 7.9.

The number of workers originating in each category of household is provided in the satellite accounts associated with the social accounts, but the total number of people had to be estimated. To do this, I made use of information on the money value of animal products consumed by each category of household and the per capita fat intake from animal products for each category of household (see the second column of and the notes to table 7.9 for details about the assumptions underlying these calculations). The resulting estimates of dependents, or people per worker, are shown in the third column of table 7.9 and appear to be reasonable. Next, crude estimates were made for another parameter, number of people per household. On the basis of these assumptions, it was possible to estimate the number of households of each category and the average number of workers per household. These are also shown in table 7.9. In addition to providing a necessary overview, this table also furnishes information that will be needed for the analysis of scenarios (in chapter 8).

According to table 7.9, the greatest dependency ratios (people, including children and the elderly, per worker) are highest in the poorest households, while the affluent households have the highest numbers of workers in the labor force. To have more confidence in this important finding, it would be necessary to improve the estimates of key parameters underlying table 7.9, and some insights into the reality are provided by figure 7.4, which shows the distribution of households by size (in 1980). Urban areas had a slightly higher proportion of one-person households but a substantially higher proportion of households with seven or more people, especially those with ten or more people. These are presumably the most humble, who are obliged to fit large numbers of people into small spaces; they

TABLE 7.9. ESTIMATED HOUSEHOLD DEMOGRAPHICS IN INDONESIA IN 1985

Households	(1) Workers	(2) People	(3) = (2) ÷ (1) People per Worker	(4) People per Household	(5) = (2) ÷ (4) Households	(6) Workers per Household
1 Landless agricultural	4.7	14.4	3.1		3.3	1.5
2 Small farmer	15.1	47.0	3.1		10.7	1.5
3 Medium farmer	5.2	16.2	3.1		3.7	1.4
4 Bigger farmer	6.1	13.3	2.2	4.4	3.0	2.0
5 Rural low-status	9.4	22.8	2.4		5.2	1.8
6 Rural outside the labor force	2.0	7.8	3.9		1.8	1.2
7 Rural high-status	5.6	8.4	1.5		1.9	2.9
8 Urban low-status	9.7	18.5	1.9		3.7	2.6
9 Urban outside the labor force	1.7	5.2	3.1	5.0	1.0	1.5
10 Urban high-status	6.4	10.3	1.6		2.1	3.0
Total (or average)	65.9	163.9	2.5	4.6	35.9	1.8

Source: (1) BPS 1991, table 3.2.2.

(2) Calculated from tables 3.3.1 and 3.3.2 in BPS 1991 showing household money outlays (including imputed values) for all categories of animal products in the diet, and from different surveys; and from table 3.3.7 showing fat intake from animal products (in grams) per capita per day for each household category. It was reasoned that its outlays for each category of households would be equal to the product of three terms: population, grams of fat per capita, and cost per gram. One household category was selected as numeraire. Then the ratio of a given household category's population relative to that of the numeraire was estimated as the ratio of their outlays divided by the ratio of fats per capita (since the cost per gram is assumed to be the same for both). The total national population in 1985 was 164 million. (4) Averages in 1980 of 4.7 in rural areas and 5.3 in urban areas were computed from Way 1984, pp. 187, 312. (Note that the median, not the average, is reported on p. 312.) Since the average for the country as a whole in 1985 is determined as 4.6 (last row), these figures were scaled down to 4.4 and 5.0, respectively. The total number of households in 1985 is estimated from BPS 1992, p. 149.

Note: The household classification is from BPS 1991. Totals may not add due to rounding.

may constitute a subset of urban lower-income households that could profitably be disaggregated from the other categories. Estimates of people per household for the social accounting household categories are shown in table 7.9, column 4.

The estimates in table 7.9 indicate over 10 million people in about 2 million high-status urban households and over 8 million people in another 2 million high-status households in other areas of the country, for a total of over 18 million people in 1985. A decade

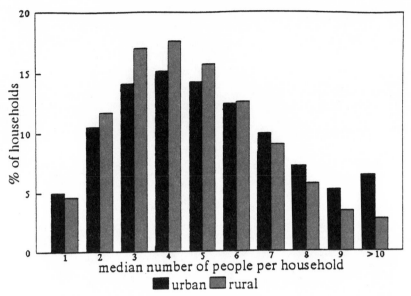

Figure 7.4. Distribution of Urban and Rural Households by Size in Indonesia in 1980
Source: Calculated from Way 1984, p. 312.

earlier it had been estimated that only about 1.7 million people in Indonesia lived like the upper middle class of Europe and the United States. Of those, 1.3 million were urban dwellers, including foreigners such as those on the staffs of international agencies, and the remaining 400,000 were mainly estate owners or large traders in Java or Sumatra. Another 17 million were characterized as able to own a motorcycle but not a car (Business International Asia/Pacific 1975, 174–76). Even though this source is from the early 1970s, it becomes clear that "high-status" in table 7.9 refers to the most comfortable among the ordinary working people and not by any means to a middle-class lifestyle by international standards.

My objective is to use the data in the social accounts along with table 7.9 to describe each of the ten kinds of households. The social accounts are in money units only, so I start with the supporting information in physical units. The social accounting document reports the number of each of sixteen categories of workers who are members of each household type. I have reorganized these data to show the breakdown by rural and urban workers in table 7.10. Here we see that a small number of urban workers, most but not all of whom are agricultural workers (the first two employment cate-

TABLE 7.10. HOUSEHOLDS BY PREVALENCE OF URBAN AND RURAL WORKERS IN INDONESIA IN 1985 (THOUSANDS OF WORKERS)

	Households										
	1	2	3	4	5	6	7	8	9	10	
Workers	Landless Agricultural	Small Farms	Medium Farms	Larger Farms	Rural Nonfarm Low	Rural Outside the Labor Force	Rural Nonfarm High	Urban Low	Urban Outside the Labor Force	Urban High	Total
a. Urban Workers											
1 Paid agricultural	280	18	1	0	0	0	0	56	15	11	381
2 Unpaid agricultural	11	428	58	79	0	0	0	33	26	21	656
3 Paid production	64	55	12	10	0	0	0	3,255	346	371	4,113
4 Unpaid production	16	51	5	5	0	0	0	1,516	169	828	2,590
5 Paid clerical and service	38	34	4	7	0	0	0	1,778	542	2,359	4,762
6 Unpaid clerical and service	38	93	8	9	0	0	0	2,789	467	1,702	5,106
7 Paid professional and technical	6	9	3	4	0	0	0	198	129	1,028	1,377
8 Unpaid professional and technical	1	3	0	0	0	0	0	56	16	113	189
Total	454	691	91	114	0	0	0	9,681	1,710	6,433	19,174
b. Rural Workers											
1 Paid agricultural	3,127	410	81	81	301	186	59	0	0	0	4,244
2 Unpaid agricultural	241	11,597	4,360	5,371	531	847	341	0	0	0	23,289
3 Paid production	334	576	162	101	3,196	273	265	0	0	0	4,908
4 Unpaid production	114	636	167	126	1,776	169	1,334	0	0	0	4,324
5 Paid clerical and service	148	233	60	56	788	146	972	0	0	0	2,404

6 Unpaid clerical and service	224	848	236	194	2,580	319	1,595	0	0	0	5,996
7 Paid professional and technical	26	78	33	35	188	74	964	0	0	0	1,399
8 Unpaid professional and technical	2	13	6	6	86	12	89	0	0	0	214
Total	4,216	14,392	5,105	5,970	9,447	2,028	5,619	0	0	0	46,779
c. Total Workers											
1 Paid agricultural	3,407	428	82	81	301	186	59	56	15	11	4,625
2 Unpaid agricultural	252	12,025	4,418	5,450	531	847	341	33	26	21	23,945
3 Paid production	398	631	174	111	3,196	273	265	3,255	346	371	9,021
4 Unpaid production	130	687	172	131	1,776	169	1,334	1,516	169	828	6,914
5 Paid clerical and service	186	267	64	63	788	146	972	1,778	542	2,359	7,166
6 Unpaid clerical and service	262	941	244	203	2,580	319	1,595	2,789	467	1,702	11,102
7 Paid professional and technical	32	87	36	39	188	74	964	198	129	1,028	2,776
8 Unpaid professional and technical	3	16	6	6	86	12	89	56	16	113	403
Total	4,670	15,083	5,196	6,084	9,447	2,028	5,619	9,681	1,711	6,433	65,953

Source: Calculated from BPS, 1992, table 3.2.2.
Note: Totals may not add due to rounding.

gories), belong to households whose principal livelihood is working the land (the first four categories of households). These urban-based agricultural households account for about 7 percent (1,350,000 out of 19,174,000) of all urban workers and about 4 percent of all workers in agricultural households. Aside from these people, all urban workers are members of the three categories of urban households, and all rural workers belong to agricultural or other rural households. While we do need to keep in mind that some urban households are mainly engaged in agriculture, including subsistence gardening, the figures suggest that since households are distinguished on the basis of urban or rural location, there is no need to also distinguish urban from rural workers. This consideration reduces the number of categories from 16 to 8.

I next examine the prevalence of paid and unpaid workers in the different categories of households. Table 7.11 shows that in 1985 only 36 percent of Indonesian workers were paid a salary, while 64 percent were paid in kind, were involved in the production of goods and services that are deemed similar to marketed items but are produced and consumed at home, or were small or large proprietors. In the accounts, an income is imputed for these workers, and proprietors will generally also receive capital-type income. Less than 10 percent of workers' income in agricultural households that own or operate land takes the form of money, and these households account for more than half of all Indonesian households (see table 7.9). Landless agricultural households, by contrast, receive 86 percent of income from a money wage. Even among the high-status, nonagricultural rural households, only 40 percent of workers earn a money wage. In urban areas, as one would expect, most workers are paid a salary. Yet even among high-status, urban households, over 40 percent do not.

Table 7.11 also shows the magnitudes of income that are involved (section e). Out of a total household income of 63 trillion rupiahs in 1985, about one-third accrued to paid workers, another third was the imputed wages for the services of unpaid workers, and the final third was earned as capital income. The proportions varied widely over the different categories of households. For both urban and rural households outside of the labor force, the contributions of paid earnings to household income was much lower than the number of paid workers would suggest (comparison of sections d and e); clearly, workers in these households receive by far the lowest wages. It is less surprising that a similar comparison shows the high-status

TABLE 7.11. HOUSEHOLDS BY PREVALENCE OF PAID AND UNPAID WORKERS AND BY EARNINGS IN INDONESIA IN 1985

	Households										
	1	2	3	4	5	6	7	8	9	10	
Workers	Landless Agricultural	Small Farms	Medium Farms	Larger Farms	Rural Nonfarm Low	Rural Outside the Labor Force	Rural Nonfarm High	Urban Low	Urban Outside the Labor Force	Urban High	Total
a. Paid Workers (thousands)											
1 Agricultural	3,407	428	82	81	301	186	59	56	15	11	4,625
3 Production	398	631	174	111	3,196	273	265	3,255	346	371	9,021
5 Clerical and service	186	267	64	63	788	146	972	1,778	542	2,359	7,166
7 Professional and technical	32	87	36	39	188	74	964	198	129	1,028	2,776
Total	4,024	1,414	356	295	4,473	679	2,260	5,287	1,033	3,769	23,588
b. Unpaid Workers (thousands)											
2 Agricultural	252	12,025	4,418	5,450	531	847	341	33	26	21	23,945
4 Production	130	687	172	131	1,776	169	1,334	1,516	169	828	6,914
6 Clerical and service	262	941	244	203	2,580	319	1,595	2,789	467	1,702	11,102
8 Professional and technical	3	16	6	6	86	12	89	56	16	113	403
Total	646	13,669	4,840	5,790	4,974	1,348	3,359	4,394	679	2,664	42,364
c. Total Workers (thousands)											
1 Agricultural	3,659	12,453	4,501	5,531	832	1,033	400	88	42	32	28,570
3 Production	529	1,319	346	242	4,972	442	1,599	4,771	515	1,199	15,935
5 Clerical and service	448	1,208	308	266	3,368	466	2,567	4,567	1,009	4,061	18,268
7 Professional and technical	35	104	41	45	274	87	1,053	254	145	1,141	3,179
Total	4,670	15,083	5,196	6,084	9,447	2,028	5,619	9,681	1,711	6,433	65,953
d. Paid Out of Total Workers											
1 Agricultural	0.93	0.03	0.02	0.01	0.36	0.18	0.15	0.63	0.36	0.33	0.16
3 Production	0.75	0.48	0.50	0.46	0.64	0.62	0.17	0.68	0.67	0.31	0.57
5 Clerical and service	0.42	0.22	0.21	0.24	0.23	0.31	0.38	0.39	0.54	0.58	0.39
7 Professional and technical	0.93	0.84	0.87	0.87	0.69	0.86	0.92	0.78	0.89	0.90	0.87
Average	0.86	0.09	0.07	0.05	0.47	0.34	0.40	0.55	0.60	0.59	0.36
e. Earnings (billions of rupiahs)											
Paid	2,302	1,003	286	229	2,904	370	3,131	4,941	995	6,742	22,903
Unpaid (imputed)	197	5,532	1,955	2,437	2,016	420	1,897	2,870	318	1,893	19,535
Capital	325	2,513	2,357	6,361	1,264	1,194	819	2,744	1,378	1,745	20,700
Total	2,824	9,048	4,598	9,027	6,184	1,984	5,847	10,555	2,691	10,380	63,138

Source: Calculated from BPS 1992: workers, table 3.2.2; earnings, table 3.2.4.

Note: Totals may not add due to rounding.

households, both rural and urban, to have the workers with the highest wage rates.

In all the agricultural households, 80–90 percent of the workers are employed in agricultural jobs, and the rest do manual or service-type labor, with few professionals among them (table 7.11, section c). There are striking differences among the three categories of rural, nonagricultural households, however. In the low-status households, more than half are employed in paid manual or unpaid service work—no doubt the male and female "heads of household," respectively—whereas in the high-status households, most of the manual workers are unpaid, as they are small proprietors. Rural high-status households include 35 percent of the nation's paid professionals; many of them have highly desirable jobs as part of the extensive government bureaucracy. Rural households that are considered outside the labor force, like other rural nonagricultural households, have a substantial share of paid manual and unpaid service workers, but most are identified as unpaid agricultural workers. They have the lowest percentage of paid jobs outside of the agricultural households and little supplementary capital income.

Low-status urban households, like nonagricultural rural households, are mainly supported by paid manual workers and unpaid service workers; the rest of their numbers are unpaid manual workers and paid service workers. They and the low-status rural households, accounting together for about 30 percent of the labor force and 25 percent of the households, provide most of the nation's manual laborers and a large share of the service workers, mainly the unpaid ones.

Rural and urban high-status households, based on a very inclusive definition of high-status, together account for 20 percent of the labor force. About 60 percent of the urban workers receive salaries; these are overwhelmingly in service and to a lesser extent in professional jobs. The unpaid workers in the urban high-status households are also employed mainly in service jobs, but a third of them are reported as doing manual work.

The satellite accounts to the social accounts include a tabulation of workers by industry (see the activity classification in appendix B, table B.1). Using this information, a matrix multiplication makes it possible to determine the industries in which members of each kind of household are employed; this is shown in table 7.12. (The calculation involves the table of employees by household and that of employees by industry.)

Most food production is attributable to households that own or

TABLE 7.12. WORKERS BY HOUSEHOLD CATEGORY AND BY EMPLOYING INDUSTRY IN INDONESIA IN 1985 (THOUSANDS OF WORKERS)

Workers	1 Landless Agricultural	2 Small Farms	3 Medium Farms	4 Larger Farms	5 Rural Nonfarm Low	6 Rural Outside the Labor Force	7 Rural Nonfarm High	8 Urban Low	9 Urban Outside the Labor Force	10 Urban High	Total
1 Food crops	2,389	10,429	3,801	4,673	668	843	341	53	26	21	23,245
2 Nonfood crops	861	1,113	390	475	155	122	63	19	6	9	3,212
3 Livestock	120	404	143	175	29	33	14	7	3	4	931
4 Forestry & hunting	66	119	42	51	23	12	12	5	1	3	334
5 Fish	232	409	131	161	33	32	15	26	9	9	1,056
6 Fuel extraction	5	7	2	1	31	3	11	57	9	28	156
7 Other mining	10	27	7	5	89	10	46	35	5	13	248
8 Food & tobacco	63	166	44	31	552	58	231	352	41	102	1,640
9 Textiles & apparel	47	128	33	24	378	41	181	496	58	142	1,528
10 Wood & construction	186	444	119	83	1,618	161	543	1,037	122	279	4,592
11 Paper & other manufacturing	26	45	12	8	171	17	44	382	51	123	879
12 Chemicals & other manufacturing	42	91	24	17	338	34	118	335	47	130	1,178
13 Utilities	3	5	1	1	18	2	8	30	5	13	85
14 Trade	256	855	223	186	2,382	302	1,557	2,409	446	1,687	10,304
15 Restaurants	20	58	14	12	146	19	106	348	64	245	1,033
16 Hotels	2	3	1	1	10	2	12	30	8	35	104
17 Ground transport	70	186	48	35	556	61	267	722	86	255	2,286
18 Other transport & communications	12	22	6	5	74	9	40	185	34	121	507
19 Banking & insurance	3	4	1	1	12	2	14	50	14	65	166
20 Real estate & business services	11	17	5	4	65	8	38	116	26	103	393
21 Public administration	125	220	66	66	645	140	1,264	1,083	330	1,719	5,658
22 Services	140	432	109	88	1,044	144	909	1,904	321	1,327	6,417
Total	4,688	15,186	5,223	6,104	9,037	2,055	5,834	9,681	1,711	6,433	65,952

Source: Calculated from BPS 1992, table 3.3.1.

Note: Totals may not add due to rounding.

operate land, while landless agricultural households account for more substantial shares of labor in nonfood crops, fish, and forest products. Nonagricultural rural households all have a substantial involvement in trade, probably some combination of commercial and barter activities; the low-status households also produce wood products. In the high-status households, 38 percent of the workers are employed in public administration or the provision of personal services. In all categories of urban households, over one-fourth of the workers are also involved in trade; the other main industries are public administration, personal services, and wood products. Of the manufacturing industries, only paper and chemicals draw more than 10 percent of their employees from the high-status urban households, although those households provide 30 percent or more of the employees in hotels, banks, and public administration.

Personal consumption (measured in rupiahs per household) of goods and services was computed for the different categories of households. These consumption patterns are shown in table 7.13 in comparison to a hypothetical household consuming an average amount of each of the goods and services. In the countryside, only the bigger farm households and the high-status nonfarm households consume more than the nationwide average, leaving two-thirds of the population at far below the national average except for consumption of forest products and hunting. The relative consumption by that two-thirds of paper, electricity, commercial trade, transportation, and banking is especially low. Even the bigger farmers use electricity, commercial trade, and motorized transport relatively little.

The total value of consumption is about the same for low-status urban households as for the bigger farm households but the composition is rather different. The urban households spend less on food and natural materials (like wood) but use electricity, commercial trade, restaurants—actually the modest food stands that dot the streets in many neighborhoods—transportation, banking, and public services. The nonagricultural high-status households stand out among rural households for their greater use of paper and banking services.

All categories of urban households use the kinds of services that are typical of cities—electricity, transportation, banks, etc. In addition they receive substantial amounts of public services (provided through public administration), probably mainly public education and health services. Over the ten categories of households, the total value of consumption varies by less than six to one (table 7.13): less

Table 7.13. Household Consumption Relative to an Average Household in Indonesia in 1985

| | 1 | 2 | 3 | 4 | 5 | 6 | 7 | 8 | 9 | 10 | |
| | | | | | | Households | | | | | |
Workers	Landless Agricultural	Small Farms	Medium Farms	Larger Farms	Rural Nonfarm Low	Rural Outside the Labor Force	Rural Nonfarm High	Urban Low	Urban Outside the Labor Force	Urban High	Total
1 Food crops	0.61	0.86	0.95	1.87	0.68	0.76	1.39	1.06	1.10	1.61	1.00
2 Nonfood crops	0.63	1.02	0.82	1.21	0.73	0.88	1.62	1.04	1.10	1.52	1.00
3 Livestock	0.29	0.42	0.65	1.52	0.52	0.80	2.08	1.51	1.96	3.75	1.00
4 Forestry & hunting	1.13	1.28	1.03	1.54	0.90	0.92	1.01	0.45	0.30	0.25	1.00
5 Fish	0.58	0.71	0.88	1.85	0.75	0.93	1.62	1.22	1.18	1.72	1.00
6 Fuel extraction	0.00	0.00	0.00	0.00	0.00	0.00	0.00	0.00	0.00	0.00	0.00
7 Other mining	0.64	0.94	1.04	1.94	0.70	0.80	1.26	0.99	0.93	1.14	1.00
8 Food & tobacco	0.67	0.63	0.79	1.66	0.79	0.85	1.64	1.41	1.26	1.93	1.00
9 Textiles & apparel	0.45	0.38	0.64	1.54	0.64	0.93	2.68	1.44	2.05	2.84	1.00
10 Wood & construction	0.40	0.46	0.73	1.70	0.78	0.74	3.02	1.07	1.29	2.68	1.00
11 Paper & other manufacturing	0.21	0.21	0.49	1.41	0.72	0.56	3.66	1.08	1.72	4.54	1.00
12 Chemicals & other manufacturing	0.49	0.28	0.64	1.74	0.69	0.87	2.08	1.74	1.93	2.94	1.00
13 Utilities	0.25	0.08	0.20	0.52	0.35	0.65	1.41	2.66	3.57	5.87	1.00
14 Trade	0.21	0.11	0.32	0.76	0.62	0.79	1.94	2.63	2.67	4.53	1.00
15 Restaurants	0.58	0.23	0.49	1.27	0.82	0.97	1.79	2.11	1.98	3.20	1.00
16 Hotels	0.29	0.16	0.47	1.42	0.48	0.65	2.87	1.42	2.88	4.67	1.00
17 Ground transport	0.22	0.14	0.26	0.66	0.62	0.78	1.91	2.66	2.75	4.54	1.00
18 Other transport & communications	0.21	0.09	0.27	0.82	0.53	0.72	1.80	2.38	2.67	5.47	1.00
19 Banking & insurance	0.24	0.23	0.64	1.84	0.65	0.75	3.23	1.00	1.21	4.30	1.00
20 Real estate & business services	0.46	0.24	0.50	1.27	0.53	0.77	1.37	2.03	2.94	4.20	1.00
21 Public administration	0.47	0.57	0.48	1.06	0.64	0.83	1.67	1.62	2.32	3.33	1.00
22 services	0.32	0.18	0.49	1.37	0.61	0.60	3.00	1.54	2.24	4.28	1.00
Total (in rupiah)	0.51	0.50	0.67	1.50	0.69	0.81	1.87	1.53	1.73	2.85	1.00
Consumption per household (thousands of rupiahs)	838	816	1,092	2,448	1,333	1,329	3,058	2,508	2,838	4,656	1,631

Source: Calculated from BPS 1992, table 3.3.1; number of households from table 7.9.
Note: See appendix C for value of rupiah.

than four to one in rural areas and less than two to one in urban areas. The range is from about $400 per household per year for the smallest farmers to almost $2,500 for the highest-status urban residents. According to an Indonesian colleague, the upper middle class annual income would begin at the equivalent of about $30,000 in Jakarta and $12,000 in other cities (personal communication from Budy Prasetyo Resosudarmo, 1996). While the highest-income households have clearly not been distinguished (and maybe not even taken into account) and the representation of the most marginal may be very incomplete, the data suggest relatively modest differences in the material standards of living among the vast majority of households.

To complete this story, transfer payments (payments or receipts for taxes, welfare, money sent to a rural household from a relative in the city, etc.), which intermediate between the earnings of a household's members and the means available for the household's consumption or savings, need to be examined. The reported amounts of transfer payments suggest that most categories of households receive more transfer income than they pay (most of the difference being accounted for by the taxation of industry), with the notable exception of the agricultural households, which are the only ones to pay more in taxes to the government than they receive in return from the government.

Improving the Social Accounts for Indonesia

This chapter has provided a qualitative description based on the anthropological literature as well as various descriptive statistics including social accounting data to draw a picture of the households of Indonesia. The first round of recommendations for improving the accounts is focused on the classification of households.

The wealthiest households are invisible in all of the statistics because the highest-status categories are defined to include households of rather modest means. Thus it has not been possible to distinguish the work and consumption practices of even the upper middle classes, not to mention the true business and military elite. At least one more category should be added in both the urban and the rural setting. The most affluent agricultural households can be identified by ownership of larger parcels of land (see table 7.7), by agricultural techniques, or by major crop.

Nearly a third of all households fall into a single category: the smallest farm households, owning or operating less than half an acre of land. These need to be disaggregated, and one good choice would be to distinguish irrigated paddy farmers. Possibly seminomadic cultivators should also be represented explicitly.

Regional differences in lifestyles are substantial, and three categories of urban households could be distinguished: those on Java, those on Kalimantan, and all others. The population of Jakarta is nearly as large as that of the entire island of Kalimantan and could be considered as a separate category of urban households. Because of the substantially greater fertility of soil on Java, it could be useful to distinguish paddy farmers on and off Java.

Eight percent of all households appear to be outside of the labor force (or "unclassified"), but it is not clear whether this is a temporary or permanent situation or how it is different from unemployment, for which the source documents do not include adequate figures. Those counted as employed include the full gamut, from individuals working a few hours a week to those holding more than one regular job. The proportion of those working substantially more or less than standard full time is large enough to require some concept of full-time equivalency. One approach would be to classify workers as part-time or full-time. While the distinction is rough, it can be easily estimated and would represent a substantial improvement over present practices.

One of the main lessons of the classification proposed in table 3.1 of chapter 3 is that a bottom-up classification is generally not symmetric and can be a perfectly adequate and even superior approach to classification. For example, if urban residents of Jakarta or wet paddy growers are distinguished on the basis of their unique characteristics and large numbers, there is no reason that other cities or other crops also need to be singled out. Taking advantage of this principle, I propose revising the ten-category household classification of the Indonesian social accounts in the direction indicated in table 7.14. The present classification of labor has sixteen categories—agricultural, production, service, and professional, all of which are paid or unpaid and rural or urban. I suggest that the rural-or-urban distinction be dropped, as the analysis has shown it to be unnecessary, and replaced by the distinction as to part or full time. Thus, the number of labor categories would remain unchanged.

The proposed household classification (table 7.14) has seven categories of households whose members make their living mainly from agriculture. This makes fourteen categories if their

TABLE 7.14   PROPOSED HOUSEHOLD CLASSIFICATION FOR INDONESIA

Agricultural Households: Java, Other Islands

a1	shifting cultivation
a2	agricultural labor
a3	small farm, irrigated paddy
a4	small farm, other crops
a5	medium farm
a6	bigger farm
a7	large or modern farm

Rural, Nonagricultural Households: Java, Other Islands

r1	rural, low status
r2	rural, higher status
r3	rural affluent

Urban: Jakarta, Other Java, Kalimantan, Other Islands

u1	urban, low status
u2	urban, large household
u3	urban, higher status
u4	urban, upper middle class
u5	modern elite

Note: This classification includes 14 agricultural; 6 rural, nonagricultural; and 20 urban categories for a total of 40 categories. The existing classification is shown in appendix B.

location on or off Java is indicated. Swidden agriculture, which involves the periodic fallowing of land, is distinguished as a separate category, and the smallest farms are subdivided to irrigated paddy and other crops. A category is added for the largest and most modern operations.

The two categories of urban and rural households outside the labor force have been eliminated pending a better understanding as to the reasons for this status. Instead, classifications for the truly affluent have been added to both the urban and rural categories. The rural, nonagricultural categories are divided by residence on Java or the other islands.

The very large urban household is added as a new category, along with an urban upper middle class and an urban elite. It is proposed that the urban categories be disaggregated for Jakarta and urban areas elsewhere on Java, on Kalimantan, and on other islands.

The proposed household classification thus has forty categories. This number should be compared to the sixty-six production activities in the official input–output table (BPS 1989). In a country that today has over 40 million households and only a fraction as many business establishments, there is no reason except for customary practices to have fewer household than industrial categories. This forty-category classification can be conceived (and drawn) as a four-level tree. At the first level is the rural–urban distinction. At the second level rural households are divided into those that are mainly agricultural and those that are not. The third level introduces two different sorts of geographic distinctions, and there are three types of detail at the final level. This tree is less symmetric than the standard one used in social accounts (figure 3.3) but more so than, say, the subdivisions of the animal kingdom. It features repetitions that will probably be reduced as this kind of work proceeds.

The first step in implementing the scheme of table 7.14 should be simply to estimate how many households fall into each category, following the example of table 7.9. Then an "activity analysis" is needed for each one of them. By this I refer to the classification of household activities that were listed in chapter 3 (table 3.2) and to a qualitative description of how each kind of household carries them out. In the process, there will surely be changes made to the household classification and the classification of activities.

The ultimate objective is to arrive at a household classification that makes sense for use in the collection of many kinds of socioeconomic data, including work, consumption, income, nutrition, education, health, leisure, and so on. The existence of a classification and the coding of survey information as to the category of household will make it possible to make use of the information in this way. Of course, one of the principal uses of the information by household will be the expanded input–output analysis, to which I now turn.

Notes

1. Total fertility (average number of children born to a woman) fell from 5.6 in 1967–70 to 3.0 in 1991 and is expected to reach 2.2 around 2000 (Wirakartakusumah 1993, 5–6).

2. Infant mortality fell from 106 per thousand in 1980 to 73 per thousand in 1990 (Wirakartakusamah 1993, 5–8).

3. These calculations assume that (1) all cars and motorcycles are owned by households and that (2) no household owns more than one. Since some vehicles are owned by government or business and some households own more than one vehicle, the percentage of households owning at least one vehicle is an upper bound.

4. These potential problems also affect qualitative descriptions and index numbers, but they become impossible to ignore when the separate pieces are integrated.

5. Foreign estimates of the Indonesian population are 5–10 percent higher than the Indonesian figures (Kuipers 1993, 83), but the reasons for the discrepancies are unknown and cannot necessarily be attributed to the systematic exclusion of specific subgroups.

Chapter 8

Scenario about Lifestyle Changes in Indonesia

This chapter reports on an experiment that draws together the material that has been described in the preceding chapters. I have designed a scenario that reflects the kinds of changes that could take place in the Indonesian economy over the period from 1985 to 2000 and analyze the implications for households.

The description of the Indonesian economy provided by the social accounting matrix for 1985, introduced in chapter 4, is one starting point for the exercise. The other starting point is a set of development scenarios for the Indonesian economy that my colleagues and I formulated over the course of several years (Duchin, Hamilton, and Lange 1993; Duchin and Lange 1993). The work was done for BAPPENAS, the Indonesian Ministry of Planning, and focused on three kinds of challenges: unemployment, competition over land (especially for agriculture and tree plantations), and availability of water. For present purposes, I will pick up only that strand of the story directly related to employment.

The scenarios were analyzed using a database that benefited from detailed case studies about technological choices in individual sectors of the economy and a dynamic input–output model of the entire Indonesian economy. The framework included only one household category, however, and had limited feedback between household activities and the rest of the economy.

The basic idea behind the various scenarios was to anticipate and resolve the kinds of problems that might arise, especially of a social or environmental nature, assuming the country was able to maintain—or restore—high rates of economic growth through investments in particular technologies in selected sectors. On the social side, a principal concern was whether enough jobs could be created to employ new entrants into the labor force while also absorbing the large numbers who might otherwise be unemployed or underemployed. The basic conclusion was that, even though the expanding manufacturing activities were substantially less labor intensive than agriculture and other traditional activities, the overall projected rate of growth would require many additional workers. The challenge seemed to lie not so much in an inadequate number of jobs as in whether the available labor force would be able and willing to do the kinds of work called for. The new scenario is intended to explore what kinds of people would be holding the new jobs.

Description of the Scenario

The scenario analyzed here is a composite of those formulated for the earlier studies. It was designed to capture their empirical content (within a static, one-region framework) while shedding more light on the changes directly affecting households.

The scenario is based on assumptions regarding investment, exports, imports, and technologies. It assumes that investment in durable structures and capital goods grows at an average annual rate of 4.7 percent between 1985 and 2000, with the highest growth in the demand for construction, machinery, and industrial materials (#7, 9, and 10 in the classification reported in appendix B, table B.1). Exports grow at an average annual rate of 5.5 percent, with textiles (#8) expanding at 10 percent a year but the largest earner of foreign exchange in 1985, petroleum and other mining output (#5), expanding at a much lower rate. Imports grow even faster than exports, at an average annual rate of 7.8 percent, effectively reducing the balance of trade surplus that was reported for 1985. The fastest-growing imports are manufactured items, notably transport equipment and metal products (#9) and fertilizers and other chemicals (#10).

The technological changes represented in the present, simplified version of the scenario assume the adoption of techniques that rely more on capital and less on labor compared to present practices. I have not attempted to represent the changing use of energy and materials, which was an important aspect of the original work. The growth in investment is presumed to be accompanied by increases in the return on capital; to compensate, labor requirements per unit of output decline by 50 percent for agricultural workers and by 10 to 30 percent for some other categories of workers. Requirements (per unit of output) for the most qualified workers are not expected to fall.

The material advantages associated with investment, increased imports, and labor savings can be enjoyed by foreign consumers (through a decline in the overall price level and thus in particular of exported items), owners of capital, and different categories of domestic households. I have assumed an increase in consumption coefficients of 10–20 percent for many items, especially for the lowest-status categories of households, to assure a relative improvement in their situation.

A comparative static computation for this scenario was made for the years 1985 and 2000 using the mathematical framework described in chapter 6.

Results

Computations were made for 1985 (using the information in the social accounts) and 2000 (using the scenario assumptions) with both the quantity and price models closed for households. The outcomes for 1985 are shown in column 1 of table 8.1; the first seventeen figures show the levels of these activities, measured in 1985 prices. The next thirteen figures are the earnings of labor and the other factors, also in 1985 prices; and the last twelve are the incomes of the institutions, including the ten categories of households. All unit prices for 1985 are by definition equal to 1.0.

Scenario results for 2000 are reported in columns 2 through 4. The changes in the volumes of output, in constant 1985 prices, are shown in column 2; the new relative prices in column 3; and the resulting values (change in volume times price change) in column 4.

There is an overall decline in prices, but one of the most striking results is how little they change. The intention of the scenario was for the domestic economy to benefit from the improvements in efficiency rather than allowing the price level to fall, and the assump-

TABLE 8.1. QUANTITY AND PRICE RESULTS FOR ACTIVITIES, FACTORS, AND
INSTITUTIONS IN INDONESIA IN 1985 AND 2000

		1985 Quantity (billion rupiahs) (1)	2000 Relative to 1985 Quantity (2)	Price (3)	Value (4)
Activities (output)					
1	Food crops	16,957	1.82	0.75	1.37
2	Nonfood crops	6,537	1.98	0.84	1.66
3	Livestock and fishery products	8,933	2.04	0.89	1.82
4	Forestry and hunting	2,286	2.36	0.93	2.20
5	Oil and other mining	17,501	1.90	0.98	1.87
6	Food, beverages, and tobacco	18,934	1.94	0.84	1.63
7	Wood and construction	3,990	2.54	0.91	2.32
8	Textiles and apparel	21,343	2.57	0.94	2.42
9	Paper, transportation, and metal processing	9,876	1.77	0.95	1.68
10	Chemicals, cement, etc.	23,444	2.06	0.96	1.99
11	Utilities	1,803	2.09	0.96	2.01
12	Restaurants and hotels	20,990	2.06	0.94	1.93
13	Road, air, and water transport, and communications	8,817	2.06	0.96	1.98
14	Banking, insurance, and real estate	8,099	2.12	0.97	2.06
15	Public services	10,593	1.97	0.97	1.92
16	Personal services	5,101	2.03	0.95	1.92
17	Trade and transportation margins	18,020	2.01	0.94	1.89
Factors (worker earnings)					
18	Paid agricultural workers	2,565	0.95	0.99	0.94
19	Unpaid agricultural workers	9,348	0.93	0.95	0.89
20	Paid production workers	6,676	1.90	0.99	1.89
21	Unpaid production workers	3,019	1.74	0.98	1.71
22	Paid clerical and service workers	8,415	2.02	0.98	1.99
23	Unpaid clerical and service workers	6,780	1.85	0.99	1.83
24	Paid professional and technical workers	5,247	2.00	0.98	1.95
25	Unpaid professional and technical workers	391	1.96	0.98	1.92
26	Unincorporated capital	20,756	2.19	0.96	2.11
27	Domestic incorporated capital	8,390	2.13	0.99	2.10
28	Government incorporated capital	12,605	1.98	0.99	1.96
29	Foreign incorporated capital	12,276	1.96	0.99	1.94
30	Net indirect taxes	2,790	2.01	0.98	1.97
Institutions (household incomes)					
31	Landless agricultural	2,933	1.31	1.00	1.30
32	Small farms	9,466	1.45	0.97	1.41
33	Medium farms	4,702	1.67	0.92	1.53
34	Larger farms	9,296	1.85	0.93	1.72
35	Rural nonfarm low	7,088	1.90	1.01	1.92
36	Rural outside the labor force	2,707	1.91	1.01	1.94
37	Rural nonfarm high	7,209	1.95	0.96	1.87
38	Urban low	11,843	1.96	1.00	1.95
39	Urban outside the labor force	3,781	2.02	1.01	2.04
40	Urban high	12,908	1.99	0.98	1.95
41	Companies	29,113	2.01	0.99	1.98
42	Government	18,702	1.99	0.98	1.94

Source:(1) Solution to the quantity model for 1985 (X_{1985}); (2) solution to the quantity model
for 2000 divided by (1)(X_{2000}/X_{1985}); (3) solution to the price model for 2000 $(P_{2000}$; prices for
1985 are all equal to 1.0.); (4) product of (2) and (3).
Note: See appendix C for value of the rupiah.

tions about increased consumption were adjusted in order to obtain that outcome.

According to table 8.1, there is a modest decline in the number of agricultural workers (factors 18 and 19) even though the quantity of agricultural production (activities 1–3) increases substantially (column 2). The volume of consumption of agricultural households (institutions 31–34) increases between 31 percent for households of agricultural laborers and 85 percent for those with the biggest farms (column 2). But the corresponding incomes increase only from 30 percent to 72 percent (column 4) because the assumed structural changes lowered the cost of the consumption bundles of the households on medium and larger farms the most (column 3).

The six categories of nonagricultural households (institutions 35–40) all increase their volumes of consumption more than the agricultural households, and this is especially true for the urban and highest-status households (column 2). Again, these changes in total income are attenuated (column 4) because of the effects of changes in relative prices (column 3).

Note that I have been able in this analysis to complement the usual computation of changes in incomes—which are actually changes in physical volumes because they are implicitly measured in constant prices—by an assessment of changes in prices and thus in effective incomes. The power of the price computation is partly obscured in this particular scenario because substantial changes in prices have been excluded by design. In essence, this computation permits us to ask: How much can the volume of household consumption increase in the absence of substantial price changes? The answer is that overall it increases by 65 percent (computed from rows 31 to 40 in columns 1 and 2).

But this increase in consumption is shared among a larger number of workers and households, on the one hand, and more consumption per household, on the other. I now look into this breakdown.

The number of workers of each kind in 1985 is shown in table 8.2 along with the average wage per worker. Making use of this information, which is not part of the social accounts, I am able to calculate the number of workers in 2000 at just over 97 million (see table 8.2). While the unit wages change very little under this scenario, the average wage still increases because of the faster growth of higher-wage occupations.

TABLE 8.2. WORKERS AND WAGES IN INDONESIA IN 1985 AND 2000

	1985		2000	
Workers	Workers (thousands)	Wage per Worker (thousands of rupiahs)	Workers (thousands)	Wage per Worker (thousands of rupiahs)
18 Paid agricultural	4,625	555	4,394	550
19 Unpaid agricultural	23,945	390	22,318	372
20 Paid production	9,021	740	17,103	736
21 Unpaid production	6,914	437	12,029	429
22 Paid clerical and service	7,165	1,174	14,505	1,154
23 Unpaid clerical and service	11,102	611	20,553	602
24 Paid professional and technical	2,776	1,890	5,558	1,845
25 Unpaid professional and technical	403	969	791	951
Total	65,952	—	97,250	—
Average	—	644	—	705

Source: For 1985, number of workers from BPS 1991, p. 24; wage per worker from factor earnings in 1985 (table 8.1) divided by number of workers. For 2000, number of workers from quantity change (table 8.1 column 2) multiplied by workers in 1985; wage per worker in 2000 from wage per worker in 1985 multiplied by price change (table 8.1 column 3).
Notes: 1. See appendix C for value of the rupiah.
    2. Totals may not add due to rounding.

Assuming that the number of workers per household does not change between 1985 and 2000, I can now compute the number of households of each type in 2000 and the change in consumption per household. Table 8.3 shows an increase of 41 percent in the number of households, an increase of 32 percent in the quantity of consumption of the average household, and (taking account also of the price changes) an increase of 79 percent in the value of consumption. By combining the input–output computation with a small amount of additional information, I have been able to distinguish demographic changes from actual improvements in the standard of living.

The average agricultural household operating more than a hectare of land consumes substantially more than the other agricultural households (table 8.3). The number of the former does not increase under this scenario, while the latter do grow by 6–15 percent each. The number of urban households increases the most, such that they account for 25 percent of all households (or 28 percent of the population) in 2000 compared to only 19 percent of the

TABLE 8.3. Household Consumption in Indonesia in 1985 and 2000

Households	1985 (1) Number of households (millions)	1985 (2) Consumption per household (thousands of rupiahs)	2000 (3) Number of households (millions)	2000 (4) Consumption per household (thousands of rupiahs)	2000 relative to 1985 (5) Number of households	2000 relative to 1985 (6) Quantity of consumption per household	2000 relative to 1985 (7) Price of consumption bundle	2000 relative to 1985 (8) Value of household consumption
31 Landless agricultural	3.3	889	3.8	1,011	1.15	1.14	1.00	1.30
32 Small farms	10.7	885	11.7	1,173	1.09	1.33	0.97	1.41
33 Medium farms	3.7	1,271	3.9	2,013	1.06	1.58	0.92	1.53
34 Larger farms	3.0	3,099	3.1	5,548	1.02	1.79	0.93	1.72
35 Rural nonfarm low	5.2	1,363	9.3	1,448	1.78	1.06	1.01	1.92
36 Rural outside the labor force	1.8	1,504	2.5	2,068	1.40	1.38	1.01	1.94
37 Rural nonfarm high	1.9	3,794	3.5	4,016	1.82	1.06	0.96	1.87
38 Urban low	3.7	3,201	6.9	3,364	1.88	1.05	1.00	1.95
39 Urban outside the labor force	1.0	3,781	1.9	4,020	1.89	1.06	1.01	2.04
40 Urban high	2.1	6,146	4.0	6,422	1.92	1.04	0.98	1.95
Total	35.9	—	50.6	—	1.41	—	—	1.79
Average	—	1,976	—	2,600	—	1.32	0.98	—

Notes: 1. Consumption per household in 1985 calculated as household income (table 8.1) divided by number of households table 7.9. (No savings are assumed.)
2. Changes in number of households calculated on the following assumptions: unchanged distribution of factors over households (in social accounting matrix) and unchanged total number of workers per household. Quantity of consumption per household in 2000 is quantity of consumption (table 8.1) divided by number of households. Change in price from table 8.1.
3. See appendix C for value of the rupiah.
4. Totals may not add due to rounding.

households (or 21 percent of the population) in 1985 (see tables 8.3 and 7.9). The volume of consumption per household increases most for the agricultural households, especially those operating land (33–79 percent), and least for the high-status urban households (4 percent). Thus, those categories of households whose material means are growing the most are also the ones whose numbers are stagnating. These kinds of fundamentally important, partially off-setting results have not previously been investigated in the analysis of social accounting data.

Until this point I have followed standard practice in implicitly assuming that the definition of a household category is fixed. But this particular scenario assumes a substitution of capital for labor in the production sectors, a shift that can be expected to affect the sources of household income. The consequences are revealed in table 8.4, which confirms the increased importance of capital income for all categories of households (last column). The great-est shift is for landless agricultural households, who receive 20 percent of their income in 2000 from capital, compared to 11 per-cent in 1985. (This result is based on the assumption that they retain their share, relative to other households, of capital income.) The least change in the sources of income is experienced by urban households, especially the high-status ones that continue to receive most of their income from paid clerical and professional work (last row).

Under the assumptions of this scenario, landless agricultural households in 2000 receive less than half of their income from paid agricultural labor, 14 percent from paid manual work, and as much as 20 percent as capital income (Table 8.4). The other agri-cultural households now receive 42 percent, 67 percent, and 83 percent, respectively, of their income from capital. The economic base of these households has thus changed substantially. Since the profits earned from agriculture in the countryside are often invested not in agriculture but in such activities as the transport of goods, rice milling, and the extension of credit, it is not clear that these should still be considered agricultural households: some should no doubt be reclassified as rural but nonagricultur-al. The point here is that under alternative scenarios, the pattern of factor ownership and the sources of income of a particular household category can be expected to change along with its con-sumption practices. The results of an analysis should be inter-preted accordingly.

TABLE 8.4. CHANGING COMPOSITION OF HOUSEHOLD INCOME IN INDONESIA BETWEEN 1985 AND 2000

| | | | | | Workers | | | | | |
Households	Paid Agricultural 18	Unpaid Agricultural 19	Paid Production 20	Unpaid Production 21	Paid Clerical & Service 22	Unpaid Clerical & Service 23	Paid Professional & Technical 24	Unpaid Professional & Technical 25	Unincorporated Capital 26	Total
1985										
31 Landless agricultural	0.66	0.02	0.10	0.01	0.05	0.04	0.01	0.00	0.11	1.00
32 Small farms	0.03	0.53	0.05	0.03	0.02	0.06	0.01	0.00	0.28	1.00
33 Medium farms	0.01	0.38	0.03	0.01	0.01	0.04	0.01	0.00	0.51	1.00
34 Larger farms	0.01	0.25	0.01	0.00	0.00	0.01	0.00	0.00	0.70	1.00
35 Rural nonfarm low	0.02	0.02	0.32	0.09	0.09	0.21	0.04	0.01	0.20	1.00
36 Rural outside the labor force	0.05	0.11	0.06	0.03	0.04	0.07	0.04	0.00	0.60	1.00
37 Rural nonfarm high	0.01	0.02	0.03	0.13	0.23	0.16	0.27	0.01	0.14	1.00
38 Urban low	0.00	0.00	0.26	0.06	0.17	0.20	0.04	0.00	0.26	1.00
39 Urban outside the labor force	0.00	0.00	0.11	0.03	0.18	0.08	0.07	0.00	0.51	1.00
40 Urban high	0.00	0.00	0.04	0.05	0.36	0.11	0.25	0.02	0.17	1.00
2000										
31 Landless agricultural	0.49	0.02	0.14	0.01	0.07	0.06	0.02	0.00	0.20	1.00
32 Small farms	0.02	0.34	0.07	0.03	0.03	0.07	0.01	0.00	0.42	1.00
33 Medium farms	0.01	0.21	0.04	0.01	0.01	0.04	0.01	0.00	0.67	1.00
34 Larger farms	0.00	0.13	0.01	0.00	0.00	0.01	0.00	0.00	0.83	1.00
35 Rural nonfarm low	0.01	0.01	0.31	0.08	0.10	0.20	0.04	0.01	0.23	1.00
36 Rural outside the labor force	0.03	0.05	0.06	0.02	0.04	0.07	0.04	0.00	0.69	1.00
37 Rural nonfarm high	0.00	0.01	0.03	0.12	0.24	0.16	0.28	0.01	0.16	1.00
38 Urban low	0.00	0.00	0.25	0.06	0.18	0.19	0.04	0.00	0.29	1.00
39 Urban outside the labor force	0.00	0.00	0.10	0.03	0.18	0.07	0.07	0.00	0.54	1.00
40 Urban high	0.00	0.00	0.04	0.05	0.36	0.10	0.25	0.02	0.18	1.00

Source: 1985 figures calculated from table 8.1 (in appendix B); 2000 income levels obtained from table B.3 (product of columns 1 and 5); assumes an unchanged distribution of workers across households.

Note: Totals may not add due to rounding.

Conclusions

Now I return to the initial question posed in this chapter about staffing the future work requirements of the Indonesian economy. The computation reported here estimates a workforce of 97.25 million for 2000. The plausibility of this figure is examined in table 8.5. The first column of the table shows population and employment in 1990 according to official sources, which report unemployment at 2.5 percent. An estimate of "hidden unemployment" is shown in the second column (underlying assumptions are described in Duchin, Hamilton, and Lange [1993]). The third column shows projected employment in 2000 based on growth rates for the total population and working age population, and an increased labor force participation rate to reflect more women in paid work, prepared at the Demographic Institute of the University of Indonesia (Wirakartakusumah 1993). The result of these last assumptions is an economically active labor force in 2000 of 97.67 million (compared to employment requirements in 2000, according to the scenario, of 97.25 million). In terms of total numbers, all new entrants to the labor force could be employed and all of the hidden unemployment of 1990 could be absorbed as well, under the assumptions of the scenario analyzed here.

Next, we can examine which kinds of households are furnishing

TABLE 8.5. POPULATION, LABOR FORCE, AND EMPLOYMENT IN INDONESIA IN 1985, 1990, AND 2000

	(1) 1990	(2) 1990 Full-time equivalent	(3) 2000 (independent projection)	(4) 1985	(5) 2000 (scenario computation)
Population (millions)	179.25	179.25	208.7	163.9	—
Population aged 10 and over (A)	135.71	135.71	165.3	—	—
Participation rate (B) (%)	57.33	54.73	59.08	—	—
Economically active labor force (millions) (AxB/100)	77.80	74.27	97.67	—	—
• working	75.85	59.15		65.9	97.25
• unemployed	1.95	15.12		—	—
Rate of unemployment (%)	2.50	20.36		—	—

Source: (1) and (2) from Duchin, Hamilton, and Lange 1993; (3) applies growth rates for population and work-age population, and participation rate from Wirakartakusumah 1993, p. 15, to column (2); (4) from table 7.9; and (5) from present computations.

these workers. Table 8.6 shows the numbers of workers by household category and by type of work in 1985 and 2000 and the changing distribution of workers within a household. The latter figures naturally tell a story compatible with that of table 8.4, which showed the changing distribution of sources of income; however, here the numbers of workers is not weighted by their respective salaries. Table 8.6 shows that the proportion of agricultural workers in landless agricultural households falls from 78 percent in 1985 to 64 percent in 2000; the decline in numbers is less steep than the corresponding share of incomes.

These figures are displayed from another point of view in table 8.7, which shows the distribution over households and types of work of those workers added to the labor force between 1985 and 2000 under the assumptions of the scenario. The overwhelming majority of the additional jobs are for production and clerical workers, and over half of all additions are to low-status urban or rural but nonagricultural households.

The bottom portion of the table shows the distribution of additional workers for each household category. Unpaid clerical work and paid production work account for most of the new jobs for most categories of households. Today landless agricultural households send 78 percent of their workers into the fields. All of the new jobs available for them will be in production and clerical work, and the situation is similar for the other categories of agricultural households. In other words, in less than a generation many of them will be expected to do the same kinds of work as most urban and other rural workers, a substantial change in lifestyles.

Recommendations

The results of the analysis tell a coherent story about the future contraction of agricultural workers in Indonesia, and show how most of those who might otherwise have been expected to work in the fields will instead be needed in offices and factories if the pursuit of modernization continues.

It is easy to see the advantages of using the forty-household classification described in table 7.14 over the ten categories used in this analysis. On the basis of more detailed results it would be possible to target real households for different kinds of support services and training. It would also be valuable to provide a more detailed classification of kinds of work as a basis for designing training programs.

TABLE 8.6. NUMBERS OF WORKERS BY HOUSEHOLD CATEGORIES AND TYPE OF WORK IN INDONESIA IN 1985 AND 2000

Households	Workers								
	Paid Agricultural 18	Unpaid Agricultural 19	Paid Production 20	Unpaid Production 21	Paid Clerical & Service 22	Unpaid Clerical & Service 23	Paid Professional & Technical 24	Unpaid Professional & Technical 25	Total
1985 Workers (thousands)									
31 Landless agricultural	3,407	252	398	130	186	262	32	3	4,670
32 Small farms	428	12,025	631	687	267	941	87	16	15,083
33 Medium farms	82	4,418	174	172	64	244	36	6	5,196
34 Larger farms	81	5,450	111	131	63	203	39	6	6,084
35 Rural nonfarm low	301	531	3,196	1,776	788	2,580	188	86	9,447
36 Rural outside the labor force	186	847	273	169	146	319	74	12	2,028
37 Rural nonfarm high	59	341	265	1,334	972	1,595	964	89	5,619
38 Urban low	56	33	3,255	1,516	1,778	2,789	198	56	9,681
39 Urban outside the labor force	15	26	346	169	542	467	129	16	1,711
40 Urban high	11	21	371	828	2,359	1,702	1,028	113	6,433
Total	4,625	23,945	9,021	6,914	7,166	11,102	2,776	403	65,953
Distribution of Workers by Household Category									
31 Landless agricultural	0.73	0.05	0.09	0.03	0.04	0.06	0.01	0.00	1.00
32 Small farms	0.03	0.80	0.04	0.05	0.02	0.06	0.01	0.00	1.00
33 Medium farms	0.02	0.85	0.03	0.03	0.01	0.05	0.01	0.00	1.00
34 Larger farms	0.01	0.90	0.02	0.02	0.01	0.03	0.01	0.00	1.00
35 Rural nonfarm low	0.03	0.06	0.34	0.19	0.08	0.27	0.02	0.01	1.00
36 Rural outside the labor force	0.09	0.42	0.13	0.08	0.07	0.16	0.04	0.01	1.00
37 Rural nonfarm high	0.01	0.06	0.05	0.24	0.17	0.28	0.17	0.02	1.00
38 Urban low	0.01	0.00	0.34	0.16	0.18	0.29	0.02	0.01	1.00
39 Urban outside the labor force	0.01	0.00	0.34	0.16	0.18	0.29	0.02	0.01	1.00
40 Urban high	0.01	0.02	0.20	0.10	0.32	0.27	0.08	0.01	1.00
Total	0.07	0.36	0.14	0.10	0.11	0.17	0.04	0.01	1.00

2000 Workers (thousands)

									Total
31 Landless agricultural	3,236	235	755	226	377	484	65	5	5,384
32 Small farms	407	11,207	1,197	1,196	540	1,742	175	32	16,496
33 Medium farms	78	4,118	330	299	129	452	71	11	5,489
34 Larger farms	77	5,080	211	227	128	376	79	11	6,189
35 Rural nonfarm low	286	495	6,060	3,091	1,595	4,777	376	169	16,848
36 Rural outside the labor force	177	790	518	295	296	591	148	24	2,839
37 Rural nonfarm high	56	318	502	2,321	1,968	2,953	1,930	175	10,222
38 Urban low	53	31	6,171	2,638	3,600	5,163	397	110	18,163
39 Urban outside the labor force	14	25	656	294	1,097	865	259	31	3,241
40 Urban high	10	20	703	1,441	4,776	3,150	2,058	222	12,380
Total	4,394	22,318	17,103	12,029	14,505	20,553	5,558	791	97,250

Distribution of Workers by Household Category

									Total
31 Landless agricultural	0.60	0.04	0.14	0.04	0.07	0.09	0.01	0.00	1.00
32 Small farms	0.02	0.68	0.07	0.07	0.03	0.11	0.01	0.00	1.00
33 Medium farms	0.01	0.75	0.06	0.05	0.02	0.08	0.01	0.00	1.00
34 Larger farms	0.01	0.82	0.03	0.04	0.02	0.06	0.01	0.00	1.00
35 Rural nonfarm low	0.02	0.03	0.36	0.18	0.09	0.28	0.02	0.01	1.00
36 Rural outside the labor force	0.06	0.28	0.18	0.10	0.10	0.21	0.05	0.01	1.00
37 Rural nonfarm high	0.01	0.03	0.05	0.23	0.19	0.29	0.19	0.02	1.00
38 Urban low	0.00	0.00	0.34	0.15	0.20	0.28	0.02	0.01	1.00
39 Urban outside the labor force	0.00	0.01	0.20	0.09	0.34	0.27	0.08	0.01	1.00
Total	0.05	0.23	0.18	0.12	0.15	0.21	0.06	0.01	1.00

Source: Author's calculations.
Note: Totals may not add due to rounding.

TABLE 8.7. ADDITIONAL WORKERS BY HOUSEHOLD CATEGORY AND TYPE OF WORK IN INDONESIA IN 2000 RELATIVE TO 1985

Households		Paid Agricultural 18	Unpaid Agricultural 19	Paid Production 20	Unpaid Production 21	Paid Clerical & Service 22	Unpaid Clerical & Service 23	Paid Professional & Technical 24	Unpaid Professional & Technical 25	Total
							Workers			
Additional Workers (thousands)										
31	Landless agricultural	-170	-17	357	96	191	223	33	3	714
32	Small farms	-21	-817	566	509	273	801	88	16	1,413
33	Medium farms	-4	-300	156	127	65	208	36	5	293
34	Larger farms	-4	-370	100	97	65	173	39	6	105
35	Rural nonfarm low	-15	-36	2,864	1,314	807	2,197	188	83	7,401
36	Rural outside the labor force	-9	-58	245	125	150	272	74	12	811
37	Rural nonfarm high	-3	-23	237	987	995	1,358	966	86	4,603
38	Urban low	-3	-2	2,916	1,122	1,821	2,374	198	54	8,481
39	Urban outside the labor force	-1	-2	310	125	555	398	130	15	1,530
40	Urban high	-1	-1	332	613	2,416	1,449	1,030	109	5,947
Total		-231	-1,628	8,082	5,115	7,339	9,451	2,781	387	31,297
Proportion of the Additions										
31	Landless agricultural			0.40	0.11	0.21	0.25	0.04	0.00	1.00
32	Small farms			0.25	0.23	0.12	0.36	0.04	0.01	1.00
33	Medium farms			0.26	0.21	0.11	0.35	0.06	0.01	1.00
34	Larger farms			0.21	0.20	0.14	0.36	0.08	0.01	1.00
35	Rural nonfarm low			0.38	0.18	0.11	0.29	0.03	0.01	1.00
36	Rural outside the labor force			0.28	0.14	0.17	0.31	0.08	0.01	1.00
37	Rural nonfarm high			0.05	0.21	0.22	0.29	0.21	0.02	1.00
38	Urban low			0.34	0.13	0.21	0.28	0.02	0.01	1.00
39	Urban outside the labor force			0.20	0.08	0.36	0.26	0.08	0.01	1.00
40	Urban high			0.06	0.10	0.41	0.24	0.17	0.02	1.00
Total				0.24	0.15	0.22	0.29	0.08	0.01	1.00

Source: Table 8.6.

Note: Proportion of additions calculated as the number of additional workers divided by the total number of additions (positive figures only) to the household category. Totals may not add due to rounding.

I have not incorporated into this exercise the assumptions about specific technological changes that were developed in the course of case studies about forests and forest products, rice production, textiles, electric power, and other activities. It is clear, however, from past work that these kinds of assumptions can be concrete enough and sufficiently well documented to provide the basis for scenarios with empirical content that are more than numerical exercises. While this chapter has demonstrated the enormous, still largely untapped potential of extending the conceptual and analytic approach of structural economics to households, case studies will be needed to provide more of the empirical grounding that is essential to ensure usefully detailed conclusions. It is much easier to do a case study about, say, small farmers growing paddy under irrigation on islands other than Java (one of the categories in table 7.14) than one on the far more varied group of all small farmers (a social accounting category). (This is surely true from the point of view of an expert on households, like an anthropologist.) That is why a better classification must be the first step in this direction.

Case studies of specific categories of households need to give explicit attention to their prospects for providing different types of workers. Case studies of specific factors, like paid clerical workers or income from capital, also need to address the complementary issue of the types of households that furnish them. A portion of the extended input–output matrix (the submatrix called W in chapter 6) shows the distribution of each factor over the different types of households and other institutions, and another (T) represents transfers of income. It is precisely these two submatrices that distinguish a social accounting matrix from the basic input–output matrix. In the present analysis, as in all of the social accounting studies that have been done to date, no assumptions were made about changes in these submatrices. This subject is an important focus for future work.

Chapter 9
Concluding Remarks

My goal in this book is to elicit strategic thinking not only about technological choices but also about people's lifestyle options, in rich and in poor countries, in the interest of better articulating the social, environmental, and economic objectives of reasonable citizens of the planet. This entails bringing more empirical, social content into the formalistic practices of contemporary economics, providing a conceptual grounding for the vast quantities of data that are or could be collected by modern statistical offices, and imposing more structure on the content-rich social science descriptions of how people live. I believe that structural economics represents the most powerful framework we have for analyzing not only technological choices and technological changes but also lifestyle choices and lifestyle changes because it makes it possible to bring all of these pieces together.

One of the temptations of data-based modeling is the call for ever more data of broader scope, more detail, or higher precision. Another temptation is to elaborate the mathematical framework by adding equations more quickly than the empirical work can absorb them. Such equations generally lend themselves more to stating and proving abstract theorems than to quantification. The discipline I have adopted for avoiding these excesses is a style of theorizing that uses the development of classification schemes to structure the data requirements and insists on a close congruence between the logic of the equations and the meaning of the data. Thus, while the data are often crudely estimated, there are no instances where one variable "proxies" for another.

I have not elaborated in this volume on the classification for environmental variables and the mathematical equations relating them to production and household activities. Both are at very early stages of development in which the classifications, the equations, and the empirical feedback have barely begun to influence each other.

I suggest a couple of priorities for further research that maintains a fruitful balance between theory and practice. One is to regard the design and quantification of new scenarios as a valuable scholarly contribution. If a literature on substantively rich scenarios existed, there would be far less tolerance for the often trivial statements that are commonly examined in the name of "hypothesis testing."

Another priority is the development of case studies about specific types of households. This research would be analogous to that of economists who specialize in, say, steel and related industries or agriculture. A household specialty might focus on alternative lifestyles of the elderly in the United States, for example, or the various kinds of rice farmers throughout Indonesia.

The Economy of the Dominican Republic

I have used the case of Indonesia as an example throughout this work, and my understanding of that society was vastly increased by the exercise. Subsequently, I worked in the Dominican Republic with economists at the Central Bank. Their main concern was to anticipate the economic and social effects of opening up their small, highly protected economy to foreign trade. This would be accomplished by lifting various tariffs and other barriers to encourage imports while investing in improving efficiency to promote exports in selected sectors. Implementing the scenario involved identifying specific opportunities for expanding imports or exports and quantifying the underlying changes in tariffs or input structure (Duchin and Nauphal 1996).

The results suggested that opening the economy would involve a shift in jobs away from agricultural and the least skilled production workers toward professionals and other white-collar workers. The steepest drop in prices was in the real cost of the consumption goods and services purchased by the lowest-income households, providing a partial offset for their loss of employment opportunities. My Dominican colleagues were disappointed to find that the level of taxes would not increase. We traced this result to the fact that most taxes were levied on petroleum refining, which contracted, and on those manufacturing activities that could be expected to grow the most slowly.

A second scenario was designed to examine whether a shift in public outlays from construction projects toward public health and education would provide not only direct services but also jobs for the lowest-income households. The impact on the economy, perhaps surprisingly, was to stimulate small increases in the production of most goods and services. Job opportunities improved, especially for informal workers, retailers, and vendors. We agreed that the most important follow-up would be to disaggregate microenterprises from "formal"establishments producing similar outputs and then revisit both scenarios for a refined assessment of the effects on the informal economy. The experience in Indonesia made it possible for my team to move quickly in the Dominican Republic to help implement its first-ever social accounting matrix and to formulate scenarios. The substantial differences in the challenges facing the two economies are reflected in the specific questions addressed. Despite the differences in size and natural wealth, however, a strong common element emerged in the concern in both countries about employment and the ability of the poorest households to cope with change. This concern led to the desire for a more detailed description of the informal sector.

Some Loose Ends

I have touched on many subjects in this volume—classifications, mathematical equations, databases, a description of the Indonesian economy, scenario formulation, and scenario analysis. In each case, I had to decide at a certain point that it would not be practical to attempt further refinement at the present time despite my keen awareness of many of the limitations. Here are a few examples:

I have described structural economics partly in terms of important extensions to input–output economics, such as the operational dynamic model or the model of the world economy. Yet I have used a static, one-country formulation in the closure for households. There is no conceptual barrier to a more ambitious integration, and in Indonesia we actually implemented a dynamic model. However, the potential to learn from the static model closed for households has barely been tapped. I believe that it is still too early to expect empirical significance from a dynamic version of the mathematical formalism.

I have argued for the superiority of a bottom-up classification scheme over the usual symmetric, top-down variety, but in the empirical analyses I have been obliged to compromise with the existing classifications. I once believed that simply showing people the classification in table 3.1 would free their imaginations enough that they would come up with at least a crude version of the same for their own countries, but I now know that this remains a very challenging exercise. In the Dominican Republic, I was pleased that it proved possible to collect data for as many as six occupations and six household categories.

I have identified unemployment and underemployment as a major challenge for the Indonesian (and Dominican) economy, and the mathematical equations are able to represent these phenomena explicitly. Yet the empirical exercises I report do not make use of this capability. This is an example of an area where a little further thought (for example, what assumptions to make about consumption in households that include unemployed workers) would have permitted a richer analysis. As in many other instances, however, it will have to await another opportunity.

Another loose end is the fact that the various data objects used for examples, notably the input–output table and the social accounting data for Indonesia, are not necessarily consistent. They come from different sources, subject to different definitions and conventions. Here, too, with further analysis I could have identified and resolved the various discrepancies.

While there will be ample opportunity to strengthen the new framework described in this volume, it has already begun to demonstrate its promise. Over the past several years my colleagues and I have provided training sessions in several countries, including Indonesia and the Dominican Republic, and used them to stimulate a dialogue about a structural approach to economic development and a scenario-based approach to development strategy. The analysis provided conclusions that could not have been obtained through standard economic approaches; in all cases, our colleagues in those countries continue to work with these frameworks. A concerted effort toward building an intellectual community in this area and a

cumulative body of work will require the creation of university programs. These would include courses, ranging from the general to the
technical, about technology and lifestyle choices and about the interdependency of economic, social, and environmental phenomena
within a framework that does not prejudge the appropriateness of
alternative development strategies.

Growth versus Qualitative Change

Finally, I want to speak about economic growth. In order to establish the importance of technological choices and lifestyle options, I
devoted several paragraphs in chapter 3 to disputing the position
that economic growth is a necessary social objective and that failure
to achieve it must be a disaster. Yet the scenario I analyzed (and,
quite frankly, almost every scenario I have ever analyzed) explicitly
assumes a growing economy. The fact is that in the early 1990s our
Indonesian colleagues had no interest in scenarios with less than a
6 percent average annual rate of expansion. Using the frameworks
that are familiar to economists, it is difficult to make a case for the
potential attractiveness of a scenario in terms other than growth.
Structural economics, by contrast, can provide a detailed description
of changes in the presence or absence of growth. Any of the scenarios serves as an example—say, the shift in government outlays from
construction to education and health services. The change in structure can be represented whether or not there is a change in scale
because of the detailed classification scheme and detailed data.

Especially in the rich, industrialized world, an economy that
does not grow (leaving aside the ambiguities surrounding the definition of growth) can meet the needs and desires of its citizens provided that their satisfaction does not rely mainly on the expansion
of production and consumption. The quality of people's lives
involves satisfaction from the various activities that make up their
households' lifestyles. But while it is common to group households
in terms of their incomes or the value of goods and services they purchase, such groupings rarely take into account how they use their
time or derive pleasure, as from home-cooked or restaurant meals,
listening to music or watching television, bowling or hiking.

With an appropriately detailed household classification scheme,
one can begin to associate attitudes and behaviors with economic
variables. Of the forty categories of American households that are
described in table 3.1, the following categories have virtually identi-

cal household incomes: upper-middle-class retirement communities; fringe-city areas of singles complexes, garden apartments, and trim bungalows; new immigrant neighborhoods, primarily in the nation's port cities; mid-scale, mid-size towns; working-class rowhouse districts; small towns based on light industry and farming; and crossroads villages serving the nation's lumber and breadbasket needs. Yet they probably differ substantially in the ways they carry out the household activities that are listed in table 3.2. The data are available to tell these stories, to examine the ranges of behaviors, and to explore the implications if new behaviors were adopted by different categories of households. The adoption of new behaviors, if the options and their implications were more explicit, could be similar to the spread of successful technological practices and innovations from one sector to another.

The challenge is to describe lifestyles in terms not only of employment and consumption patterns but also of attitudes and prospects for changes in behaviors. This is similar to describing the process for manufacturing, say, paper in order to reveal the plausibility and potential attractiveness of the cogeneration of heat and electricity. It is a daunting challenge, but the effort is rewarding, and the payoff for success may be substantial. I believe that structural economics can help us take it on.

Appendix A: Industrial Classification for the United States at a Moderate Level of Detail

1   Livestock and livestock products
2   Other agricultural products
3   Forestry and fishery products
4   Agricultural, forestry, and fishery services
5   Metallic ores mining
6   Coal mining
7   Crude petroleum and natural gas
8   Nonmetallic minerals mining
9   New construction
10   Maintenance and repair construction
11   Ordnance and accessories
12   Food and kindred products
13   Tobacco products
14   Broad and narrow fabrics, yarn and thread mills
15   Miscellaneous textile goods and floor coverings
16   Apparel
17   Miscellaneous fabricated textile products
18   Lumber and wood products
19   Furniture and fixtures
20   Paper and allied products, except containers

21 Paperboard containers and boxes

22 Newspapers and periodicals

23 Other printing and publishing

24 Industrial and other chemicals

25 Agricultural fertilizers and chemicals

26 Plastics and synthetic materials

27 Drugs

28 Cleaning and toilet preparations

29 Paints and allied products

30 Petroleum refining and related products

31 Rubber and miscellaneous plastics products

32 Footwear, leather, and leather products

33 Glass and glass products

34 Stone and clay products

35 Primary iron and steel manufacturing

36 Primary nonferrous metals manufacturing

37 Metal containers

38 Heating, plumbing, and fabricated structural metal products

39 Screw machine products and stampings

40 Other fabricated metal products

41 Engines and turbines

42 Farm, construction, and mining machinery

43 Materials handling machinery and equipment

44 Metalworking machinery and equipment

45 Special industry machinery and equipment

46 General industrial machinery and equipment

47 Miscellaneous machinery, except electrical

48 Computer and office equipment

49 Service industry machinery

50 Electrical industrial equipment and apparatus

51 Household appliances

52 Electric lighting and wiring equipment

53 Audio, video, and communication equipment

54 Electronic components and accessories

55 Miscellaneous electrical machinery and supplies

56 Motor vehicles (passenger cars and trucks)

57 Truck and bus bodies, trailers, and motor vehicle parts

58   Aircraft and parts

59   Other transportation and equipment

60   Scientific and controlling equipment

61   Ophthamalic and photographic equipment

62   Miscellaneous manufacturing

63   Railroads and related services, passenger ground transportation

64   Motor freight transportation and warehousing

65   Water transportation

66   Air transportation

67   Pipelines, forwarders, and related services

68   Communications except radio and TV

69   Radio and TV broadcasting

70   Electric services (utilities)

71   Gas production

72   Water and sanitary services

73   Wholesale trade

74   Retail trade

75   Finance

76   Insurance

77   Owner-occupied dwellings

78   Real estate and royalties

79   Hotels and lodging places

80   Personal and repair services (except auto)

81   Computer and data processing services

82   Legal, engineering, accounting, and related services

83   Other business and professional services, except medical

84   Advertising

85   Eating and drinking places

86   Automotive repair and services

87   Amusements

88   Health services

89   Educational and social services

90   Federal government enterprises

91   State and local government enterprises

Source: *Survey of Current Business*, May 1994, p. 64.
Note: This numbering scheme is a simplified version of that used in the
most recent input–output table. In the source document, the codes range is
1 through 79 because they include, for example, 73A, 73B, 73C, and 73D.

Appendix B: Social Accounting Classifications and Matrix for Indonesia

This Appendix describes the social accounting matrix (SAM) used in the analysis reported in chapter 8 in terms of the activities, factors, and institutions that it comprises. This SAM, based on the one provided by the Central Bureau of Statistics of Indonesia (BPS 1991, table 1) and more detailed figures included in that document, has been reorganized following the conventions of an input–output approach, with activities in the upper-left-hand quadrant, factor inputs below, and institutional consumption to the right. I have reserved the name "Other" for transactions that do not function like activities, factors, or institutions. This functional criterion involves treating capital investment and international trade as a border for the table while moving certain other transactions into the body of the table.

The inter-industry portion of the new table has seventeen rather than sixteen activities because trade and transport margins are treated as an economic activity. The number of factors is thirteen rather than twelve because net indirect taxes are treated as a factor payment. Imports have been moved from a row to be combined with exports to form a column of net exports. The new SAM has been disaggregated using the most detailed supporting information. Thus, the number of institutions is twelve instead of eight, and the number of households is increased to ten.

The classifications of the individual activities, factors, institutions, and other transactions are provided in table B.1.

TABLE B.1. CLASSIFICATIONS FOR ACTIVITIES, FACTORS, AND INSTITUTIONS IN THE STRUCTURAL MATRIX FOR INDONESIA USED IN THIS STUDY

Activities (output)

1	Food Crops	Farm food crops
2	Nonfood Crops	Farm nonfood crops
3	Livestock and Fishery Products[a]	Livestock and products; fishery, drying and salting of fish
4	Forestry and Hunting	Forestry and hunting
5	Oil and Other Mining[a]	Coal and metal ore, petroleum and natural gas mining; other mining and quarrying
6	Food, Beverages and Tobacco	Food, beverages, and tobacco manufacturing industries
7	Wood and Construction	Wood and wood products industries and construction sector
8	Textiles and Apparel	Spinning, textiles, leather and wearing apparel manufacturing industries
9	Paper, Transportation, and Metal Processing	Paper and printing industries, manufacture of transport equipment, metal products and other manufacturing industries
10	Chemicals, Cement, etc.	Chemical, fertilizer, clay products, cement and basic metal manufacturing industries
11	Utilities	Electricity, gas and water supply
12	Restaurants and Hotels[b]	Restaurants; hotels and lodging places
13	Road, Air, and Water Transport, and Communications[a]	Road transport and railways; air transport, water transport and communication
14	Banking, Insurance, and Real Estate[a]	Banking and insurance; real estate and business services
15	Public Services	Public administration and defense, social and related community services and recreational and cultural services
16	Personal Services	Personal, household and other services
17	Trade and Transportation Margins	Wholesale and retail trade, services allied to transport, storage, warehousing

Factors (worker earnings)

Labor[c]

18	Paid Agricultural	Agricultural workers
19	Unpaid Agricultural	Agricultural workers
20	Paid Production	Production, transport equipment operators, and manual workers
21	Unpaid Production	Production, transport equipment operators, and manual workers
22	Paid Clerical and Service	Clerical, sales and service workers
23	Unpaid Clerical and Service	Clerical, sales and service workers
24	Paid Professional and Technical	Professional, managerial, and noncivilian workers
25	Unpaid Professional and Technical	Professional, managerial, and noncivilian workers

(continues)

TABLE B.1. (*continued*)

Nonlabor
26 Unincorporated Capital[d]   Land, owner-occupied housing, and other urban
                                        and rural capital
27 Domestic Incorporated Capital
28 Government Incorporated Capital
29 Foreign Incorporated Capital
30 Net Indirect Taxes

Institutions (household incomes)

Households
31 Landless Agricultural   Agricultural employees
32 Small Farms   Agricultural operators or land owners of < 0.5
                                        hectare
33 Medium Farms   Agricultural operators or land owners of 0.5–1.0
                                        hectare
34 Larger Farms   Agricultural operators or land owners of > 1.0
                                        hectare
35 Rural Nonfarm Low   Low status, nonagricultural self-employed,
                                        clerical, retail sales, personal services, and
                                        transport and manual workers
36 Rural Outside the Labor   Nonlabor force and unclassified households
    Force
37 Rural Nonfarm High   High status, nonagricultural self-employed,
                                        clerical and sales, services, managers, supervisors,
                                        technicians, teachers and noncivilians
38 Urban Low   Low status, nonagricultural self-employed,
                                        clerical, retail sales, personal services, and
                                        transport and manual workers
39 Urban Outside the Labor   Nonlabor force and unclassified households
    Force
40 Urban High   High status, nonagricultural self-employed,
                                        clerical and sales, services, managers, supervisors,
                                        technicians, teachers, and noncivilians

Nonhousehold
41 Companies
42 Government

Other

43 Capital Account
44 Rest of World

Source: Based on BPS 1990, p. 90.
Notes: [a] Disaggregated to 2 activities in the most detailed matrix.
          [b] Disaggregated to 3 activities in the most detailed matrix.
          [c] Distinguished by urban or rural place of work in the most detailed matrix.
          [d] Disaggregated to 4 categories in the most detailed matrix.

The formats of the official table and the one used in this analysis are shown in table B.2, which indicates the dimensions of each block.

Table B.3 displays the full SAM.

TABLE B.2. STRUCTURE OF THE SOCIAL ACCOUNTING MATRIX

a. Original Social Accounting Matrix

		Factors	Institutions	Activities	Other	
		1	2	3	4	
Factors	1			S21 (12x16)	S14 (12x4)	S1
Institutions	2	S32 (8x12)	S33 (8x8)		S24 (8x4)	S2
Activities	3		S13 (16x8)	S11 (16x16)	S34 (16x4)	S3
Other	4	S41 (2x17)	S42 (2x13)	S43 (2x12)	S44 (4x4)	S4
Total		S1′	S2′	S3′	S4′	

b. Social Accounting Matrix Used in This Study

		Factors	Institutions	Activities	Investment/ Savings and Imports/Exports	
		1	2	3	4	
Activities	1	S11 (17x17)		S13 (17x12)	S14 (17x2)	S1
Factors	2	S21 (13x17)			S24 (13x2)	S2
Institutions	3		S32 (12x13)	S33 (12x12)	S34 (12x2)	S3
Other	4		S42 (2x13)	S43 (2x12)	S44 (2x)	S4
Total		S1′	S2′	S3′	S4′	

☐ No Transactions   ▨ Transactions

Source: CBS 1991.

TABLE B.3. SOCIAL ACCOUNTING MATRIX OF INDONESIA, 1985 (BILLIONS OF RUPIAHS)

			Production Activities					
			1	2	3	4	5	6
Activities	1	Food Crops	592	4	53	0	0	7,795
	2	Nonfood Crops	13	649	62	0	0	2,604
	3	Livestock and Fishery Products	64	10	1,850	0	0	232
	4	Forestry and Hunting	2	11	21	10	2	8
	5	Oil and Other Mining	0	0	8	0	641	8
	6	Food, Beverages and Tobacco	0	0	490	0	0	1,316
	7	Wood and Construction	13	10	14	1	34	35
	8	Textiles and Apparel	24	67	35	16	107	24
	9	Paper, Transportation, and Metal Processing	37	75	62	62	151	266
	10	Chemicals, Cement, etc.	850	353	191	46	277	258
	11	Utilities	0	7	13	3	5	36
	12	Trade, Restaurants, and Hotels	0	6	7	5	97	43
	13	Road, Air, and Water Transport	8	29	7	6	112	39
	14	Banking, Insurance, and Real Estate	81	74	58	19	550	187
	15	Public Services	0	5	3	0	7	5
	16	Personal Services	10	58	14	40	173	41
	17	Trade and Transportation Margins	2,340	1,214	1,926	674	764	2,402
Factors	18	Paid Agricultural	1,503	730	282	50	0	0
	19	Unpaid Agricultural	7,360	1,109	762	117	0	0
	20	Paid Production	5	16	7	8	320	636
	21	Unpaid Production	5	6	2	6	60	317
	22	Paid Clerical and Service	2	14	8	6	268	93
	23	Unpaid Clerical and Service	9	1	2	2	7	12
	24	Paid Professional and Technical	0	8	4	2	216	16
	25	Unpaid Professional and Technical	3	0	0	0	16	4
	26	Unincorporated Capital	3,902	1,586	2,762	591	387	715
	27	Domestic Incorporated Capital	6	81	185	430	4	135
	28	Government Incorporated Capital	22	318	15	44	3,317	916
	29	Foreign Incorporated Capital	0	70	50	136	9,955	98
	30	Net Indirect Taxes	105	29	41	12	30	695
Institutions	31	Landless Agricultural Household	0	0	0	0	0	0
	32	Small Farms	0	0	0	0	0	0
	33	Medium Farms	0	0	0	0	0	0
	34	Larger Farms	0	0	0	0	0	0
	35	Rural Nonfarm Low Household	0	0	0	0	0	0
	36	Rural Household Outside the Labor Force	0	0	0	0	0	0
	37	Rural Nonfarm High Household	0	0	0	0	0	0
	38	Urban Low Household	0	0	0	0	0	0
	39	Urban Household Outside the Labor Force	0	0	0	0	0	0
	40	Urban High Household	0	0	0	0	0	0
	41	Companies	0	0	0	0	0	0
	42	Government	0	0	0	0	0	0
Ex	43	Capital Account	0	0	0	0	0	0
	44	Rest of World	422	372	16	3	1,157	212
		Total	17,378	6,909	8,949	2,289	18,658	19,145
			1	2	3	4	5	6

				Production Activities							
7	8	9	10	11	12	13	14	15	16	17	
2	47	0	2	0	290	0	0	39	0	0	1
282	1	2	370	0	156	0	0	4	0	0	2
29	0	8	0	0	865	2	0	53	0	0	3
2	1,599	6	13	0	21	0	0	0	2	0	4
0	1,316	5	6,473	104	0	0	0	0	0	0	5
4	28	3	47	0	1,112	13	2	62	0	0	6
1,261	16	32	70	0	78	14	4	42	147	0	7
21	1,516	48	78	50	240	114	437	86	44	0	8
54	2,222	2,921	357	95	222	193	162	270	797	0	9
529	5,870	1,148	3,206	816	558	1,438	43	346	600	0	10
22	22	40	163	287	277	31	43	52	163	0	11
5	85	18	149	2	266	533	80	34	18	14,404	12
8	40	34	133	15	366	268	145	36	52	3,616	13
38	436	80	269	14	913	302	608	91	222	0	14
2	10	4	16	2	46	26	87	213	6	0	15
4	21	33	184	20	207	1,090	82	35	26	0	16
540	881	2,735	4,545	0	0	0	0	0	0	0	17
0	0	0	0	0	0	0	0	0	0	0	18
0	0	0	0	0	0	0	0	0	0	0	19
316	2,527	413	556	68	125	887	134	458	200	0	20
263	645	59	77	7	73	725	5	13	757	0	21
40	185	127	279	42	1,504	372	936	3,984	556	0	22
8	11	1	5	2	6,102	22	21	37	536	0	23
8	200	108	152	33	99	154	229	3,947	72	0	24
5	58	6	25	3	25	14	7	74	150	0	25
117	726	280	1,802	32	3,080	1,140	2,864	218	553	0	26
305	1,564	776	1,052	30	2,042	519	702	195	117	0	27
72	281	206	3,487	153	820	880	1,261	258	15	0	28
8	761	147	420	26	457	0	82	0	0	0	29
47	274	636	-487	0	1,048	79	165	45	70	0	30
0	0	0	0	0	0	0	0	0	0	0	31
0	0	0	0	0	0	0	0	0	0	0	32
0	0	0	0	0	0	0	0	0	0	0	33
0	0	0	0	0	0	0	0	0	0	0	34
0	0	0	0	0	0	0	0	0	0	0	35
0	0	0	0	0	0	0	0	0	0	0	36
0	0	0	0	0	0	0	0	0	0	0	37
0	0	0	0	0	0	0	0	0	0	0	38
0	0	0	0	0	0	0	0	0	0	0	39
0	0	0	0	0	0	0	0	0	0	0	40
0	0	0	0	0	0	0	0	0	0	0	41
0	0	0	0	0	0	0	0	0	0	0	42
0	0	0	0	0	0	0	0	0	0	0	43
149	4	6,393	3,797	0	549	531	905	718	246	0	44
4,139	21,346	16,269	27,241	1,803	21,539	9,348	9,004	11,310	5,347	18,020	
7	8	9	10	11	12	13	14	15	16	17	

					Factors of Production								
	18	19	20	21	22	23	24	25	26	27	28	29	30
Activities 1	0	0	0	0	0	0	0	0	0	0	0	0	0
2	0	0	0	0	0	0	0	0	0	0	0	0	0
3	0	0	0	0	0	0	0	0	0	0	0	0	0
4	0	0	0	0	0	0	0	0	0	0	0	0	0
5	0	0	0	0	0	0	0	0	0	0	0	0	0
6	0	0	0	0	0	0	0	0	0	0	0	0	0
7	0	0	0	0	0	0	0	0	0	0	0	0	0
8	0	0	0	0	0	0	0	0	0	0	0	0	0
9	0	0	0	0	0	0	0	0	0	0	0	0	0
10	0	0	0	0	0	0	0	0	0	0	0	0	0
11	0	0	0	0	0	0	0	0	0	0	0	0	0
12	0	0	0	0	0	0	0	0	0	0	0	0.	0
13	0	0	0	0	0	0	0	0	0	0	0	0	0
14	0	0	0	0	0	0	0	0	0	0	0	0	0
15	0	0	0	0	0	0	0	0	0	0	0	0	0
16	0	0	0	0	0	0	0	0	0	0	0	0	0
17	0	0	0	0	0	0	0	0	0	0	0	0	0
Factors 18	0	0	0	0	0	0	0	0	0	0	0	0	0
19	0	0	0	0	0	0	0	0	0	0	0	0	0
20	0	0	0	0	0	0	0	0	0	0	0	0	0
21	0	0	0	0	0	0	0	0	0	0	0	0	0
22	0	0	0	0	0	0	0	0	0	0	0	0	0
23	0	0	0	0	0	0	0	0	0	0	0	0	0
24	0	0	0	0	0	0	0	0	0	0	0	0	0
25	0	0	0	0	0	0	0	0	0	0	0	0	0
26	0	0	0	0	0	0	0	0	0	0	0	0	0
27	0	0	0	0	0	0	0	0	0	0	0	0	0
28	0	0	0	0	0	0	0	0	0	0	0	0	0
29	0	0	0	0	0	0	0	0	0	0	0	0	0
30	0	0	0	0	0	0	0	0	0	0	0	0	0
Institutions 31	1,865	60	273	22	128	113	37	2	325	0	0	0	0
32	266	4,782	486	234	175	506	77	9	2,513	0	0	0	0
33	52	1,733	153	55	44	164	37	3	2,357	0	0	0	0
34	52	2,277	95	38	41	120	41	3	6,361	0	0	0	0
35	140	131	1,955	533	570	1,298	239	54	1,264	0	0	0	0
36	103	217	118	52	78	145	72	6	1,194	0	0	0	0
37	30	108	184	756	1,340	961	1,577	74	819	0	0	0	0
38	41	18	2,692	682	1,818	2,121	390	49	2,744	0	0	0	0
39	9	11	295	90	493	210	197	8	1,378	0	0	0	0
40	7	12	427	557	3,727	1,142	2,581	182	1,745	0	0	0	0
41	0	0	0	0	0	0	0	0	57	8,390	12,538	7,484	0
42	0	0	0	0	0	0	0	0	0	0	67	0	2,790
Ex 43	0	0	0	0	0	0	0	0	0	0	0	0	0
44	0	0	0	0	0	0	0	0	0	0	0	4792	0
Total	2,565	9,348	6,676	3,019	8,415	6,780	5,247	391	20,756	8,390	12,605	12,276	2,790
	18	19	20	21	22	23	24	25	26	27	28	29	30

	Institutions												Other		Total	
31	32	33	34	35	36	37	38	39	40	41	42	43	44		
453	2,060	792	1,302	797	301	612	931	279	784	0	0	99	144	17,378	1
68	360	99	122	126	50	104	133	41	108	0	4	78	1,474	6,909	2
203	860	411	760	481	222	544	801	273	919	0	0	54	307	8,949	3
40	147	41	51	51	17	21	19	4	6	0	0	71	125	2,289	4
0	0	0	0	0	0	0	0	0	0	0	0	301	9,799	18,658	5
941	2,871	1,242	2,187	1,780	637	1,368	2,347	610	1,775	0	0	119	191	19,145	6
64	176	103	207	146	71	228	244	101	266	0	58	41	665	4,139	7
15	55	30	58	45	14	65	46	16	64	0	382	16,300	1,351	21,346	8
41	130	107	253	220	57	418	246	114	573	0	504	5,399	266	16,269	9
146	277	216	487	329	138	369	619	198	577	0	330	168	6,857	27,241	10
12	13	10	23	26	16	39	147	57	179	0	117	0	0	1,803	11
223	295	226	499	516	206	478	1,021	304	939	0	696	0	384	21,539	12
72	136	99	223	314	136	372	1,020	313	1,064	0	286	0	400	9,348	13
153	283	219	485	329	151	388	798	328	1,028	0	377	0	523	9,004	14
173	688	200	370	381	163	369	715	296	811	0	6,711	0	2	11,310	15
78	142	134	313	236	78	434	444	188	684	0	413	127	35	5,347	16
0	0	0	0	0	0	0	0	0	0	0	0	0	0	18,020	17
0	0	0	0	0	0	0	0	0	0	0	0	0	0	2,565	18
0	0	0	0	0	0	0	0	0	0	0	0	0	0	9,348	19
0	0	0	0	0	0	0	0	0	0	0	0	0	0	6,676	20
0	0	0	0	0	0	0	0	0	0	0	0	0	0	3,019	21
0	0	0	0	0	0	0	0	0	0	0	0	0	0	8,415	22
0	0	0	0	0	0	0	0	0	0	0	0	0	0	6,780	23
0	0	0	0	0	0	0	0	0	0	0	0	0	0	5,247	24
0	0	0	0	0	0	0	0	0	0	0	0	0	0	391	25
0	0	0	0	0	0	0	0	0	0	0	0	0	0	20,756	26
0	0	0	0	0	0	0	0	0	0	0	0	0	247	8,390	27
0	0	0	0	0	0	0	0	0	0	0	0	0	538	12,605	28
0	0	0	0	0	0	0	0	0	0	0	0	0	66	12,276	29
0	0	0	0	0	0	0	0	0	0	0	0	0		2,790	30
13	17	3	12	13	7	5	13	13	11	0	2	0	0	2,933	31
12	105	8	37	34	17	11	46	43	37	0	62	0	6	9,466	32
3	8	5	11	15	10	7	6	9	5	0	19	0	5	4,702	33
9	40	8	30	30	16	11	30	29	24	0	36	0	6	9,296	34
11	50	10	36	71	21	14	39	39	32	0	501	0	79	7,088	35
7	30	12	21	22	77	8	24	24	20	199	242	0	36	2,707	36
1	2	0	8	9	2	3	22	4	9	1,098	178	0	23	7,209	37
14	59	12	40	44	26	16	65	49	41	0	822	0	101	11,843	38
13	53	26	36	40	23	15	44	107	37	452	213	0	32	3,781	39
2	5	1	28	4	4	11	9	9	29	1,722	591	0	112	12,908	40
0	0	0	0	0	0	0	0	0	0	331	0	0	313	29,113	41
89	173	141	266	155	96	96	372	32	397	11,482	2,517	0	30	18,702	42
77	432	543	1,430	874	150	1,202	1,642	300	2,487	13,567	3,283	0	0	25,987	43
0	0	0	0	0	0	0	0	0	0	263	358	3,231	0	24,118	44
2,933	9,466	4,702	9,296	7,088	2,707	7,209	11,843	3,781	12,908	29,113	18,702	25,987	24,117	487,806	
31	32	33	34	35	36	37	38	39	40	41	42	43	44		

Source: BPS 1991, table 1.
Note: Totals may not add due to rounding.

Appendix C: Exchange Rates for the Indonesian Currency

The basic unit of currency in Indonesia is the rupiah. The exchange rate was fixed at Rp 415 to US$1 from 1971 until 1978, when the rupiah was devalued to Rp 625. Thereafter, the rate floated slightly. Two major devaluations occurred in 1983 and 1986, bringing the exchange rate to Rp 1,641 at the end of 1986. A policy of more gradual depreciation at about 5 percent per year was followed through 1992 (Frederick and Worden 1993, p. 428).

The following exchange rates are reported against the US dollar: Rp 1,125 (1985 average), Rp 1,132 (end of August 1986), Rp 1,633 (end of September 1986), Rp 1,640 (end of April 1987), Rp 1,669 (May 17, 1988), Rp 2,010 (February 1992) (Thorbecke and van der Pluijm 1993, p. xiv). It was Rp 2,600 in July 1996 and Rp 2,700 in July 1997.

A dramatic loss of value of many Asian currencies began in the summer of 1997. By February 1998, one dollar was worth Rp 7,000–9,000.

References

Adelman, Irma, and J. Edward Taylor. 1990. "Is Structural Adjustment with a Human Face Possible?" *Journal of Development Studies* 26, no. 4, (April):387–407.

Appelbaum, E., F. Duchin, and D. Szyld. 1995. "Closing Input–Output Models for Households," unpublished.

Ayres, R. 1978. *Resources, Environment & Economics: Applications of the Materials/Energy Balance Principle.* New York: John Wiley & Sons.

Ayres, R., and L. Ayres. 1994. "Chemical Industry Wastes: A Materials Balance Analysis," Working Paper, Center for the Management of Environmental Resources, INSEAD, Fontainebleau, France.

———. 1996. "The Life-Cycle of Chlorine: Part I, II, III, & IV." Working Paper, Center for the Management of Environmental Resources, INSEAD, Fontainebleau, France. Parts I and II have been published in the *Journal of Industrial Ecology*, 1, no. 1, 81–94 and 1, no. 2, 65–89.

Ayres, R., and A. Kneese. 1969. "Production, Consumption, and Externalities." *American Economic Review* 59, no. 3 (June):282–97.

Biesiot, W. and H. C. Moll, eds. 1995. "Reduction of CO^2 Emissions by Lifestyle Changes," Research Report #80. Center for Energy and Environmental Studies, University of Groningen, the Netherlands.

Borges, Jorge Luis. 1964. "The Analytical Language of John Wilkins," in *Other Inquisitions 1937–1952.* Austin: University of Texas Press, pp. 101–5.

Boulding, K. 1966. "The Economics of the Coming Spaceship Earth," in *Resources for the Future: Environmental Quality in a Growing Economy* (Baltimore: Johns Hopkins Press); also in H.E. Daly, ed., 1973, *Economics, Ecology, Ethics* (San Francisco: W.H. Freeman), pp. 253–63.

BPS (Biro Pusat Statistik; Indonesian Central Bureau of Statistics). 1985. *Inter-Census Population Survey,* SUPAS.

———. 1987. *National Economic and Social Survey.* SUSENAS.

———. 1989. *Indonesian Input–Output Table.* Jakarta: Biro Pusat Statistik.

———. 1991. *Social Accounting Matrix Indonesia 1985. Volume I.* Jakarta: Biro Pusat Statistik.

————. 1992. *Statistik Indonesia: Statistical Yearbook of Indonesia, 1991.* Jakarta: Biro Pusat Statistik.

Business International Asia/Pacific Ltd. 1975. "Indonesia: Business Opportunities in a Resource-Rich Economy." Hong Kong: Business International Asia/Pacific Ltd.

Carter, A. P. 1970. "A Linear Programming System Analyzing Embodied Technological Change," in A. Brody and A. P. Carter, eds., *Contributions to Input–Output Analysis,* chapter 4, pp. 77–98. Amsterdam: North Holland Publishing.

Central Bureau of Statistics of Norway. 1992. *Natural Resources and the Environment (1991).* Oslo, Norway.

Chenery, H. B. 1975. "The Structuralist Approach to Development Policy." *American Economic Review* 65, no. 2:310–16.

Chickering, A. Lawrence, and Mohamed Saladine, eds. 1991. *The Silent Revolution: The Informal Sector in Five Asian and Near Eastern Countries.* San Francisco: ICS Press.

Civardi, Marisa B., and Renata T. Lenti. 1988. "The Distribution of Personal Income at the Sectoral Level in Italy: A SAM Model." *Journal of Policy Modeling* 10, no. 3:453–68.

Costa, P. 1988. "Using Input–Ouput to Forecast Freight Transport Demand," in L. Bianco and A. La Bella, eds., 1988, *Freight Transport Planning and Logistics,* pp. 49–A20. Lectures and Notes in Economics and Mathematical Systems 317. Berlin: Springer-Verlag.

————. 1992. "Sentieri di crescita settoriale dell'economia italiana oltre il 2000," in P. Costa, ed., *Settori e regioni nell'economia italiana verso il 2000,* pp. 19–55. Milan, Italy: F. Angeli.

Daly, H. 1968. "On Economics As a Life Science." *Journal of Political Economy* 76, no. 3 (May/June): 392–406; also in H.E. Daly, ed., 1973, *Economics, Ecology, Ethics.* San Francisco: W.H. Freeman, pp. 238–52.

————. 1977. *Steady-State Economics.* San Francisco: W.H. Freeman.

Dawson, Barry, and John Gillow. 1994. *The Traditional Architecture of Indonesia.* London: Thames and Hudson.

de Haan, M., and S. J. Keuning. 1996. "Taking the Environment into Account: The NAMEA Approach." *The Review of Income Wealth,* Series 42, no. 2.

de Haan, M., S. Keuning, and P. Bosch. 1993. *Integrating Indicators in a National Accounting Matrix Including Environmental Accounts.* Netherlands Central Bureau of Statistics, no. NA-060.

de Soto, Hernando. 1989. *The Other Path: The Invisible Revolution in the Third World.* New York: Harper & Row.

Drake, Christine. 1989. *National Integration in Indonesia: Patterns and Policies.* Honolulu: University of Hawaii Press.

Duchin, F. 1988. "Analyzing Structural Change in the Economy," in Maurizio Ciaschini, ed., *Input–Output Analysis: Current Developments,* chapter 8, pp. 113–28. London: Chapman and Hall.

————. 1990. "Technological Change and International Trade." *Economic Systems Research* 2, no. 1: 47–52. Also in Jorge Niosi, ed., 1991, *Technology and National Competitiveness,* chapter 1, pp. 3–10. Montreal: McGill-Queens University Press.

————. 1994. "Household Use and Disposal of Plastics: An Input-Output Case Study for New York City." Report to the AT&T Industrial Ecology Faculty Fellowship Program.

Duchin, F., C. Hamilton, and G. Lange. 1993. "Environment and Development in Indonesia: An Input–Output Analysis of Natural Resource Issues." Final report, supported by the Natural Resource Management Project of the United States Agency for International Development (USAID).

Duchin, F., and G. Lange. 1992a. "Input–Output Modeling: Development and the Environment in Indonesia." Final Report, supported by the Environmental Programming Support Services Project of the Canadian International Development Agency (CIDA), March.

———. 1992b. "Technological Choices, Prices, and Their Implications for the U.S. Economy, 1963–2000." *Economic Systems Research* 4, no. 1: 53–76.

———. 1993. "Development and the Environment in Indonesia: An Input–Output Approach." Final report, supported by the Environmental Programming Support Services Project of the Canadian International Development Agency (CIDA).

———. 1994. *The Future of the Environment: Ecological Economics and Technological Change.* New York: Oxford University Press.

———. 1995. "The Choice of Technology and Associated Changes in Prices in the U.S. Economy." *Structural Change and Economic Dynamics* 6, no. 3: 335–57.

———. 1998. "Prospects for the Recycling of Plastics in the United States," In *Structural Change and Economic Dynamics* 9, no. 3.

Duchin, F., and K. Nauphal. 1996. "Incorporation of the Institutional Accounts for the Dominican Republic into the Input–Output Framework." Report to the Central Bank of the Dominican Republic (July).

Duchin, F., and D. Szyld. 1985. "A Dynamic Input–Output Model with Assured Positive Output." *Metroeconomica* 37 (October):269–82.

Durning, A. T. 1992. *How Much Is Enough? The Consumer Society and the Future of the Earth.* New York: W.W. Norton.

———. 1996. "The Car and the City: 24 Steps to Safe Streets and Healthy Communities." *Northwest Environment Watch*, no. 3 (April).

Edler, D. 1990. *Ein Dynamisches Input–Output Modell zur Abschätzung der Auswirkungen Ausgewählter Neuer Technologien auf die Beschäftigung in der Bundesrepublik Deutschland* (A Dynamic Input-Output Model for the Assessment of the Effects of Selected New Technologies on Employment in West Germany). Berlin: Duncker & Humblot.

Edler, D., R. Filip-Köhn, F. Meyer, R. Staglin, and H. Wessels. 1990. "Intersectoral Effects of the Use of Industrial Robots and CNC-Machine Tools: An Empirical Input-Output Analysis," in R. Schettkat and M. Wagner, eds., *Technological Change and Employment: Innovation in the German Economy*, pp. 293–314. Berlin: de Gruyter.

Ehrlich, P., and J. Holdren. 1974. "Impact of Population Growth." *Science* 171: 1212–17.

Eldredge, N. 1995. *Dominion.* New York: Holt.

Engwicht, David. 1993. *Towards an Eco-City (Reclaiming Our Cities and Towns: Better Living with Less Traffic).* Philadelphia: New Society Publishing.

Frederick, William H., and Robert L. Worden, eds. 1993. *Indonesia: A Country Study.* Washington, D.C.: United States Library of Congress, Federal Research Division.

Geertz, Clifford. 1973. "Thick Description: Toward an Interpretive Theory of Culture," in *The Interpretation of Cultures*, pp. 3–30. New York: Basic Books.

Geertz, Hildred. 1963. *Indonesian Cultures and Communities.* New Haven, Conn.: HRAF Press.

Georgescu-Roegen, Nicholas. 1951. "Some Properties of a Generalized Leontief Model," in T.C. Koopmans, ed., *Activity Analysis of Production and Allocation,* chapter 10, pp. 165–73. New York: J. Wiley & Sons.

Gowdy, John. Forthcoming 1998. "Evolution, Environment, and Economics," in J. van der Bergh, ed., *Environmental and Resource Economics.* Cheltenham: Edward Elgar.

Guinness, Patrick. 1994. "Local Society and Culture," in H. Hill, ed., *Indonesia's New Order: The Dynamics of Socio-economic Transformation.* Honolulu: University of Hawaii Press.

Hanbury-Tenison, Robin. 1975. *A Pattern of Peoples: A Journey among the Tribes of Indonesia's Outer Islands.* New York: Charles Scribner's Sons.

Hannon, B., R. Costanza, and R. Ulanowicz. 1991. "A General Accounting Framework for Ecological Systems." *Theoretical Population Biology* 40, no. 1:78–104.

Hannon, B., and F. Puleo. 1975. "Transferring from Urban Cars to Buses: The Energy and Employment Impacts," in R.H. Williams, ed., *The Energy Conservation Papers,* chapter 3. Cambridge, Mass.: Ballinger.

Hanson, Kenneth A., and Sherman Robinson. 1991. "Data, Linkages, and Models: U.S. National Income and Product Accounts in the Framework of a Social Accounting Matrix." *Economic Systems Research* 3, no. 3:215–32.

Herendeen, R.A., and C.W. Bullard. 1975. "The Energy Cost of Goods and Services." *Energy Policy* 3, no. 4:268–78.

Hidayat, Tirta. 1991. "The Construction of a Two-Region Social Accounting Matrix for Indonesia and Its Application to Some Equity Issues," Ph.D. thesis, Cornell University.

Hill, Hal, and Anna Weidemann. 1989. "Regional Development in Indonesia: Patterns and Issues," in H. Hill, ed., *Unity and Diversity: Regional Economic Development in Indonesia Since 1970,* pp. 3–54. Singapore: Oxford University Press.

Hirsch, F. 1976. *Social Limits to Growth.* Cambridge, Mass.: Harvard University Press.

Homan, Peter, Reimar Schefold, Vincent Dekker, and Nico de Jonge, eds. 1990. *Indonesia in Focus.* Meppel (Netherlands): Edu' Actief Publishing.

Hull, Terence H. 1994. "Fertility Decline in the New Order Period: The Evolution of Population Policy 1965–1990," in H. Hill, ed., *Indonesia's New Order: The Dynamics of Socio-economic Transformation,* pp. 123–44. Honolulu: University of Hawaii Press.

Huq, Muzammel, and Maheen Sultan. 1991. "'Informality' in Development: The Poor As Entrepreneurs in Bangladesh," in Chickering and Saladine, eds., *The Silent Revolution.* San Francisco: ICS Press.

Idenburg, A.M. 1993. *Gearing Production Models to Ecological Economic Analysis: A Case Study, within the Input–Output Framework, of Fuels for Road Transport.* Enschede, Netherlands: Faculty of Public Administration, University of Twente (doctoral dissertation).

Johnson, Karin, Wendy Gaylord, and Gerald Chamberland. 1993. *Indonesia: A Study of the Education System.* Washington, D.C.: American Association of Collegiate Registrars and Admissions Officers and National Association of Financial Services Auditors.

Keuning, Steven J. 1985. "Segmented Development and the Way Profits Go." *Review of Income and Wealth*, series 31, no. 4 (December):375–96.

———. 1989a. "Evaluating Multidimensional Inequality within a Social Accounting Framework: With an Application to Indonesia," unpublished paper. Voorburg: Netherlands Central Bureau of Statistics, National Accounts Research Division.

———. 1989b. "Measuring Welfare with a Social Accounting Matrix, with Special Reference to Indonesia." *Netherlands Review of Development Studies* 2:121–41.

———. 1991. "Proposal for a Social Accounting Matrix Which Fits into the Next System of National Accounts." *Economic Systems Research* 3:233–48.

———. 1993a. "An Information System for Environmental Indicators in Relation to the National Accounts," in W. de Vries, G. den Bakker, M. Gircour, S. Keuning, and A. Lenson, eds., *The Value-Added of National Accounting,* chapter 17, pp. 287–305. Voorburg: Netherlands Central Bureau of Statistics.

———. 1993b. "Productivity Changes and Shifts in the Income Distribution." Paper presented at the Tenth International Conference on Input-Output Techniques, Sevilla, Spain, March 29–April 3, 1993.

———. 1994. "The SAM and Beyond: Open SESAME!" *Economic Systems Research* 6, no. 1: 21–50.

———. 1995. *Accounting for Economic Development and Social Change.* Rotterdam, Netherlands: Erasmus University (dissertation).

Keuning, S., and W. de Ruijter. 1988. "Guidelines to the Construction of a Social Accounting Matrix." *Review of Income and Wealth*, series 34, no. 1 (March): 71–100.

Keuning, S., and E. Thorbecke. 1989. "The Impact of Budget Retrenchment on Income Distribution in Indonesia: A Social Accounting Matrix Application." OECD Development Technical Centre, Paper no. 3.

Koentjaraningrat, ed. 1967. *Villages in Indonesia.* Ithaca: Cornell University Press.

Kuipers, Joel C. 1993. "The Society and Its Environment," in William H. Frederick and Robert L. Worden, eds., *Indonesia: A Country Study,* Washington, D.C.: U.S. Library of Congress, Federal Reserve Division, pp. 69–136.

Lange, G., and F. Duchin. 1994. *Integrated Environmental-Economic Accounting, Natural Resource Accounts, and Natural Resource Management in Africa.* Washington, D.C.: Winrock International Environmental Alliance.

Lave, L., E. Cobas-Flores, C.T. Hendrickson, and F. C. McMichael. 1995. "Life-Cycle Assessment: Using Input–Output Analysis to Estimate Economy-Wide Discharges." *Environmental Science & Technology* 29:420–26.

Leontief, W. 1936. "Quantitative Input and Output Relations in the Economic System of the United States." *Review of Economics and Statistics* 18, no. 3 (August):105–25.

———. 1937. "Interrelation of Prices, Output, Savings and Investment: A Study in Empirical Application of Economic Theory of General Inter-dependence." *Review of Economics and Statistics* 19, no. 3 (August):109–32.

———. 1952. "Some Basic Problems of Structural Analysis." *The Review of Economics and Statistics* 34, no. 1:1–9.

———. 1953. "Dynamic Analysis," in W. Leontief, eds., *Studies in the Structure of the American Economy,* pp. 53–90. New York: Oxford University Press; reprinted 1977, White Plains, N.Y.: International Arts & Science Press.

———. 1970. "The Dynamic Inverse," in A.P. Carter and A. Brody, eds., *Contributions to Input–Output Analysis,* pp.17–43. Amsterdam: North Holland Publishing;

reprinted in W. Leontief, 1977, *Essays in Economics, Volume Two*, White Plains, N.Y.: M.E. Sharpe.

———. 1973. "Structure of the World Economy: Outline of a Simple Input-Output Formulation," in *Les Prix Nobel, 1973*. Stockholm: Nobel Foundation. Reprinted in *American Economic Review* 64, no. 6, (December 1974).

———. 1986a. "Domestic Production and Foreign Trade: The American Capital Position Reexamined," in W. Leontief, ed., *Input–Output Economics*, chapter 5, pp. 65–93. New York: Oxford University Press. First published in *Proceedings of the American Philosophical Association* 97, no. 4 (September 1953).

———. 1986b. *Input–Output Economics*, 2nd ed. New York: Oxford University Press.

———. 1986c. "Technological Change, Prices Wages, and Rates of Return on Capital in the U.S. Economy," in W. Leontief, ed., *Input–Output Economics*, pp. 392–418. New York: Oxford University Press.

———. 1986d. "Wages, Profits Prices, and Taxes," in W. Leontief, ed., *Input–Output Economics*, pp. 55–64. New York: Oxford University Press.

Leontief, W., A. P. Carter, and P. A. Petri. 1977. *The Future of the World Economy*. New York: Oxford University Press.

Leontief, W., and P. Costa. 1996. *Il trasporto merci e l'economia italiana. Scenari di Interazione al 2000 ed al 2015*. Venice, Italy: Marsilio.

Leontief, W. and F. Duchin. 1983. *Military Spending: Facts and Figures and Prospects for the Future*. New York: Oxford University Press.

Leontief, W., and F. Duchin. 1986. *The Future Impact of Automation on Workers*. New York: Oxford University Press.

Leontief, W., J. Koo, S. Nasar, and I. Sohn. 1983. *The Future of Non-fuel Minerals in the U.S. and World Economy*. Lexington, Mass.: D.C. Heath, Lexington Books.

Leontief, W., J. Mariscal, and I. Sohn. 1983. "Prospects for the Soviet Economy to the Year 2000." *Journal of Policy Modeling* 5, no. 1, pp. 1–18.

Mantra, Ida Bagus. 1990. *Urbanization in Indonesia*. Nagoya: United Nations Centre for Regional Development.

Margulis, Lynn, and Karlene Schwartz. 1982. *Five Kingdoms: An Illustrated Guide to the Phyla of Life on Earth*. New York: W.H. Freeman.

Mishan, E.J. 1969. *The Costs of Economic Growth*. New York: Penguin Books.

Mitchell, Susan. 1995. "Birds of a Feather," in *American Demographics* (February):40–48.

Mollison, B. 1988. *Permaculture: A Designer's Manual*. Tyalgum, New South Wales, Australia: Tagari Publications.

Morris, David, and Irshad Ahmed. 1992. *The Carbohydrate Economy: Making Chemicals and Industrial Materials from Plant Matter*. Washington, D.C.: Institute for Local Self Reliance.

Morrison, Christian, and Erik Thorbecke. 1990. "The Concept of Agricultural Surplus." *World Development* 18, no. 8: 1081–95.

Nakicenovic, Nebojsa. 1994. "Energy Gases: The Methane Age and Beyond," in *The Future of Energy Gases*, U.S. Geological Survey Professional Paper 1570.

New North American Industrial Classification System (NAICS) Website: http:/www.census.gov/epcd/www/naicsusr.html#NEWSECTORS

Parikh, J., K. Parikh, S. Gokarn, J. P. Painvly, B. Saha, and V. Shukla. 1991. "Consumption Patterns: The Driving Force of Environmental Stress." Report prepared for the United Nations Conference on Environment and Development, Indira Gandhi Institute of Development Research, Bombay.

Plate, Klaus, ed. 1994. *City Traffic: From EGO-Mobility to ECO-Mobility (A Study of the Cities of Heidelberg, Bautzen, Cambridge, and Montpellier)*. Final Report to the European Union Project on Exchange of Experiences in Transport Planning. Dusseldorf: GEMINI.

Pyatt, G. 1988. "A SAM Approach to Modeling." *Journal of Policy Modeling* 10, no. 3: (Fall):327–52.

———. 1991. "Fundamentals of Social Accounting." *Economic Systems Research* 3, no. 3:315–341.

Pyatt, G., and E. Thorbecke. 1976. *Planning Techniques for a Better Future*. Geneva: International Labor Office.

Robinson, S., and D. Roland-Holst. 1988. "Macroeconomic Structure and Computable General Equilibrium Models," *Journal of Policy Modeling* 10, no. 3 (Fall):353–76.

Rogner, H. 1993. "Global Energy Futures: The Long-Term Perspective for Eco-Restructuring." Paper presented at United Nations University Symposium on Eco-Restructuring, Tokyo, July 5–7.

Round, J. 1991. "A SAM for Europe: Problems and Perspectives," *Economic Systems Research* 3, no. 3:249–68.

Rutz, Werner. 1987. *Cities and Towns in Indonesia: Their Development, Current Positions and Fuctions with Regard to Administration and Regional Economy*. No. 4 in the series "Urbanization of the Earth," Wolf Tietze-Helmstedt, ed. Berlin: Gebruder Borntraeger.

Schumacher, E.F. 1973. *Small Is Beautiful: A Study of Economics As If People Mattered*. New York: Harper & Row.

Scitovsky, T. 1976. *The Joyless Economy*. New York: Oxford University Press.

Stone, R. 1970. "Demographic Input-Output: An Extension of Social Accounting," in A. P. Carter and A. Brody, eds., *Contributions to Input-Output Analysis*, vol. 1, pp. 293–319. Amsterdam: North-Holland Publishing.

———. 1971. *Demographic Accounting and Model Building*. Paris: Organization for Economic Cooperation and Development.

———. 1986. "Social Accounting: The State of Play." *Scandinavian Journal of Economics*, pp. 453–72.

Subramanian, S., and E. Sadoulet. 1990. "The Transmission of Production Fluctuations and Technical Change in a Village Economy: A Social Accounting Matrix Approach," *Economic Development and Cultural Change*, 39, no. 1 (October): 131–67.

Thorbecke, Erik. 1989. "The Social Accounting Matrix Framework to Capture the Interdependence between Domestic and Foreign Variables." Prepared for the Conference on Large-Scale Social Science Models, National Center for Supercomputing Applications, University of Illinois, September.

———. 1992. *Adjustment and Equity in Indonesia*. In the series "Adjustment and Equity in Developing Countries," C. Morrisson, ed. Paris: Organization for Economic Cooperation and Development.

Thorbecke, E., and T. van der Pluijm. 1993. *Rural Indonesia: Socio-Economic Development in a Changing Environment*. New York: New York University Press.

Timmer, Peter. 1975. "The Choice of Technique in Indonesia," in P. Timmer, J. W. Thomas, L. T. Wells, and D. Morawetz, eds., *The Choice of Technology in Developing Countries: Some Cautionary Tales*, Harvard Studies in International Affairs, no. 32, pp. 1–30. Cambridge: Center for International Affairs, Harvard University.

Todd, J. 1991. "Ecological Engineering, Living Machines and the Visionary Land-scape," in C. Etnier and B. Guterstam, eds., *Ecological Engineering for Wastewater Treatment.* Gothenburg, Sweden: Bokskogen.

Tsing, Anna. 1993. *In the Realm of the Diamond Queen.* Princeton, N.J.: Princeton University Press.

United Nations. 1993. *Integrated Environmental and Economic Accounting (Interim Version).* Studies in Methods, Handbook of National Accounting, series F, no. 61. New York, N.Y.: United Nations, Statistical Division.

U.S. Department of the Census. 1994. *Statistical Abstract of the United States*, table no. 707. Washington, D.C.: United States Bureau of the Census.

U.S. Department of Labor, Bureau of Labor Statistics (BLS). 1990. *Consumer Expenditure Survey.* Washington, D.C.: BLS.

Way, Peter. 1984. *Detailed Statistics on the Urban and Rural Population of Indonesia, 1950–2010.* Washington, D.C.: United States Bureau of the Census, Center for International Research.

WCED (World Commission on Environment and Development). 1987. *Our Common Future* (Brundtland Report). New York: Oxford University Press.

Weiss, M. J. 1988. *The Clustering of America.* New York: Harper & Row.

Wirakartakusumah, M. D. 1993. "Demographic Transitions in Indonesia and its Implications in the 21st Century." Unpublished paper, Demographic Institute, Faculty of Economics, University of Indonesia.

Index

Heterick Memorial Library
Ohio Northern University

	DUE	RETURNED		DUE	RETURNED
1.			13.		
2.			14.		
3.			15.		
4.			16.		
5.			17.		
6.			18.		
7.			19.		
8.			20.		
9.			21.		
10.			22.		
11.			23.		
12.			24.